# WINDOWS 2000

# IIS 5.0:
# A Beginner's Guide

**ROD TRENT**

Osborne/**McGraw-Hill**

New York   Chicago   San Francisco   Lisbon
London   Madrid   Mexico City   Milan
New Delhi   San Juan   Seoul   Singapore
Sydney   Toronto

Osborne/**McGraw-Hill**
2600 Tenth Street
Berkeley, California 94710
U.S.A.

To arrange bulk purchase discounts for sales promotions, premiums, or fund-raisers, please contact Osborne/**McGraw-Hill** at the above address.

**IIS 5.0: A Beginner's Guide**

1234567890 CUS CUS 01987654321

ISBN 0-07-213372-4

| | |
|---|---|
| **Publisher** | **Indexer** |
| Brandon A. Nordin | Irv Hershman |
| **Vice President & Associate Publisher** | **Computer Designers** |
| Scott Rogers | Melinda Moore Lytle |
| **Acquisitions Editor** | George Toma Charbak |
| Francis Kelly | **Illustrators** |
| **Acquisitions Coordinator** | Michael Mueller |
| Alexander Corona | Alex Putney |
| **Technical Editor** | Lyssa Sieben-Wald |
| Jim Kelly | **Cover Series Design** |
| **Copy Editor** | Amparo Del Rio |
| Rachel Lopez | **Cover Production Artist** |
| **Proofreader** | Will Chan |
| Stefany Otis | |

This book was composed with Corel VENTURA™ Publisher.

I could never write a book (or do anything else, for that matter) and not dedicate it to my beautiful and loving wife (and mother of my three wonderful children: Alex, Rachel, and Bubbub) who gives me the support and strength to accomplish it. At the end of the day, when my brain no longer functions, she revives my weary psyche. I would like also like to dedicate this book to my Dad, Porter Trent, who watched his son grow up and helped him to make those decisions that formed a unique individual.

# ABOUT THE AUTHOR

**Rod Trent**, MCP, MCSE, CNE, A+, is the author of several best-selling books, whitepapers, and magazine articles. He has more than 14 years of experience in the computing industry. He is the owner of myITforum.com, which offers training and consulting services as well as a world-popular Web site dedicated to organizing and supporting the technology community.

# CONTENTS

# INTRODUCTION

IS 5.0 is the latest release of Microsoft's Internet Information Server. For companies that want to give their business immediate exposure on the Internet, and/or want to automate and Web-enable internal processes, IIS 5.0 is a simple yet powerful solution.

Microsoft has developed IIS 5.0 with the business world in mind, incorporating the latest features found on the most popular Web sites. IIS 5.0 provides the best Web services available and offers more features than most organizations will decide to use. Over the next few chapters, identify what IIS 5.0 can do for your company and focus on those areas that are most critical to your organization.

This book covers those concepts, features, and functions that are built into IIS 5.0, and shows you how to extend IIS through Windows Script Host, ASP, and add-on applications. Whether you are a Web administrator for a corporation or a technician working for an Internet services company, *IIS 5.0: A Beginner's Guide* will help you quickly become educated on Internet services as represented in the latest release of Microsoft's Internet Information Server.

# Who Should Read this Book

Despite what the title suggests, *IIS 5.0: A Beginner's Guide* is a book for Web server administrators with varying levels of expertise. If you are just getting started with IIS 5.0, the book offers insight into setting up, configuring, and deploying a secure Web site using Microsoft's Web server software. It offers step-by-step tutorials for understanding and then creating Web solutions using the latest Internet technologies such as HTML, DHTML, JScript, VBScript, and ASP. And, once the knowledge of the Web technologies are tucked away, the book goes on and applies this working insight to actual applications that rely on Microsoft's .NET initiative. For beginner's, the book allows a quick path to proficiency in using and maintaining IIS 5.0. And, as you leave the beginner status, the book grows to enhance your next steps to becoming an expert.

For those individuals already familiar with IIS 5.0, *IIS 5.0: A Beginner's Guide* includes walk-throughs for upgrading from earlier versions. The book also goes into detail about the differences between the versions and gives critical information on the familiar processes that have changed in the new release. Before picking through the new version to identify those things you will need to alter how you manage the Web server, sift through this book. The logically inlaid information will allow you to get up-to-speed faster.

# What This Book Covers

To better understand the content included in *IIS 5.0: A Beginner's Guide*, it will help to read through a brief outline of each chapter. As you will read, the book's logical layout takes you from the first steps to the last step of comprehension.

▼ **Chapter 1, Installing IIS 5.0**   Before delving into the specific services that IIS 5.0 provides, you need to become comfortable with the installation options available to you. Chapter 1 outlines how IIS 5.0 is installed and gives you insight into areas you should watch out for.

■ **Chapter 2, IIS Interfaces**   Administrative access to IIS 5.0 can be completed in two different ways: through the Microsoft Management Console (MMC) snap-in and via a powerful Web interface. Chapter 2 describes these two access tools and helps you decide which one is right to use in different situations.

■ **Chapter 3, FTP Service Reference**   The FTP service of IIS 5.0 is a powerful tool, allowing Web site visitors to download and upload files.

Use Chapter 3 as a reference to create a secure area on the Web server to accommodate user file needs.

■ **Chapter 4, WWW Service Reference**   The main focus of IIS 5.0 is to provide a robust Web server. This chapter describes this service in detail, allowing you to step through the options available.

■ **Chapter 5, SMTP Service Reference**   Not only does IIS 5.0 offer the best in Web and file services, but it goes even further to give you the ability to install a dominant Internet mail delivery system. By including this feature, you can easily integrate e-mail services with your Web pages. Chapter 5 provides a complete reference for the e-mail services.

■ **Chapter 6, NNTP Service Reference**   News servers provide a popular forum for individuals that want to interact with people all over the world. Whether they need support or they want a place to socialize, IIS 5.0 provides for this by including the NNTP service. This chapter gives you the ability to understand NNTP and its available options.

■ **Chapter 7, Server Properties Reference**   Beyond specific service properties and options, IIS 5.0 includes explicit server selections that allow you to configure site-wide settings. Chapter 7 provides a comprehensive reference for these settings.

■ **Chapter 8, MMC Utilities Reference**   In addition to site-wide settings, IIS 5.0 provides access to much-needed utilities built into the right-click menus of the interface. Utilities such as Backup and Restore, Restart IIS, and the Permissions Wizard are covered in Chapter 8.

■ **Chapter 9, Active Server Pages**   Active Server Pages (ASP) is the crux of creating interactive and reactive Web sites. By utilizing ASP, you can construct Web sites that make the visitor want to visit again and again. Not only does Chapter 9 build your knowledge of this great technology, it also starts you out with the basics of Web building: HTML. Create your own HTML page from scratch in a few minutes.

■ **Chapter 10, Database Connectivity**   Data is the most critical aspect of any company. Without the storage of years upon years of data, it would be as if the company was starting from scratch. Reading Chapter 10, you learn how to give access to data storage through a Web page.

■ **Chapter 11, More Web Technologies**   The Internet is in constant change. Every day a new Web technology emerges and, for Web professionals, it pays to keep on top of the current offerings. This chapter describes, in depth, the latest Web technologies and how they can make your life easier.

- **Chapter 12, Upgrading from IIS 4.0**    If your company has benefited from the use of Microsoft's earlier version of IIS, you'll want to read this chapter. Find out how to safely migrate your current IIS 4.0 Web site to the new IIS 5.0 version.

- **Chapter 13, Windows 2000 Benefits for IIS 5.0**    A key component of IIS 5.0 is its level of integration with Windows 2000. Windows 2000 is the next generation of operating systems; it improves performance, stability, security, and organization of the IIS. Chapter 13 describes these key components and helps you understand the benefits Microsoft has developed.

- **Chapter 14, IIS 5.0 and Microsoft Exchange 2000**    IIS 5.0 provides a level of service for applications never before experienced. Microsoft, with their .NET initiative, has conceded that all products must be Web-enabled. Chapter 14 helps you see the benefit of .NET and how it applies to Microsoft Exchange 2000. For those tasked with deploying Microsoft Exchange 2000, it also gives you special tips for optimizing the IIS 5.0 environment for this enterprise e-mail and collaboration tool.

- **Chapter 15, IIS Performance and Troubleshooting**    A default installation of IIS 5.0 may not prepare your Web site to run optimally. Chapter 15 takes you through the key areas where performance can be tweaked. In IIS 5.0, performance and troubleshooting generally go hand-in-hand, so this chapter also focuses on sections of IIS that are important to monitor.

- **Chapter 16, Client Connection Issues**    A Web site will never see traffic if the client cannot connect to it. This chapter looks at some common issues the client may experience and gives you the knowledge to fix them. It also lists the most common Web browser error codes and helps you determine if the error is a client problem, or if the issue exists on the IIS 5.0 server, itself.

- **Chapter 17, IIS 5.0 Certification Requirements**    Certification for Microsoft's Web server has changed dramatically over the past months. Chapter 17 digs into the current methods for becoming a Web certification professional, and outlines the requirements for Microsoft's new Web tests.

■ **Appendix A, Windows 2000 Events for IIS 5.0**   IIS 5.0 relies heavily on the features included in Windows 2000. Because of this, it's not surprising that errors generated by IIS are recorded by Windows 2000 in its own error recording mechanisms. Appendix A lists the Windows 2000 error numbers associated with IIS 5.0 and explains their importance.

■ **Appendix B, IIS Registry Settings**   IIS 5.0 uses the new Metabase heavily for storing its properties, but there is still some registry information you need to be aware of for optimizing IIS 5.0. This appendix lists all of the registry information included for IIS 5.0.

▲ **Appendix C, WebDAV Publishing**   WebDAV is installed when you install IIS 5.0, but you have to perform specific steps to take advantage of this key Web publishing tool. Appendix C covers WebDAV and shows you how to take advantage of collaborative publishing in your organization.

# IIS 5.0 Product Overview

To achieve a full understanding of the benefits of the new version of Internet Information Server (IIS), it helps to visualize the differences between earlier versions, as well as to identify the new technologies. There are several Internet server offerings on the market, but none as comprehensive and easy to setup and use as IIS 5.0.

## Subtle Differences Between IIS 4.0 and IIS 5.0

For those individuals already familiar with previous versions of IIS, IIS 5.0 does not incorporate any major changes in the way the Web services work. However, there are a few additions to IIS 5.0 that might immediately make organizations decide to upgrade to the latest version.

## Availability

IIS 4.0 was an add-on to the Windows NT operating system through the download or purchase of the Windows NT Option Pack. IIS 5.0 is included as an installation option as part of the Windows 2000 operating system. Not only is this a convenient option for those organizations already rolling out Microsoft's latest operating system, but also it helps solidify Microsoft's dedication to the Internet and Internet-based services.

> **NOTE:** There are several Microsoft products that require IIS be installed on a Windows 2000 Server to function. One example is the latest version of Microsoft Exchange (Microsoft's e-mail server application).

**Backup Procedures** IIS 5.0 uses a metabase for storing IIS configuration settings. This feature uses less disk space than previous methods (Windows registry) of storing the settings. This metabase can easily be backed up and then restored so that the IIS server returns to its original state.

**Command-Line Administration Scripts** IIS 5.0 includes a little more than 30 scripts that can be executed from the command line to automate management of the Web site. Using a similar format, custom scripts can be created to automate more functions of the IIS management. Keeping with Windows 2000 standards, the automation scripts included with IIS 5.0 use the Windows Script Host (WSH) scripting engine. WSH is similar in function and features to Microsoft's Visual Basic programming language but is run as a non-compiled ASCII text format script.

**Improved Custom Error Messages** Administrators of the IIS 5.0 site can customize the error messages that are displayed to the user of the Web site should a Web page be unavailable or an Active Server Page process incorrectly.

**Process Accounting** IIS 5.0 incorporates a technology called Process Accounting. When one server hosts more than one Web site, or Web resource, it is helpful to understand how each site is affecting the server's processing capacity. The Process Accounting feature tracks each Web site's usage of the server's CPU.

**Process Throttling** After using the Process Accounting feature of IIS 5.0, you will want to be able to manage the amount of processing power given to each Web site hosted on the server. To deal with this requirement, Microsoft developed Process Throttling. Process Throttling allows you to configure, by percentage, the amount of CPU utilization available to the individual Web sites.

**Reliable Restarts** In earlier versions of IIS, when an IIS service hung or failed to respond, a reboot of the server itself would often be the only solution. Other Windows NT services could simply be stopped and restarted; the IIS services could not. IIS 5.0 presents the Reliable Restart feature. The Reliable Restart feature allows services to be recycled faster and easier through a one-step process.

**Remote Administration** With IIS 5.0, administrators can set up Operator accounts and assign limited management privileges to individuals to help distribute administrative tasks.

**Remote Administration Through Terminal Services** Windows 2000's Terminal Services support allows administrators to remotely administer IIS 5.0 using the Microsoft Management Console over a dial-up or Point-to-Point Protocol (PPTP) connection (covered later in the book).

**User Management Delegation** User Management Delegation allows an IT or ISP administrator to delegate day-to-day management of a single Web site to another individual, even if multiple Web sites exist on a single Web server.

> **NOTE:** The Windows 2000 Active Directory (AD) services are an essential and inseparable part of the Windows 2000 network architecture, and are specifically designed for distributed networking environments. AD acts as the central authority for network security, letting the operating system readily verify a user's identity and control his or her access to network resources.

**Active Server Pages (ASP)** Active Server Pages have been around in IIS for a while. Active Server Pages use scripts for server-side processing to automate functions. These pages enable the Web site to act like a standard application. In IIS 5.0, ASP have been improved for performance.

**Active Directory (AD)** IIS 5.0 fully supports the Active Directory Services Interface version 2.0. This means that IIS 5.0 can fully function within the Windows 2000 Active Directory hierarchy, and can interact with inherent or custom AD objects.

**Application Protection** IIS 5.0 creates an area of memory for the Web services to run in that is completely separate from the rest of the server's processes. This is critical for a Web site that must run 24/7. If another process on the server fails, the IIS 5.0 services will not be affected.

**Certificate Storage** Windows 2000 provides certificate services that help validate the prominence of a secure site. IIS 5.0 takes full advantage of this feature.

**Digest Authentication** Digest Authentication is another Windows 2000 feature that IIS 5.0 relies on. Digest Authentication is a secure authentication mechanism for providing secure access for users through proxy server and company firewalls.

**Fortezza**  Fortezza is a National Security Agency set of components that enable security standards. IIS 5.0 has been developed to be fully compliant with this set of industry standards.

**Kerberos v5 Authentication Protocol Compliance**  Kerberos version 5.0 is the most secure industry standard for transferring authentication tokens across the network. Authentication tokens are actually small bits of files that contain encrypted information. They are very similar (hence, the naming convention) to subway tokens where you cannot ride the L-train unless you have a token that is authorized for the trip. When a user types in personal authorization information (such as a password), several levels of authentication are actually performed in the background, so that the password information is completely encrypted and secure. IIS 5.0 fully utilizes this feature of this because Windows 2000 has been developed around this standard.

**Security Wizards**  IIS 5.0 provides a lot of features dedicated to configuring security. To ease the administration of the security features, IIS 5.0 includes security wizards, including Certificate Trust Lists, Permissions, and Web Server Certificate.

**Server-Gated Cryptography**  Server-Gated Cryptography is the technology that allows export versions of IIS to use 128-bit encryption.

**Web Distributed Authoring and Versioning (WebDAV)**  WebDAV is the Internet standard that allows file and directory access in order to manage the Web site through a standard HTTP connection. This technology provides access to the Web site for management as if the Web site were a standard network share.

**FTP Restart**  IIS 5.0 fully supports restarting a download from the last received transmission. For example, if your connection to the Internet was terminated, the interrupted download will start exactly where it left off.

**HTTP Compression**  IIS 5.0 compresses Web pages for delivery to the Web browser. Used with file caching, the compression of Web pages greatly increases the speed of Web page access.

# CHAPTER 1

## Installing IIS 5.0

Because IIS 5.0 is part of the Windows 2000 installation and not available as a separate download, before installing IIS 5.0 you must follow the hardware and software requirements for installing Windows 2000 itself. IIS 5.0 can be installed on the workstation version of Windows 2000, called Windows 2000 Professional; however, IIS has been developed to offer its services on a capable server operating system.

## IIS 5.0 INSTALLATION REQUIREMENTS

Windows NT 4.0 Workstation allowed the installation of Personal Web Services (PWS). PWS provided the capability for the non-server operating system to deliver web-type access to the contents of the computer's hard drive. PWS does not run on Windows 2000 (server or workstation) so IIS 5.0 must be installed to provide these same services. If the computer is upgraded to Windows 2000 from Windows NT 4.0, and PWS has already been installed, IIS 5.0 will be installed automatically as part of the operating system upgrade. If PWS has not been installed, IIS 5.0 must be installed manually.

**NOTE:**   If IIS 5.0 is installed on a Windows 2000 Professional workstation, there are certain components of IIS that will be unavailable because they are not supported by Microsoft on any operating system other than a server version. In the Internet Services Manager (ISM), which loads the Internet Information Server snap-in for the Microsoft Management Console (MMC), the following features will be unavailable on a Windows 2000 Professional workstation:

▼   The Operators tab is not listed on the property sheet of the Web site.

■   On the Directory Security tab, the Edit button in the IP address and domain name restrictions section appears dimmed.

▲   On the Performance tab, the Enable bandwidth throttling, Enable process throttling, and Enforce limits check boxes appear dimmed.

In addition to these features being unavailable to Windows 2000 Professional, IIS 5.0 has the following limitations running on the workstation operating system:

▼   Limited to 10 simultaneous connections.

▲   Limited to one Web and one FTP server.

IIS on a Windows 2000 Professional workstation is meant for workgroup access to resources through a Web interface.

# Hardware Requirements

Because Windows 2000 is a robust operating system, the hardware that runs it must meet stringent requirements. Part of rolling out any application is defining the best possible combination of hardware components to efficiently run it. Windows 2000 is no different. Meeting or beating the minimum requirements for Windows 2000 will ensure that IIS has capable hardware. The Microsoft reported minimum requirements are listed in the following sections.

## Microsoft Windows 2000 Professional

The following are the hardware requirements for Windows 2000 Professional:

▼   133 MHz or higher Pentium-compatible CPU

■   64 megabytes (MB) of RAM recommended minimum; more memory generally improves responsiveness (4 gigabytes [GB] RAM maximum)

■   2 GB hard disk with a minimum of 650 MB of free space (additional free hard disk space is required if you are installing over a network)

▲   Windows 2000 Professional supports single and dual CPU systems

## Microsoft Windows 2000 Server

The following are the hardware requirements for Windows 2000 Server:

▼   133 MHz or higher Pentium-compatible CPU

■   256 MB of RAM recommended minimum (128 MB minimum supported; 4 GB maximum)

- 2 GB hard disk with a minimum of 1 GB of free space (additional free hard disk space is required if you are installing over a network)

▲ Windows 2000 Server supports up to four CPUs on one machine

### Microsoft Windows 2000 Advanced Server

The following are the hardware requirements for Windows 2000 Advanced Server:

▼ 133 MHz or higher Pentium-compatible CPU

- 256 MB of RAM recommended minimum (128 MB minimum supported; 8 GB maximum)

- 2 GB hard disk with a minimum of 1 GB of free space (additional free hard disk space is required if you are installing over a network)

▲ Windows 2000 Advanced Server supports up to eight CPUs on one machine

**NOTE:**   Remember, these are the requirements reported as the lowest common denominator. Although Microsoft usually indicates that the minimums work well with the specified operating system, this does not mean that organizations can get by with the minimum. Any rollout or implementation requires careful consideration of the organization's needs as well as the political and physical structure. The hardware requirements for a company with 1,000 workstations constantly connected to the network would be considerably different from a company with 70,000 workstations across international lines in which 30 percent is mobile. Microsoft's minimums should be taken with a grain of salt.

## Microsoft Hardware Resources

Microsoft provides several resources to help determine which hardware to purchase, in addition to verifying whether the current hardware meets the Windows 2000 requirements. Spending time using these valuable resources will allow you to put together the proper hardware the first time. When rolling out your Web site, the last thing you need is to find out that incompatible hardware is keeping your implementation from continuing.

## Search for Compatible Computers

One location on Microsoft's company Web site offers an interactive Web page to identify whether a specific manufacturer's make and model of computer is compatible with Windows 2000. Some computers might already be well suited to run the new operating system; others can be made compatible by installing new hardware drivers or updating the computer's firmware. This information also is included in the results of the search utility and links to the manufacturer's Web sites are available for quick access. This interactive Web page can be found at http://www.microsoft.com/windows2000/upgrade/compat/search/computers.asp.

## Search for Compatible Hardware Devices

Going beyond the computer as a whole, Microsoft provides a Web search interface to retrieve granular information on the hardware components installed either inside the computer or attached externally. This Web site allows detailed information on the devices that are required for the computer to run and the devices that add functionality (for example, tape backup drives or uninterruptable power supplies). This interface can be found at http://www.microsoft.com/windows2000/upgrade/compat/search/devices.asp.

## Windows Hardware Compatibility List (HCL)

Microsoft has long maintained the valuable Windows HCL list for manufacturer's hardware that has been tested and certified to run on a specific Microsoft operating system. Only hardware that meets the Microsoft requirements is permitted on this list and attains the "Designed for Windows" logo. This logo certification program ensures that any hardware bearing the Microsoft logo meets or exceeds

Microsoft's standard for its Windows operating systems. The Windows HCL list can be found at the following addresses:

▼ http://www.microsoft.com/hcl/default.asp

▲ ftp://ftp.microsoft.com/services/whql/hcl/

As indicated by the preceding two Web site addresses, the HCL is available in two formats: Web-based and text versions. The Web-based version allows searching the list while connected to the Internet. The text version is retrieved from a FTP site as a text file that can be viewed in any program that reads ASCII text. This version is particularly useful for reviewing the information offline, on the computer, or as a printed hardcopy.

Here is an example of the ATI video manufacturer from the HCL that is available for download:

```
ATI Technologies, Inc.
  ATI -264VT2 PCI                      Compatible
  ATI -264VT3 PCI                      Compatible
  ATI -264VT4 PCI                      Compatible
  ATI 3D RAGE II + PCI                 Compatible
  ATI 3D RAGE II PCI                   Compatible
  ATI 3D RAGE IIC AGP                  Compatible
  ATI 3D RAGE IIC PCI                  Compatible
  ATI 3D RAGE LT PCI                   Compatible
  ATI 3D RAGE LT PRO AGP               Compatible
  ATI 3D RAGE LT PRO AGP 2X            Compatible
  ATI 3D RAGE LT PRO PCI               Compatible
```

## Software Requirements

As long as the software applications installed on the server that will run the IIS 5.0 services meet the requirements for Windows 2000, IIS should run without any problems. To verify that the applications installed on the Windows 2000 server meet Microsoft standards, and that they are completely compatible with Windows 2000, Microsoft provides several resources to help plan the Windows 2000 installation or upgrade. These are discussed in the following section.

## Search for Compatible Software

Microsoft provides a Web site specifically designed to identify software that is compatible with Windows 2000. This Web site allows the user to search for software that has been identified as able to run on Windows 2000 Professional, Windows 2000 Server, and Windows 2000 Advanced Server. The information available from the search engine is a list of applications that have been voluntarily submitted by software vendors; so, if a certain program is not listed, this does not necessarily indicate that the program does not run on Windows 2000—it might not have been submitted yet. This list is constantly updated so it should be reviewed periodically or before any new software is added. Because the software list is updated only periodically, and only when software vendors submit their information, it is sensible to contact the software vendor to find out if a particular application is compatible with Windows 2000. This information can be found at http://www.microsoft.com/windows2000/upgrade/compat/search/software.asp.

# Windows 2000–Specific Requirements

In addition to making sure that all software installed on the Windows 2000 Server is Microsoft Windows compliant, there are a couple of Windows 2000–specific items that must be installed and configured for IIS 5.0 to run. These are covered in the following sections.

## TCP/IP Protocol

The Internet and Internet-type services are heavily dependent on the TCP/IP protocol. To accommodate this network protocol standard, Windows 2000 and IIS 5.0 require that TCP/IP be installed and configured on the server. You should have an adequate working knowledge of TCP/IP before installing IIS 5.0. A good primer for networking with the TCP/IP protocol is *Windows 2000: The Complete Reference* by Kathy Ivens and Kenton Gardinier; published by

Osborne/McGraw-Hill; ISBN: 0-07-211920-9. This book covers the TCP/IP protocol as implemented in Windows 2000.

### NTFS Formatted Hard Disks

NT File System (NTFS) is the most secure file system on the market today. Developed by Microsoft, NTFS is a requirement for IIS 5.0. When the Windows 2000 server is initially set up, this option is available for selection. Hard disks, other than the one that houses the boot partition and the one that holds the system files, can be converted to NTFS at a later time.

## Additional Suggestions

In addition to the requirements for installing IIS 5.0, there are a couple of other items that are invaluable to IIS. Identifying the following requirements before your Web site goes "live" will ease the burden of changing things later.

### Database Software

One consideration that could save time and help IIS 5.0 to be fully functional is to install a database server software at the time of the IIS installation. Microsoft produces SQL Server (SQL Server 2000 is the latest version) for this purpose. SQL Server provides the easiest administration and the top performance of any database server product on the market. SQL Server also supplies unsurpassed integration with IIS. Installing a database server if storing and retrieving data through a web-type interface is a requirement for the Web site.

### Active Directory Services

One of the biggest benefits of deploying the Windows 2000 Server operating system is the ability to build the organization on a world-class directory service. Microsoft's Active Directory services (AD) is the first iteration of this type of service. AD allows organizations to centrally manage the entire networked environment. Objects within the AD can easily be moved from one location to another in a tree structure. The Active Directory Services Interface (ADSI) gives companies the vehicle to develop custom AD solutions within the organization and take advantage of the built-in AD features.

One of these features is the power to quickly publish an entire directory as a Web share. On any Windows 2000 computer that has IIS installed, Web sharing properties are available (shown in Figure 1-1) as part of the operating system's Windows Explorer interface. Folders that have been shared for Web access are immediately available for use through a Web browser in the Active Directory.

In addition to this functionality, AD and IIS work hand in hand to provide access to other objects. Using a Web page, printers that are inserted into the AD are available for viewing, management, and connection through an Internet browser. Windows 2000 dynamically lists all the printers on the server on an easily accessible Web site.

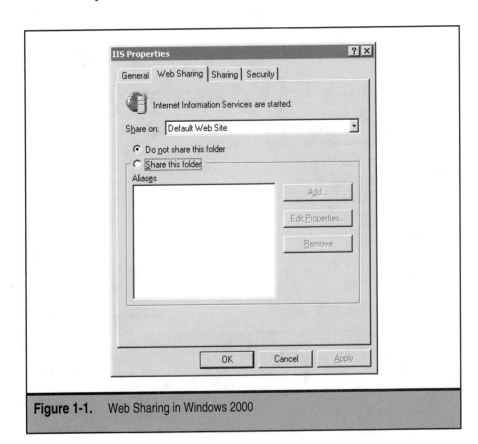

**Figure 1-1.**   Web Sharing in Windows 2000

## INSTALLING IIS 5.0

After you have gathered the requirements for a proper IIS installation, it's time to actually install the application. As with any Microsoft application, there are several ways to accomplish this—actually there are three methods for initiating the IIS 5.0 installation:

▼    IIS 5.0 can be selected as an optional component to be installed during the Windows 2000 Server installation.

■    From the Windows 2000 Server CD's main menu. As shown in Figure 1-2, IIS 5.0 can be selected for installation by clicking on the Install Add-On Components option. If AutoRun is enabled for the computer on which Windows 2000 Server

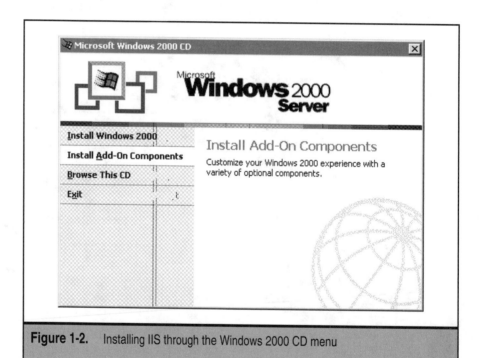

**Figure 1-2.**    Installing IIS through the Windows 2000 CD menu

will be installed, just insert the CD into the CD drive and
the menu will appear.

▲ Through the Add/Remove Windows Components option in
the Add/Remove Programs Control Panel applet (shown in
Figure 1-3). To do this, follow these steps:

1. On the Start menu, click Control Panel; then click
   Add/Remove Programs.

2. Select Add/Remove Windows Components, select the
   Internet Information Services (IIS) component, and then
   follow the on-screen instructions.

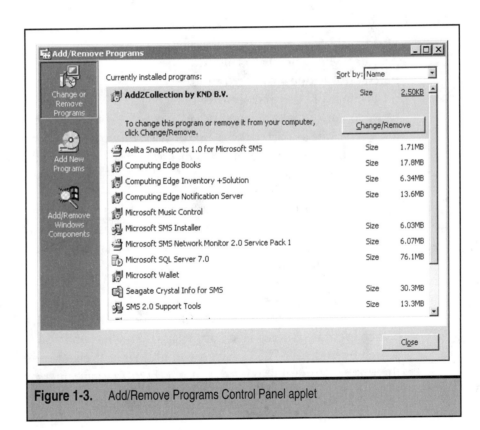

**Figure 1-3.**    Add/Remove Programs Control Panel applet

## Before Installation—Security Considerations

The Internet is bombarded by *hackers*—individuals that have nothing better to do with their time than to annoy Earth's general population. Because of these miscreants, sometimes Internet sites are illegally accessed or even put out of commission for a period of time. For the safety of the information contained on any Web site, it is a smart practice to keep current with the latest software updates. Because of Microsoft's knack for creating impressive and popular products, it is no surprise that they are the targets of the majority of these hacks. These hackers spend night and day trying to discern a way to make Microsoft look foolish.

Fortunately, Microsoft is unlike the other vendors in the market. They welcome these hacker attempts to pry into their products. And, when the hackers are successful in unlocking a doorway into a particular product, Microsoft stands alone as the vendor that can get a security patch out the door in record time.

Because of potential security breaches in IIS 5.0, it makes logical sense to verify that the latest security patches, or *hotfixes*, are applied to the Web site as part of the IIS 5.0 installation process. When planning the IIS 5.0 installation, be sure to include these patches in the rollout.

> **NOTE:**   *Hotfixes* are small patches that Microsoft releases when an application needs to have a fix applied. These fixes can be applied while the operating system is running, or "hot." These hotfixes provide in-place upgrades to certain components that need fixed.

To obtain the latest information on available security patches for IIS 5.0, visit Microsoft's Internet Information Server Security Bulletin Search Web site. Microsoft keeps this list up to date, and you can quickly search by version of IIS or by year. The current Web site address for the IIS Security Bulletin information is http://www.microsoft.com/technet/security/current.asp?productID=15.

To be completely on top of IIS security issues, sign up for Microsoft's Product Security Email Notification service. You can do this by following these steps:

1. Compose an e-mail to microsoft_security-subscribe-request@announce.microsoft.com. The subject line and the message body are not used to process the subscription request; they can be anything you like.

2. Send the e-mail.

3. You'll receive a response asking you to verify that you really want to subscribe. Compose a reply, and type **OK** in the message body. Send the reply.

4. You'll receive two e-mails: one telling you that you've been added to the subscriber list, and the other with more information on the notification service and its purpose. You'll receive security notifications whenever Microsoft sends them.

*TIP:*  In addition to keeping abreast of IIS security issues, make sure to also be aware of any reported Windows 2000 security issues. Because IIS runs on Windows 2000, some security risks posed by the operating system also might make IIS vulnerable to attack.

## Installation Walk-Through

There really is no difference in the way IIS 5.0 is installed based on the method chosen to install it. The selection of the IIS 5.0 components is the same, as is the way IIS 5.0 installs. After the installation has been initialized, the Windows Components Wizard, as shown in Figure 1-4, prompts you to allow selection of the Internet Information Services (IIS) windows component.

Selecting this component from the wizard screen selects every IIS service available. Depending on the needs of the organization, some

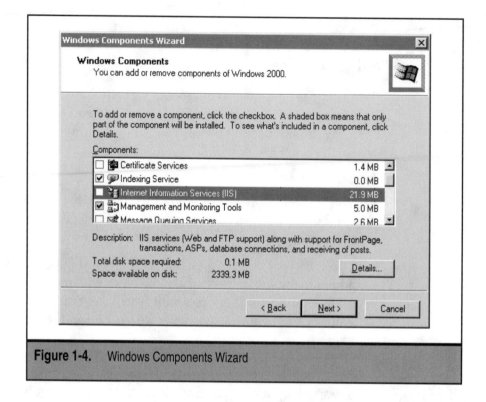

**Figure 1-4.** Windows Components Wizard

of the available services might not be needed. If they are needed later, they can be added using the same method of installation.

Clicking the Details button with the IIS component selected displays the IIS components window (shown in Figure 1-5) where each component can be selected or unselected as required. This screen allows almost total control over the specific components that will be installed.

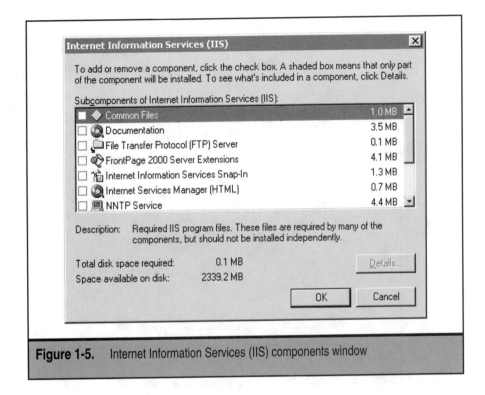

**Figure 1-5.**    Internet Information Services (IIS) components window

Based on the selected components, the Windows Components Wizard takes back control (shown in Figure 1-6) to ensure a successful installation.

**NOTE:**  When the installation is complete, remember to apply any security hotfixes identified on the IIS Security Bulletin Web site.

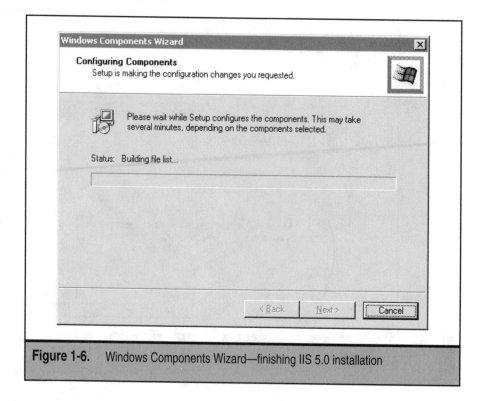

**Figure 1-6.** Windows Components Wizard—finishing IIS 5.0 installation

## IIS Services Overview

To better understand what is available as part of the IIS 5.0 installation, it helps to understand the components offered. The following list briefly describes the services available for the installation of the IIS 5.0 Web server. These services are covered in more detail in Chapters 2–7.

▼ **Common files** These are files that are required by IIS to operate the other IIS services that are installed. These common files are installed in bulk and cannot be installed independently because many of the IIS components rely on these critical files. Installation size: 1.0 MB.

■ **Documentation** Selecting the Documentation component installs the entire volume of information on IIS and the related services including publishing and site content; and Web and

FTP server administration topics, including ASP documentation and samples. Installation size: 3.5 MB.

- **File Transfer Protocol (FTP) server**  The FTP server component furnishes the IIS Web site with the ability to use the FTP protocol for uploading and downloading files. Installation size: 0.1 MB.

- **FrontPage 2000 server extensions**  The FrontPage 2000 server extensions enable authoring and administration of Web sites using Microsoft's FrontPage Web building and design application, as well as Visual InterDev. Installation size: 4.1 MB.

- **Internet Information Services snap-in**  The IIS Services snap-in is the administrative interface for monitoring and managing the IIS Web site services and additional components. This interface plugs into the Microsoft Management Console. The MMC provides a central, uniform interface for all Windows 2000 services. Snap-ins can be mixed and matched to allow a centralized console for all administrative tasks. Installation size: 1.3 MB.

- **Internet Services Manager (HTML)**  Like the IIS snap-in, the Internet Service Manager (HTML) provides for IIS administration and monitoring. The difference between the two is that this component allows administration through a Web interface (Internet browser). This is the most convenient way to access the administrative services over a slow link such as a dial-up connection. Installation size: 0.7 MB.

- **NNTP service**  The Network News Transfer Protocol (NNTP) service offers the same functionality you find on standard Internet newsgroup servers. Installing this component makes it possible for the Web site to provide a news-type service to visitors. Users can participate in discussions by posting new topics and responding to current ones. Installation size: 4.4 MB.

*TIP:* The NNTP service component enables the Details button in the Add/Remove component window. This Details button deceivingly offers no additional information about the component. Unchecking the NNTP option in the Details section removes the entire service.

- **SMTP service** The Simple Mail Transfer Protocol enables IIS 5.0 to send and receive e-mail through the Web site. Providing this feature on the Web site allows sending and receiving of messages that are designed to be Internet mail capable from applications on the client computer. Installation size: 4.9 MB.

*TIP:* The SMTP service component enables the Details button in the Add/Remove component window. This Details button deceivingly offers no additional information about the component. Unchecking the SMTP option in the Details section removes the entire service.

- **Visual InterDev RAD remote deployment support** When you select this component for installation, a security warning displays. Visual InterDev RAD (rapid application development) remote deployment support is primarily for those Web sites that will be developing Web-based applications. If this component is installed it is a smart practice to install it on a lab or test server that is used specifically for creating Web applications. When this component is in use, individuals who are given Author rights to the Web site can register new server components and modify the COM+ settings. This could place the Web server in an unusable state. Installation size: 0.1 MB.

- ▲ **World Wide Web server** The World Wide Web (WWW) server service provides admission for individuals who have access to the Web server. Without this service installed, Web pages cannot be opened and loaded by people visiting the Web site. Installation size: 1.9 MB.

*NOTE:* An installation with all services selected needs 18.0 MB of disk space.

## Service Dependencies

Several of the IIS installation services are dependent on other services to operate properly. Table 1-1 outlines these service-to-service requirements; it is particularly useful when planning IIS 5.0 space requirements. In fact, when a service is selected through the Add/Remove interface, the other required services are automatically selected.

| Service | Dependencies | Total Space |
|---|---|---|
| Common Files | None | 1.0 MB |
| Documentation | Common files, Internet Information Services snap-in, World Wide Web server | 9.0 MB |
| File Transfer Protocol (FTP) server | Common files, Internet Information Services snap-in | 2.8 MB |
| FrontPage 2000 Server Extensions | Common files, Internet Information Services snap-in, World Wide Web server | 4.7 MB |
| Internet Information Services snap-in | Common files | 2.6 MB |
| Internet Services Manager (HTML) | Common files, Internet Information Services snap-in, World Wide Web server | 5.5 MB |

**Table 1-1.** Good to Know—IIS 5.0 Service Dependencies *(continued)*

| Service | Dependencies | Total Space |
|---|---|---|
| NNTP Service | Common files, Internet Information Services snap-in, World Wide Web server | 9.1 MB |
| SMTP Service | Common Files, Internet Information Services snap-in, World Wide Web server | 8.7 MB |
| Visual InterDev RAD remote deployment support | Common files, FrontPage 2000 server extensions, Internet Information Services snap-in, World Wide Web server | 4.8 MB |
| World Wide Web server | Common files, Internet Information Services snap-in | 4.7 MB |

**Table 1-1.** Good to Know—IIS 5.0 Service Dependencies *(continued)*

Microsoft has developed an installation process that is quick and easy to configure. Understanding the function of each component can make the installation process even smoother, as you will install only those services that are required for the Web project.

Understanding all of the requirements for IIS 5.0 will allow it to install correctly the first time. While Microsoft has developed IIS to make the installation and configuration as easy as possible, paying special attention to required components will drive potential problems out of the picture.

# CHAPTER 2

## IIS Interfaces

When the IIS 5.0 installation is complete, it is time to configure the services that have been installed. This brings about the first dilemma when working with IIS: Which interface do you use to configure the Web services? The answer: It really depends on how comfortable you are with those available. The following sections describe each interface and outline the pro's and con's. Use this information to determine which interface is right for you, and which one best suits each situation.

## Internet Information Services Snap-in

Microsoft's management framework is built around the power of the Microsoft Management Console (MMC). As new products are released or become available, each includes a special component that works within the MMC interface. In the past, network administrators had to rely on various management tools that offered no integration and presented inconsistent user interfaces. The Internet Information Services snap-in (shown in Figure 2-1) is exactly as the name suggests: a *snap-in*. Snap-ins provide the actual management behavior; the MMC itself does not provide any management functionality. Administrators and other users can design custom management tools from snap-ins created by various vendors. Administrators then can save the tools they invented for later use or share them with other administrators and users.

The MMC has been around for a few years and has been used extensively by systems administrators. If you are one of these administrators, you probably are already comfortable with the MMC's interface and how it functions. If that's the case, the Internet Information Services snap-in might be your interface of choice for configuring and administering IIS.

All the Windows 2000 management tools are built around the MMC and also are snap-in components. More than likely, if you are working with IIS 5.0, you probably are already using the other Windows 2000 management components, so this common interface becomes very comfortable. The IIS 5.0 MMC snap-in provides an additional benefit over the Internet Services Manager (HTML); it allows management

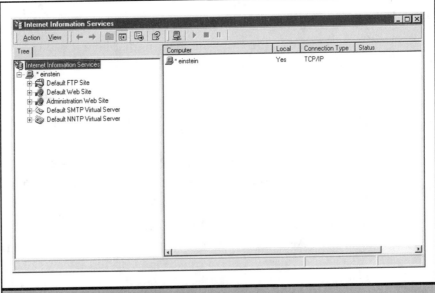

**Figure 2-1.**   Internet Information Services interface within the Microsoft
Management Console

and configuration of all the installed IIS services. The Internet Services
Manager (HTML) interface allows access only to the WWW and
FTP components and it is available only when IIS is running on a
Windows 2000 or Windows 2000 Advanced Server; it is not available
on Windows 2000 Professional.

## Working with the MMC

Because the IIS interface snaps in to the MMC, it utilizes the common
functions of the MMC. Understanding how the MMC works and how
to navigate its functions will help you quickly move around the Internet
Information Services options. The following options are available in
most MMC snap-ins:

▼   **Action menu**   The Action menu provides all of the options
you would expect to see in a standard application. Like the
File menu in most software programs, the Action menu houses
a drop-down list of available commands.

- **View menu**   The View menu allows you to change the way the information in the MMC is displayed. These options include choosing the columns that are displayed; switching between large icons, small icons, lists, and detailed lists (similar in function to the View options in Windows Explorer); and manually customizing how the information is displayed.

- **Tree pane**   The Tree pane is the leftmost window in the MMC. This tree structure allows you to quickly switch between the separate IIS services available and to expand each service to view what is available underneath. Pressing the plus (+) sign next to a service expands that service.

- **Right-click**   Right-clicking on an item in the tree pane combines the Actions and View menus into a single menu that pops up for easy selection of one of the options.

- **Contents pane**   The Contents pane is the rightmost window in the MMC. When an option is highlighted in the Tree pane, the Contents pane displays the items contained within the item without having to expand the tree.

- ▲ **Drag-and-drop**   The MMC framework allows dragging and dropping of items from one location in the Tree pane to another. This feature simplifies interaction within the MMC by reducing the number of steps needed to perform an action.

*NOTE:*   Whereas the MMC management framework allows for drag-and-drop features, the IIS snap-in does not. You cannot drag and drop items within the Internet Information Services interface.

## Customizing the MMC

Because the MMC basically is a shell, you can insert any snap-in or all snap-ins that are available. This means you can create your own management tool using the snap-ins that are installed on the computer. For example, if you have incorporated a database into your company's Intranet, you can create a management console that has both the Internet Information Services snap-in and the SQL Server Enterprise Manager built in. This gives you easy access to the tools that you use on a regular basis. Using this example, let's create a custom management tool that houses both Internet Information Services and SQL Server Enterprise Manager:

1. Run the Microsoft Management Console by selecting Start | Run; then type **MMC** and click OK.

2. When the MMC displays, click the Console menu option, and then choose Add/Remove Snap-in.

3. When the Add/Remove Snap-in window displays (shown in Figure 2-2), click the Add button.

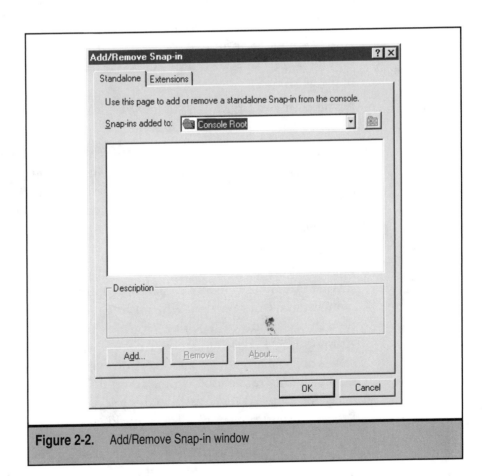

**Figure 2-2.**  Add/Remove Snap-in window

**NOTE:** If there are no snap-ins available (installed) on the computer, the window shown in Figure 2-2 will be blank.

4. A new window called Add Standalone Snap-in displays. It might take a few moments, but when the Add button is clicked, a full inventory of all of the snap-ins available on the computer is initiated. When this list is complete, you can select each snap-in that should be in your new, custom MMC and click Add. For this example, select the Microsoft SQL Enterprise Manager and Internet Information Services snap-ins. When you are done selecting, click Close. The snap-ins you have selected will be displayed back in the Add/Remove Snap-in window's list.

5. If you are satisfied with your selections, click OK to close the Add/Remove Snap-in window and return to the main MMC window. Your selections now are displayed in the Tree pane of the MMC.

6. Name your custom MMC window by clicking the Console menu option and choosing Options.

7. This new console can be named anything you like. The new console has been named My SQL IIS MMC Console, as shown in Figure 2-3. Click OK when finished modifying the name. The new name displays at the top left of the management console.

8. Save the custom console by clicking the Console menu option and selecting Save. Name the console anything you like, but make sure to name it something relative to its function. If you create many custom consoles, keeping the console name simple can save time when trying to find it later. By default, in Windows 2000 new consoles are saved to the Administrative Tools folder on the computer. You actually can save a console anywhere you like; however, saving it with the other administrative tools on the computer makes it easier for everyone to find. When saved in this folder, choosing Start | Programs | Administrative Tools quickly accesses the tools.

Using these instructions, you can effortlessly create a management console that fits how you work and what tools you work with to get the job done. You also can easily furnish these custom consoles to

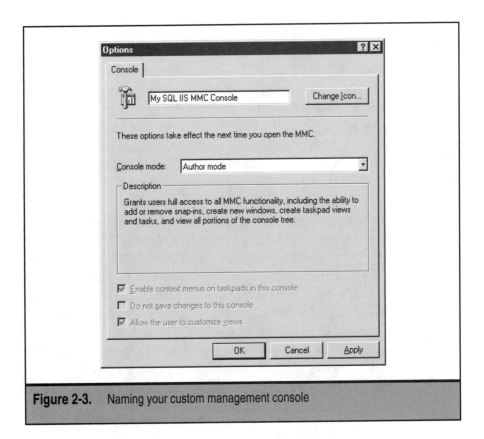

**Figure 2-3.**  Naming your custom management console

another individual by just giving him or her the file. Consoles are saved with an .MSC extension so they are immediately identifiable in the file and directory structure on the computer. These files are relatively small, so they can be e-mailed or copied to a Zip or floppy disk. Create some first-rate consoles and you might just find yourself in an IT version of Pokémon card collecting.

Note that for other people to use an MMC file that you have created, they must have the required snap-ins installed on their computer. MMC snap-ins actually are files in the operating system that have two extensions: .DLL and .OCX. Some of these snap-ins are composed of several of these files and standard installation routines make them available to the operating system.

You can't just find the snap-in files and distribute them with your custom consoles; the snap-ins actually have to be installed by the application that uses them. With the Internet Information Services snap-in, it is made available to the operating system through the IIS 5.0 installation. Similarly, the Microsoft SQL Enterprise Manager snap-in is installed using the SQL Server installation CD. If you want your custom consoles to work on another computer, make sure the correct application is installed or instruct the user to install it.

Windows 2000 provides even more features for using MMC files such as setting policies that allow only members of a specific group in the Active Directory to use a particular console or even a specific snap-in. For more information on these MMC features, check out the *Admin911: Windows 2000 Group Policy* book (ISBN: 0-07-212948-4). You can read more about this book on the Admin911 Web site: http://www.admin911.com or the Osborne/McGraw-Hill Web site: www.osborne.com.

The MMC is a powerful tool; naturally you can understand why this might be the interface of choice when managing the IIS 5.0 services. Yet, although the MMC provides many benefits, there is one significant detriment: Unfortunately, the MMC is inherently slow over a modem connection or a congested network link. If you want to administer the IIS 5.0 services while dialed into the network through a modem, be prepared to take a few high-quality drinks of coffee before completing a task.

## Internet Services Manager (HTML)

The Internet Services Manager (HTML) interface (shown in Figure 2-4) displays in any standard Web browser. This interface is particularly useful to individuals who are accustomed to browsing the Internet. The interface works the same as any Web page by allowing single-clicks of Internet-type links. These links perform actions that are processed by the IIS 5.0 server itself.

To access the Internet Services Manager (HTML) interface, open your Internet browser and type the IIS 5.0 server's Web address. This Web address is composed of the standard http:// followed

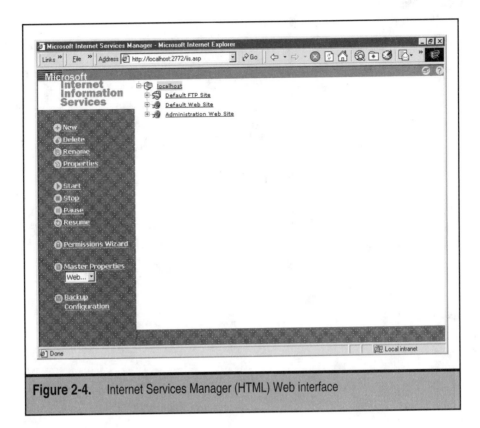

**Figure 2-4.**   Internet Services Manager (HTML) Web interface

by the server's actual name or IP address. For example, typing
**http://einstein** on my server brings up the page shown in Figure 2-5.

*TIP:*   When you open the Windows 2000 Internet Services home page,
another browser window also opens. This window, the Microsoft Internet
Information Service 5.0 documentation, provides the Web-based help file that
comes with IIS 5.0. This help documentation is completely Web enabled and
works as any other Web page running on the IIS 5.0 server. You can access this
Web version of help without opening the Welcome to Windows 2000 Internet
Services home page. To do this, open your Internet browser and type:
**http://<*servername*>/iisHelp/** in the address line.

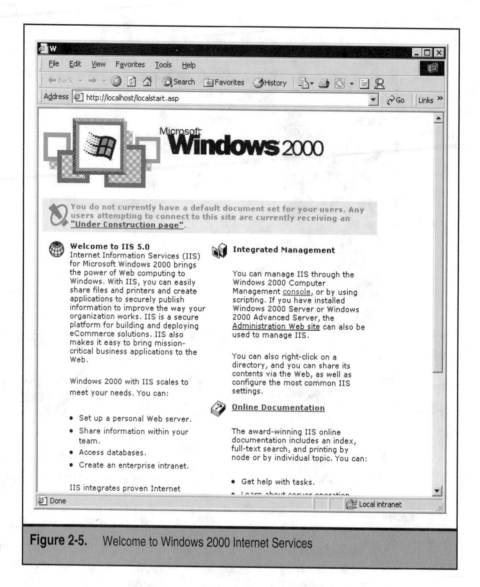

**Figure 2-5.** Welcome to Windows 2000 Internet Services

When the Welcome to Windows 2000 Internet Services home page opens, you will see several links available on the Web page. One link opens the Internet Information Services Management Console. Another opens the IIS 5.0 documentation and help file should you need access to it after it has been closed. Still another link opens the Printers Web page, which shows which printers are available for management

and connection within the Windows 2000 Active Directory.
However, the link we are targeting is the one that opens the IIS 5.0
Administration Web site. This Web site is the Internet Services
Manager (HTML) interface. Reference Figure 2-4 if you need a
quick refresher on what it looks like.

The Internet Services Manager (HTML) interface offers much the
same functionality as the Internet Information Services management
console. You can click the plus (+) sign to expand the tree information
and view the information contained within. Using the Web links in
the left-hand pane you can quickly create new items, delete old ones,
rename others, and get the properties information of any highlighted
item. You can start, stop, pause, and resume any of the services. You
can run the Permissions Wizard and even back up the IIS configuration.
This Web interface provides the same site service functions as the
Internet Information Services MMC snap-in.

If you occasionally or frequently need to manage the IIS 5.0 server
from a remote location, either through a modem dial-up line or through
a slow network connection, the Internet Services Manager (HTML) is
the quickest and cleanest interface to use. If you are like the typical
system administrator, you are on call 24 hours a day, 7 days a week.
Because critical information resides on the systems, it must be available
even when the manager of a significant department has insomnia and
decides to work at 3:00 A.M. If you must dial through a phone line to
fix a problem with the IIS 5.0 services, you will want to use Internet
Services Manager (HTML). Web technology delivers data more rapidly
to an Internet browser than to the MMC.

Even though the Internet Services Manager (HTML) interface
can save time and maybe even help you preserve your sleep, it has
some "gotchas" of which you need to be aware. These difficulties
could determine whether you use the Web version of the IIS 5.0
Services Manager or help you determine which tool is called for
in a specific situation.

If the WWW services are not running, the interface is inaccessible.
The interface offers access only to the FTP and WWW services; it does
not allow management of SMTP (Internet e-mail) and NNTP (Internet
news service).

Being familiar with the Microsoft Management Console will ultimately make working with the Internet Information Services snap-in a more rewarding experience. Once you are comfortable with how the snap-in works, it is time to become proficient in the options that are available for each installed IIS 5.0 service. Each service available in the Internet Information Services Snap-in has a Properties page that can be accessed by right-clicking it and choosing Properties from the pop-up menu.

# CHAPTER 3

## FTP Service Reference

The FTP service is the protocol used for copying files to and from remote computer systems on a network using Transmission Control Protocol/Internet Protocol (TCP/IP), such as the Internet. This protocol also allows users to use FTP commands to work with files, such as listing files and directories on the remote system.

This chapter covers the entire FTP service as it is represented in IIS 5.0. And, while Microsoft included this service in IIS 5.0, it is a standard protocol found across the entire Internet. FTP is a way of transferring files across the Internet in a secure manner.

# FTP SITE PROPERTY SHEET

The IIS interface makes working with and configuring the FTP service easy. As with all of the IIS services, configuration is one of the most important parts of setting up and maintaining the services you choose to implement. With the Default FTP Site Properties window open, there are five separate property sheets available for configuring the FTP Service. The FTP Site Property sheet has three sections available: Identification, Connection, and Enable Logging (see Figure 3-1). They are described in the following sections.

## Identification Section

The following items are available for configuration in the Identification section of the FTP Site Property sheet:

▼ **Description**   This field can accept any name you want to identify the FTP server. This name is for identification and organizational purposes.

■ **IP Address**   Any IP addresses that have been defined for use in the Network Properties of the server will be available for selection. Selecting an IP address from the drop-down menu will assign that selection to the default FTP site. This IP address will be used for connection to the server.

▲ **TCP Port** The default TCP port is 21. Across the industry this is a *de facto* standard port for FTP services. You may modify this number to any port number you like, but the client computer must be capable of identifying that this FTP server advertises the specific port. There are several FTP applications on the market that provide a client interface for accessing FTP sites. These applications can be configured to use a specified port number for a particular FTP site. For those computers that do not use an alternative FTP client software program, the Internet browser is used to access FTP sites. Internet browsers automatically look for port 21 to be available.

If you change the FTP port number for any reason, consider installing a separate FTP application on the computers in your organization. An excellent FTP client, SmartFTP, can be found at

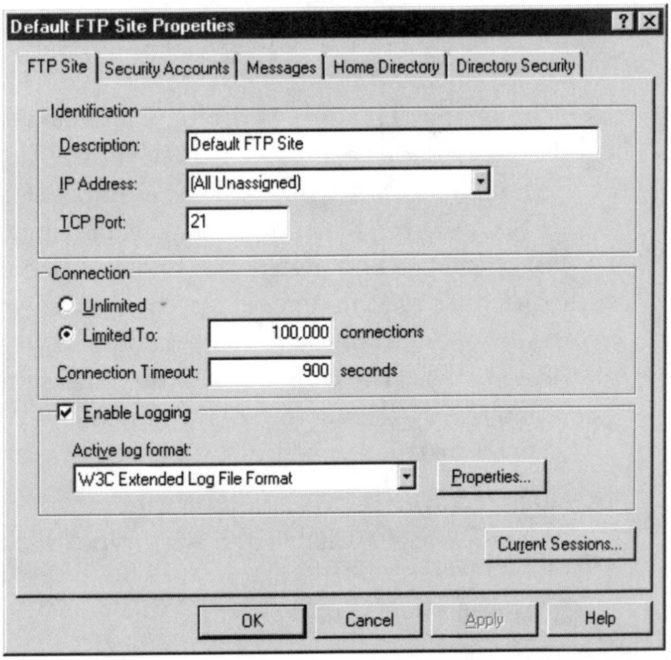

**Figure 3-1.** FTP Site properties

http://www.smartftp.com. This FTP client software has an Explorer-type interface that makes it as easy to use as performing file operations in the standard Windows interface.

## Connection Section

The Connection section of the FTP Site Properties page contains the following components:

▼ **Unlimited (Enabling)**   This selection allows a limitless number of simultaneous connections to the FTP server. Use this option if you have a server with a speedy network connection and plenty of power.

■ **Limited To**   This option allows you to set the maximum number of simultaneous connections to the FTP server. This option is useful if the server is limited in resources such as network speed and processor power. Limited To actually is the default selection for the IIS 5.0 installation. The default connection value is 100,000.

■ **Connection Timeout**   Each time a person connects to the FTP server, this counts as a connection. This connection stays live until the user terminates it. Setting the Connection Timeout option can keep the number of available connections active when users connect and then forget to disconnect. After the period of seconds specified has elapsed, the inactive connection will be dropped. At times, FTP connections also can close uncleanly, leaving the active connection in use. This setting provides fault tolerance by closing the connection after a period of time. The default installation setting is 900 seconds.

▲ **Enable Logging**   This section configures whether logging for the FTP site is available and what type of logging file format is used. The available active log formats are discussed in the following sections.

## Microsoft IIS Log Format

The Microsoft IIS log format is a file that uses standard ASCII text. These files can be opened in any file editor that can read text files such as Notepad and WordPad, both included with Windows 2000. While the Microsoft IIS log format is selected in the drop-down box, click the Properties button to customize the log file options. These options include how often the log file should be cleared, and the location and name of the log file. The Microsoft IIS log format file is not as customizable as the W3C Extended format. For most organizations, this log format will suffice for the amount of information that is stored.

## W3C Extended Log File Format (Default)

The W3C Extended Log File Format is similar to the Microsoft IIS log format file in that the format is ASCII text, but it is highly customizable in the amount of information that can be logged. With this log format selected in the drop-down box, the Properties button displays the standard General Properties tab for setting a new log creation period and log file location, but it includes an additional property sheet called *Extended Properties*. This extended logging allows retrieval of numerous items that are not available for the Microsoft IIS log file format.

Items such as the user name of the connection, the total number of bytes sent and received, and the protocol version used in the connection can give you a wealth of information about the FTP server's availability, responsiveness, capability, and overall use. This type of logging is useful to help determine when you should plan to upgrade the server based on the increase of use. It can even be used to play "big brother" with the individuals attaching to use the FTP services.

## ODBC Logging

ODBC logging is available only with Windows 2000 Server. This log file format is a fixed layout that is logged to a database such as Microsoft SQL Server. The Properties sheet of this log file format, shown in Figure 3-2, allows the manual configuration of the specific database properties. These properties are crucial for successful connectivity to an external database.

In addition to the Identification, Connection, and Enable Logging sections on the FTP Site Property sheet, a Current Sessions button is available. Clicking this button brings up a new window that displays all the live user connections to the FTP site. In addition to showing the user's names that are connected, it depicts the amount of time the user has owned the connection. If a user has been connected longer than normal or you suspect a connection has not closed out properly, you can highlight individual connections and click Disconnect. This action terminates the specific user connection. To close down all live connections, click Disconnect All. This button can be used in instances in which the FTP service must be stopped for maintenance or the server itself must be rebooted.

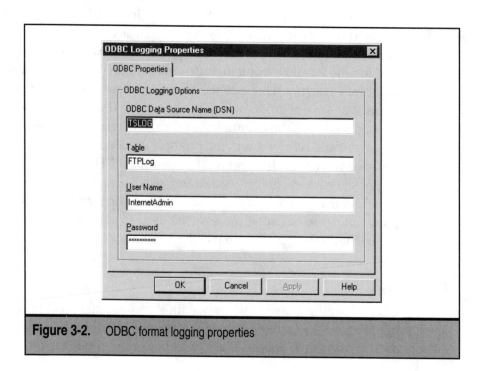

**Figure 3-2.**   ODBC format logging properties

# SECURITY ACCOUNTS PROPERTY SHEET

The Security Accounts property sheet, shown in Figure 3-3, of the default FTP properties allows you to set and configure the security for the FTP site. There are two specific sections for organizing the FTP security. These are discussed in the following sections.

## Allow Anonymous Connections Section

The Allow Anonymous Connections check box is enabled by default. This allows users to connect automatically to the FTP site using a specific user name and password that is controlled by the Windows 2000 Active Directory. By default, IIS 5.0 creates an Internet account and password

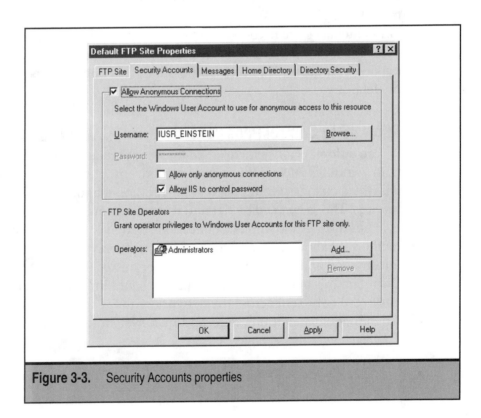

**Figure 3-3.**　Security Accounts properties

that is used by all of the IIS services. This account begins with IUSR_ and ends with the name of the Windows 2000 Server. This connection account can be changed to another account that you create manually or one that is already present in the Active Directory. Clicking the Browse button opens a window that displays a list of available Active Directory user accounts that can be selected to replace the default Internet account.

Two other options are available for configuring the Allow Anonymous Connections section: Allow Only Anonymous Connections and Allow IIS to Control Password, both of which are discussed next.

## Allow Only Anonymous Connections

When this check box is enabled, only anonymous connections can be made to the FTP site. An administrator can access the FTP site if changes or maintenance are necessary. When this option is enabled, even the administrator would be forced to use the anonymous connection, making administrative access impossible. This option is disabled by default.

## Allow IIS to Control Password

IIS can automatically synchronize the anonymous password settings with Windows 2000. If this is not enabled, any Internet account and password changes would need to be updated manually in all the IIS services. This is enabled by default; it is not recommended to disable it.

The Allow Anonymous Connections option is the most secure method for allowing access to the FTP site. It encrypts the account information and password when the user makes the connection. Disabling this method causes the user account information and password to be sent across the network without any data encryption. An individual attempting to compromise system security could easily use a protocol analyzer to retrieve user passwords and gain access to the entire system using the user's information. IIS will warn you if you try to disable this option.

## FTP Site Operators Section

The FTP Site Operators section allows you to grant administrative access to specific groups or users in the Windows 2000 Active Directory. This administrative access gives limited privileges on the specific FTP site. When multiple FTP sites are created, each site's administrative operators can be configured separately. This feature allows the FTP site and service management to be offloaded to certain individuals while others concentrate on overall IIS site management or other specific service administration.

Clicking the Add button inserts new FTP Site Operators; highlighting a listed account and clicking the Remove button revokes the rights.

# MESSAGES PROPERTY SHEET

The Messages property sheet (see Figure 3-4) allows customization of the messages that are displayed to the user when they utilize the FTP site. The Welcome message is displayed to the user when he or she initiates a successful connection to the FTP server. You can use this particular field to include site policies such as allowed connection time or specific connection information, or even to display proposed FTP outages for maintenance.

The Exit message displays text to the user as he or she disconnects from the FTP site, and the Maximum Connections message shows a custom message should the site exceed the allowed number of connections.

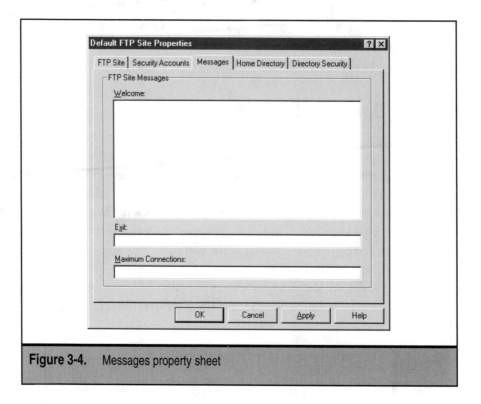

**Figure 3-4.** Messages property sheet

# HOME DIRECTORY PROPERTY SHEET

The Home Directory property sheet (see Figure 3-5) allows customization of the specific location of the FTP site. The FTP site is contained in a directory structure either on the local server or on a server share across the network. This information can be modified or verified on this property sheet. With A Directory Located On This Computer selected, the Local Path option in the FTP Site Directory section specifies a local drive letter and directory location.

When A Share Located On Another Computer is chosen, the FTP Site Directory section must contain a location to a share on another server in the common Universal Naming Convention (UNC) format: \\<servername>\<sharename>. When this option is selected, a Connect As button becomes available and a user account and password with administrative authorization to the share must be entered.

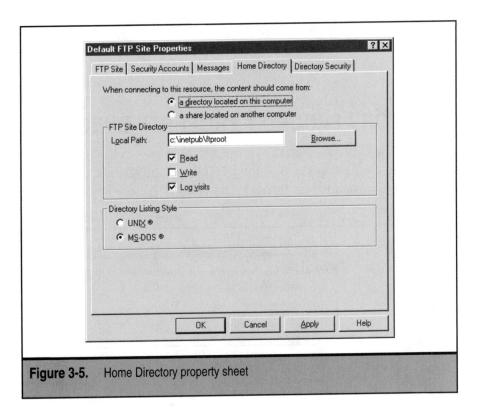

**Figure 3-5.**    Home Directory property sheet

No matter which Home Directory location is chosen, you can assign specific directory rights to the FTP directory. The Read right enables those connecting to the FTP directory to view the files that are listed there. Write access permits the connected user to upload files to the directory.

Also, part of the Home Directory property sheet provides the capability to customize how the FTP directory is displayed to the connected user. The Directory Listing Style section has two options: UNIX and MS-DOS. The difference between these formats is minimal, but should be set according to your organization's preferences or policies.

▼  **UNIX Directory Listing Style**    The UNIX directory listing style displays year dates in a four-digit format.

▲ **MS-DOS Directory Listing Style**   The MS-DOS directory
listing style displays the year dates in a two-digit format.
This is the default selection.

# DIRECTORY SECURITY PROPERTY SHEET

The Directory Security property sheet shown in Figure 3-6 allows you
to configure access to the FTP site by the specific computer's TCP/IP
network address through the TCP/IP Access Restrictions section.

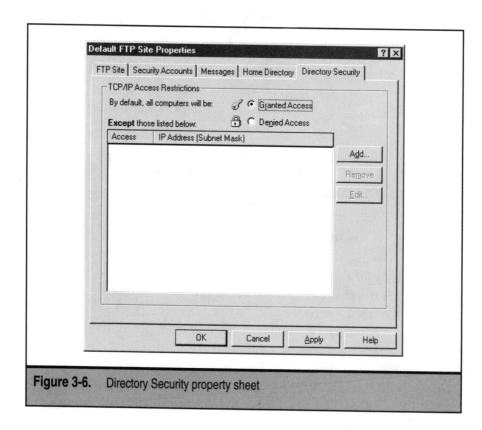

**Figure 3-6.**   Directory Security property sheet

Individual computers or entire groups can be blocked or granted access to the FTP directory. Using the TCP/IP addresses of resources on the network, either a single IP address or a group of IP addresses can be granted or denied access to the FTP site.

By providing this granular security for the FTP directory, you can exclusively limit the type of people that have access by identification or by location. When networks are rolled out across organizations, each different segment (or location) of the network receives a TCP/IP subnet address range. Each IP address in the subnet range is assigned to a device in the network of that segment. This helps to better organize and identify all of the available resources attached to the company's network. If each segment of the network possesses its own FTP site, you might want to deny access to the local FTP directory by excluding access to that specific subnet. The Directory Security property sheet allows you to provide for this type of exclusion.

# CHAPTER 4

## WWW Service Reference

The World Wide Web Server service has 10 property sheets to fully customize either the Default Web Site or any other site you install on the IIS 5.0 server. Use this chapter as a full reference for modifying WWW service properties and to understand the options that are available for configuration, performance tuning, and security.

## WEB SITE PROPERTY SHEET

The Web Site property sheet (see Figure 4-1) has three sections with which to familiarize yourself: Web Site Identification, Connections, and Enable Logging. Configuring the options on this sheet allows you to customize the general functions of the IIS 5.0 Web site.

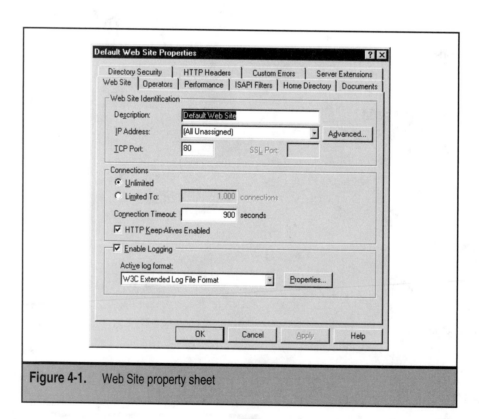

**Figure 4-1.** Web Site property sheet

# Web Site Identification Section

The following items are available for configuration in the Web Site Identification section of the Web Site Property sheet:

- ▼ **Description**   This field can accept any name you want to identify the Web server. This name is for identification and organizational purposes and is the Web site name that appears in the tree view of the IIS snap-in.

- ■ **IP Address**   Any IP addresses that have been defined for use in the Network Properties of the server will be available for selection. Selecting an IP address from the drop-down menu will assign that selection to the default Web site. This IP address will be used for connection to the server. Because IIS 5.0 has the capability to host multiple Web sites with multiple addresses and ports, the Advanced button allows you to configure the IP address, TCP port, and Host Header name for each site on the server. In the Advanced Multiple Web Site Configuration window you can add, remove, and edit any Web identities on the IIS server.

**NOTE:**   Each Web site on the IIS server must have some characteristic that sets it apart from the others—a unique combination of identification characteristics. When you configure the IP address, TCP port, and host header name for each Web site, at least one of the characteristics has to be different from the other Web sites on the server.

- ■ **TCP Port**   The default TCP port is 80. This is a *de facto* standard port across the industry for Web services. You can modify this number to any port number you like, but the client computer must be able to confirm that this Web server advertises the specific port. If you change this port number, Internet browsers will need to append the new port number to the Web site address to connect successfully. For example, if you change the port number to 70, a Web site address of http://*myserver* would need to change to http://*myserver*:70 when the site is accessed from an Internet browser. This field must contain a port number; do not leave it blank.

▲ **SSL Port**   IIS 5.0 supports the Secure Sockets Layer (SSL) port for connection to the Web site. SSL is a protocol that supplies secure data communication through data encryption and decryption. It uses RSA public-key encryption for specific TCP/IP ports. It is intended for handling commerce payments. SSL is a general-purpose encryption standard. SSL also can be used for Web applications requiring a secure link, such as e-commerce applications, or for controlling access to Web-based subscription services. The default SSL port number is 443. This is a general standard across the Internet; so, as with the TCP port for Web sites, changing this port number will generate more administration by forcing the user of the Internet browser to know the new port number to connect.

**NOTE:**   The RSA acronym derives from the last names of the inventors of the technology: Rivest, Shamir, and Adleman.

## Connections Section

The Connections section of the Web Site property page contains the following components:

▼ **Unlimited**   Enabling the Unlimited selection allows a limitless number of simultaneous connections to the IIS Web server. Use this option if you have a server with a speedy network connection and ample power. Because of the first-rate way IIS handles web connections, the Unlimited option is the default for the IIS installation.

■ **Limited To**   The Limited To option allows you to set the maximum number of simultaneous connections to the Web server. This option is useful if the server is limited in resources such as network speed and processor power. Because IIS provides superior Web performance, you might never need to limit the amount of connections to the Web site.

▲ **Connection Timeout**   Each time a person connects to the Web server, this counts as a connection. This connection stays live until the user terminates it. Setting the Connection Timeout option can keep the number of available connections active when users connect and then forget to disconnect. After the period of seconds specified has elapsed, the inactive connection will be dropped. At times, Web connections close uncleanly, leaving the active connection in use. This setting provides fault tolerance by closing the connection after a period of time. The default installation setting is 900 seconds.

## Enable Logging Section

The Enable Logging section configures whether logging for the Web site is available and what type of logging file format is used. The Active Log formats available are listed here:

▼ **Microsoft IIS Log Format**   The Microsoft IIS log format is a file that uses standard ASCII text. These files can be opened in any file editor that can read text files such as Notepad and WordPad, which are included with Windows 2000. While the Microsoft IIS log format is selected in the drop-down box, you click the Properties button to customize the log file options. These options include how often the log file should be cleared, and the location and name of the log file. The Microsoft IIS log format file is not as customizable as the W3C Extended format. For most organizations, this log format will suffice for the amount of information that is stored.

■ **NCSA Common Log Format**   NCSA common log format is a fixed (non-customizable) ASCII format, available for Web sites but not for FTP sites. It records basic information about user requests such as remote host name, user name, date, time, request type, HTTP status code, and the number of bytes received by the server. Items are separated by spaces; time is recorded as local time.

■ **W3C Extended Log File Format (Default)** The W3C Extended Log File Format is similar to the Microsoft IIS log format file in that the format is ASCII text, but it is highly customizable in the amount of information that can be logged. With this log format selected in the drop-down box, the Properties button displays the standard General Properties tab for setting a new log creation period and log file location, but it also includes an additional properties sheet called *Extended Properties.* This extended logging allows retrieval of numerous items that are not available for the Microsoft IIS log file format. Items such as the user name of the connection, the total number of bytes sent and received, and the protocol version used in the connection can supply you with a wealth of information about the Web server's availability, responsiveness, capability, and overall use.

▲ **ODBC Logging** ODBC logging is available only with Windows 2000 Server. This log file format is a fixed layout that is logged to a database, such as Microsoft SQL Server. The properties sheet of this log file format allows the manual configuration of the specific database properties. These properties are crucial for successful connectivity to an external database.

*TIP:* You can use the Log File Conversion utility (convlog.exe) to convert your Web server's log files to NCSA Common log file format. The converter also can replace IP addresses with DNS names during conversion of Microsoft IIS and Extended format log files to NCSA format, or it can be used to replace IP addresses with DNS names inside an NCSA log file. The convlog.exe file can be found in the C:\WINNT\SYSTEM32 directory.

The Log File Conversion utility is a command-line tool with the following format:

```
Usage: convlog [options] LogFile
```

It has numerous options available to easily manage how the log file is converted.

```
Options:
-i<i|n|e> = input logfile type
    i - MS Internet Standard Log File Format
    n - NCSA Common Log File format
    e - W3C Extended Log File Format
-t <ncsa[:GMTOffset] | none> default is ncsa
-o <output directory> default = current directory
-x save non-www entries to a .dmp logfile
-d = convert IP addresses to DNS
-l<0|1|2> = Date locale format for MS Internet Standard
    0 - MM/DD/YY (default e.g. US)
    1 - YY/MM/DD (e.g. Japan)
    2 - DD.MM.YY (e.g. Germany)
Examples:
convlog -ii in*.log -d -t ncsa:+0800
convlog -in ncsa*.log -d
convlog -ii jra*.log -t none
```

# OPERATORS PROPERTY SHEET

This administrative access gives limited privileges on the specific Web site. When multiple Web sites are created, each site's administrative operators can be set separately. The Operators property sheet, shown in Figure 4-2, allows you to grant administrative access to specific groups or users in the Windows 2000 Active Directory.

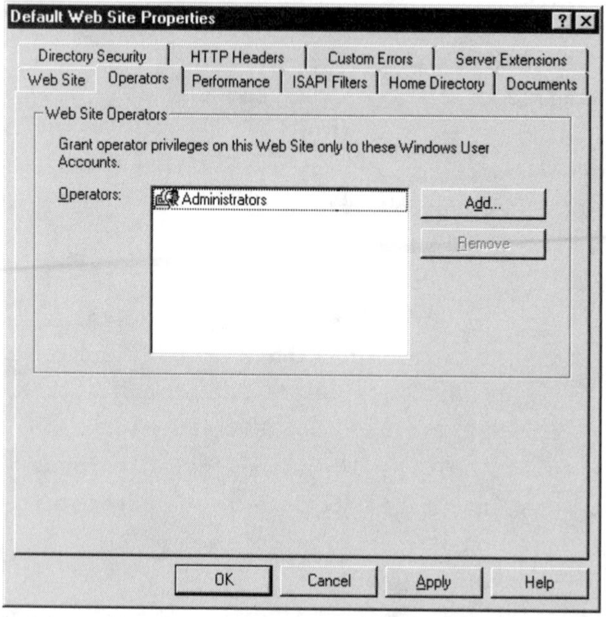

Figure 4-2.    Operators property sheet

Clicking the Add button inserts new Web site Operators.
Highlighting a listed account and then clicking the Remove button
revokes the rights for an operator already assigned to the list. By
default, the Administrators group that is local to the IIS server is
granted the Operator right.

**TIP:**   When permitting individuals or groups to administer the Web site,
following a few guidelines will help keep your Web site secure:

▼  Grant Administrator privileges only to trusted individuals.

■  Periodically change the Administrator account password.

■  Never run untrusted programs while logged on as Administrator.

▲  Use SSL security features when administering your Web server remotely.

# Performance Property Sheet

The Performance property sheet (see Figure 4-3) allows you to control how well the IIS Web server performs. As the Web site receives more connections, the overall server performance can be regulated to accommodate the increase in requests. There are three sections on this property page of which you should be aware.

## Performance Tuning Section

The Performance Tuning section allows you to adjust the Web server's performance based on the number of hits per day. The slider bar makes it easy to quickly modify the expected hits per day. There are three options for the slider bar: Fewer than 10,000, Fewer than 100,000, and More than 100,000. Based on the selection of one of these settings, IIS will automatically tune the server's performance.

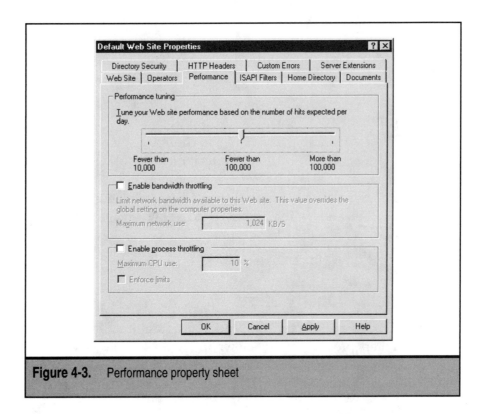

**Figure 4-3.**   Performance property sheet

You might think that bumping the slider bar up to More than 100,000 and forgetting about it would give your Web site the best performance possible, but that's not necessarily true. The Windows 2000 server actually performs much more in the background than just supplying IIS services. Additionally, estimating the hits per day well above the actual number wastes server memory and reduces the overall server performance. Using the server log files, you can calculate the estimated number of hits for the Web site; you then should place the slider bar only slightly higher than the actual number of connections.

### Enable Bandwidth Throttling Section

Bandwidth throttling allows you to control the maximum amount of bandwidth dedicated to Internet traffic on the IIS server. This feature is useful if there are other services (such as e-mail) sharing the server over a busy link. You can set the maximum network use rate by entering a number in the KB/S (kilobytes per second) field. If you have performed any other bandwidth management for the server where IIS resides, the option on this property sheet overrides all modifications.

### Enable Process Throttling Section

Process throttling allows you to configure, by percentage, the amount of server CPU (processor) utilization available to the individual Web sites. There also is an Enforce Limits check box in this section that forces the server to limit the processor utilization. If this box is not checked and the maximum CPU use percentage is exceeded, the occurrence will be logged only in the server's Event Log; no physical throttling will occur.

## ISAPI Filters Property Sheet

The Internet Server Application Programming Interface (ISAPI) Filters property sheet, shown in Figure 4-4, allows you to create your own processes based on the IIS server events. ISAPI filters are

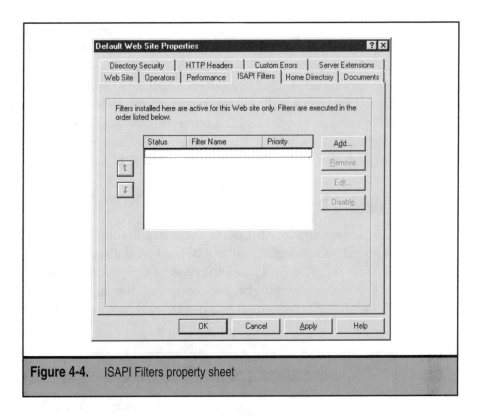

**Figure 4-4.**    ISAPI Filters property sheet

programs that respond when the Web server receives an HTTP request. You can associate an ISAPI filter with a specific Web server event. The filter is notified every time its associated event occurs. For example, a filter could be notified when a read or write event on the IIS server occurs and then, based on the filter's responsibility, the data is encrypted and returned to the client.

ISAPI filters are represented in the form of dynamic link library (DLL) files. In general, DLL files are a library of functions that are created using a development tool such as the Visual Basic or C++ programming languages. For more information on creating DLL files as ISAPI filters, search Microsoft's Developer Network (MSDN) Web site at http://msdn.microsoft.com.

The Add button on this property sheet allows you to insert a new ISAPI filter. When adding a new filter, you can name it anything you want and choose to create the filter as a file in the local file system. Alternatively, using the other available command buttons, you can remove any filters in the list, edit the filter properties, and temporarily disable any filter. In addition to the general management of the ISAPI filters, you also can change the order in which they are executed by highlighting a specific filter and clicking the up and down arrows. The filter at the top of the list is executed first, followed by the others on the list in consecutive, descending order. Reorganizing the list of filters into a logical order is useful should a specific function need to be performed before another filter is capable of completing its request.

## Home Directory Property Sheet

The Home Directory property sheet (see Figure 4-5) allows modification and management of the home directory for the specific IIS Web site. It allows customization of the specific location of the Web site and which rights the connected user has to the directory. The Web site is contained in a directory structure either on the local

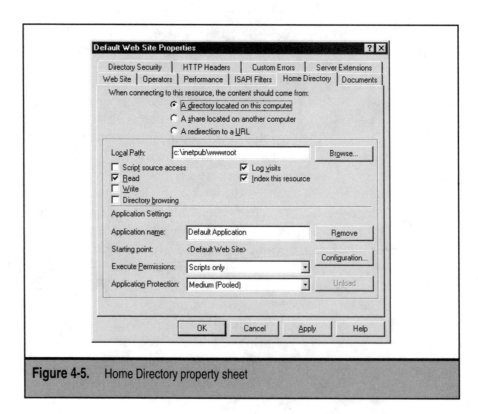

**Figure 4-5.**    Home Directory property sheet

server, on a server share across the network, or on a redirected URL. The information can be modified or verified on this property sheet.

With A Directory Located On This Computer selected, the Local Path option specifies a local drive letter and directory location. When A Share Located On Another Computer is chosen, the FTP Site Directory section must contain a location to a share on another server in the common Universal Naming Convention (UNC) format: \\ *<servername>\<sharename>*. When this option is selected, a Connect As button becomes available and a user account and password with administrative authorization to the share must be entered.

When either A Directory Located On This Computer or A Share Located On Another Computer is selected, the rights that can be assigned to the connecting user are the same. These rights include Script Source Access, Read, Write, and Directory Browsing.

## Script Source Access

Enabling this right gives users access to the source code of the scripts run on the Web site from within the home directory. Either the read or write (or both) rights must be selected for the script source access right to be available.

## Read

This right allows the user to read or download files or directories under the home directory. The read right is enabled by default for all Web sites.

## Write

Choosing to give users write access to the home directory allows them to upload files to the enabled directory.

## Directory Browsing

Because the home directory actually is a location within a file structure, enabling directory browsing permits the connected user to see the directory list. This directory listing is made available for display in a Web page format, viewable through the Internet browser.

## Log Visits

Choosing this option causes IIS to record all visits to this home directory in a log file. Note that even if this option is selected, logging for the entire Web site must be turned on or choosing to log this directory will be moot. This option is enabled by default.

## Index This Resource

Windows 2000 includes an indexing service that retrieves information on the files installed on the server and stores the list as a full-text index. This expedites any searches made to find files or folders on the server. IIS 5.0 can utilize this indexing service, minimizing the time needed to find files when searching the home directory. This option is enabled by default.

In addition to pointing the home directory location to a local directory or a network share, you also can redirect connections to the home directory to another location. This is particularly useful if you don't want connected users to have access to a specific directory underneath the home directory or if you want to send visitors to a Web page that indicates the current directory is presently under maintenance. The redirection method has three options that become available only when it is selected:

▼ **Exact URL Entered Above**   If you choose this option, you can enter the Web site address in the Redirect To field and the visitor will be whisked away to the alternate Web site.

■ **Directory Below This One**   This option assumes that you want visitors to access this home directory but you want their actual stop to be a directory underneath the main directory. When this option is selected, you need to enter only a slash and the subdirectory name (/*mysubdirectory*) in the Redirect To line. The home directory's location information is assumed and does not need to be entered.

▲ **Permanent Redirection for This Resource**   Using this option causes a message to be displayed to the visitor: |301 Permanent Redirect|. This message is a good indication to the connecting user that he or she should bookmark the new page, as the old page will be removed at some point.

## Application Settings Section

The Application Settings section is available with only A Directory Located On This Computer and A Share Located On Another Computer location options. If you have developed a Web-based application that resides in this directory structure, you can configure the settings for the application in this section. The Application Settings options include the following:

**Application Name**   With this field you can assign any name to the Web application that you want.

**Starting Point**   Although this is not an editable field, the starting point information gives you a quick reference to the specific directory for which you are making the modifications.

**Execute Permissions**   There are three types of execute permissions that can be assigned to the Web application directory: None, Scripts Only, and Scripts and Executables. The None option, of course, makes sure that nothing can be run from the application directory. This option is useful for keeping script execution from being performed while the application is being built or development modifications are being made. The Scripts Only option (the default) identifies that only scripts, such as ASP documents, can be run from the application directory. The Scripts and Executables option enables the connected user to run any type of file designated for execution. This includes standard program and utility files with an .EXE file extension.

**Application Protection**   Application protection is a safeguard against running a piece of software in the directory that could cause problems with the IIS server. By enabling some form of application protection you can ensure that other applications do not make the Web server unavailable or cause it to lock up. There are three protection grades from which you can choose: low (IIS process), medium (pooled), and high (isolated). The low level allows applications to run in the same memory space as the IIS server itself. If an application is troublesome or has not been tested properly, it has the potential to halt the IIS services with this option selected.

The medium grade (the default) places the Web application in an area of memory where other applications run. With this option selected, should the specific application from this directory fail, all applications running in the same memory space will fail but the IIS services are protected.

The high level causes this directory's application to run in its own memory space, protecting both the other running applications and the IIS server. If you have enough physical memory in the server, you can run each application in its own process.

## Documents Property Sheet

There are two specific sections on the Documents property sheet (see Figure 4-6): the Enable Default Document section and Enable Document Footer section. Read Sthrough the following sections to help understand what options are available for configuration of these components.

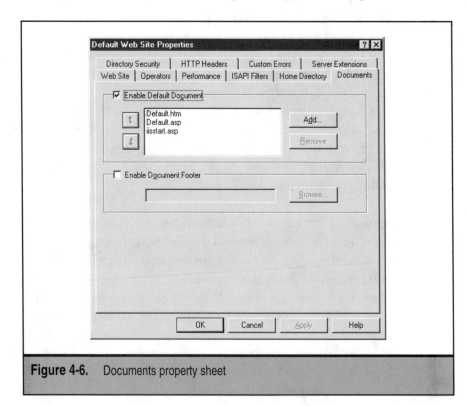

**Figure 4-6.** Documents property sheet

## Enable Default Document Section

By enabling a default document in IIS, you actually are identifying the first page that you want the connecting user to see when accessing the Web site. Most Web sites use Default.htm, Default.asp, or Index.htm. You can use this section to add any document name and to change the order in which the Internet browser searches for the specific pages. For example, if you decide that the initial page should be *MyCompanyHomePage*.htm, you would insert that into the list using the Add button and move it to the top of the list using the Up and Down arrow buttons. If you want to make a specific page name unavailable to the Internet browser, you would highlight the name in the list and click the Remove button.

Changing the default document is particularly useful if you want to develop a new start page offline, insert it into the directory, and enable it when it is operational. This allows you to work on the start page without interference from connecting users; then make it available upon completion.

## Enable Document Footer Section

By enabling a document footer, a HTML-formatted footer is inserted into every page within the directory structure. You can create the footer using any method of HTML page generation and then tell IIS where the document exists on the local server by clicking the Browse button. Footers provide functionality and a uniform look for your Web site documents; even though the content on each page is different, the footer would enable the connected user to quickly determine that the information is part of the overall site content. You can include brief copyright information or insert a company logo.

# Directory Security Property Sheet

The Directory Security property sheet shown in Figure 4-7 allows you to configure control on the particular directory structure associated with the current Web site.

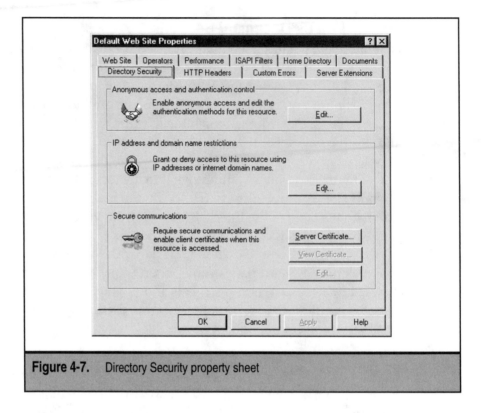

**Figure 4-7.**    Directory Security property sheet

## Anonymous Access and Authentication Control Section

This section of the Directory Security property sheet enables you to configure the way in which connecting users gain authentication to the Web site directory. Clicking the Edit button and modifying the Authentication Methods on the new configuration screen controls the directory security. As shown in Figure 4-8, several methods can be enabled and adapted for user authentication; they are described next.

## Anonymous Access

Opting for anonymous access to the Web site directory allows users to connect automatically using a specific user name and password, which are controlled by the Windows 2000 Active Directory. Clicking the Edit button displays the Anonymous User Account modification screen. By default, IIS 5.0 creates an Internet account and password that is used by all of the IIS services. This account begins with IUSR_ and ends with the name of the Windows 2000 Server. This connection

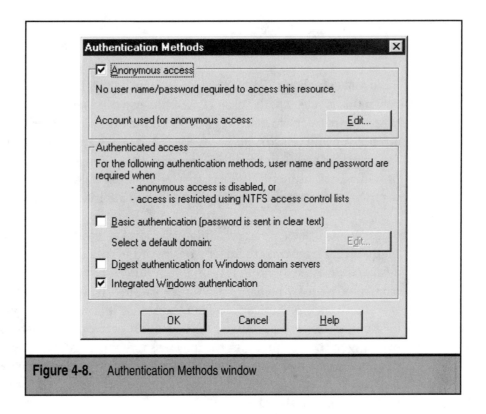

**Figure 4-8.**   Authentication Methods window

account can be changed to another account that you create manually or one that is already present in the Active Directory. Clicking the Browse button opens a window that displays a list of available active directory user accounts that can be selected to replace the default Internet account. IIS can automatically synchronize the anonymous password settings with Windows 2000 if the Allow IIS to Control Password is enabled. If this is not enabled, any Internet account and password changes would need to be updated manually in all of the IIS services. Allow IIS to Control Password is enabled by default; and it is not recommended to disable it.

## Authenticated Access

The Authenticated Access method allows even tighter security for the Web site's directory resources. This section forces the connecting user to enter an actual user name and password when Anonymous Access is disabled and directory security has been set at the file and directory structure level through Windows 2000 Server itself. There are three types of methods that can be employed: Basic Authentication, Digest Authentication, and Integrated Windows Authentication.

**Basic Authentication**   This is the lowest security level method available. When this is selected, the user's entered password is sent as clear text across the network to gain access. Should the Web site come under attack from any unscrupulous invaders, the user's password could easily be purloined and applied to access the entire network. IIS provides basic authentication as an available option for Web site security but warns against using it when you attempt to select it.

**Digest Authentication**   Digest authentication is an authentication method that transmits the user's password across the network using a *hash value*. A hash value is a small amount of binary data derived from a message by using a hashing algorithm. The hashing procedure is a one way communication. There is no feasible way of deriving the original message, or even any of its properties, from the hash value, even given the hashing algorithm. The same message will always produce the same hash value when passed through the same hashing algorithm. Messages differing by even one character can produce very different hash values.

Microsoft Internet Explorer version 5 is the only browser that currently supports Digest authentication, which works only for domains with a Windows 2000 domain controller. The domain controller must have a plain-text copy of the passwords being used because it must perform a hashing operation and compare the results with the hash sent by the browser. Because the domain controller has plain-text copies of all the passwords, it should be kept secure from physical or network attacks.

**Integrated Windows Authentication**   Integrated Windows Authentication perhaps is the most secure method for Authenticated access, providing that you have a Windows 2000 network and that the connection to the Web site will never pass through a proxy server or firewall. The integrated security provides you the capability to prompt the connecting user for the Windows 2000 domain user name and password.

For individuals who work for the company where the Web site is located, this method is as secure as the user's password. Granted, users generally cannot be relied on for creating secure passwords (passwords usually take the form of the nearest kin, a family pet, or a favorite television show) but this choice provides the top, most secure, and most uncomplicated method for intranets.

## IP Address and Domain Name Restrictions Section

The IP Address and Domain Name Restrictions section enables you to configure access to the Web site by the specific computer's TCP/IP network address or by the Internet domain name. You probably are already familiar with Internet domain names. Internet domain names describe the source location of the visiting user. For example, if someone works for Baker's Goods, his or her domain name might be bakersgood.com. If you are a competing goods services company, you might want to block the competition from seeing your weekly specials, or finding out that you will be closed for three weeks because of a rat infestation.

Individual computers or entire groups can be blocked or granted access to the Web directory using this method of restriction. Using the TCP/IP addresses of resources on the network, either a single IP address or a group of IP addresses can be granted or denied access to the Web site. You can also enter the complete Internet domain name of the client group. Clicking the Edit button displays the Restrictions window where the inclusions and exclusions can be set.

## Secure Communications Section

The Secure Communications section allows you to assign a secure server certificate to the Web site. Part of the Windows 2000 Server services, a server certificate is an encrypted file containing server identification information, which is used to verify the identity. This section cannot be configured until a server certificate has been created using the Certificate Wizard. Clicking the Server Certificate button initiates the Certificate Wizard by displaying the wizard process screen, shown in Figure 4-9.

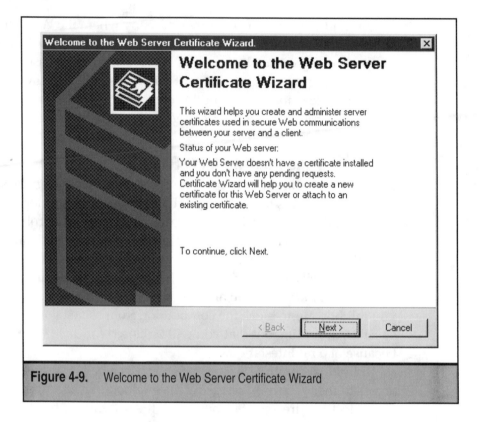

**Figure 4-9.** Welcome to the Web Server Certificate Wizard

During the IIS Certificate Wizard process, you can choose to create a brand-new certificate, assign a certificate that has been created before, or import a certificate from a backup. There are two ways to obtain a server certificate:

▼ You can issue your own server certificate.

▲ You can submit a request for a server certificate to an online certificate authority.

If you choose to issue your own server certificate, there must be a certificate authority installed on a server in the network. Windows 2000 Server provides this component as an option during its installation. It also can be installed at a later time. When a certificate authority is available on the network, the wizard process will automatically locate this service for you and immediately assign the newly created certificate to the IIS server. For more information on installing the certificate services for Windows 2000, see the Windows 2000 Server documentation. Another good reference for the Windows 2000 certificate services is *Windows 2000: The Complete Reference* (from Osborne/McGraw-Hill, by Kathy Ivens and Kenton Gardinier, ISBN: 0072119209).

Online certificate authorities provide a service of creating and issuing server certificates. These certificates serve as a common identifier for your organization on the Internet. There are several providers of certificates. They can be found by visiting the Microsoft BackOffice Security Partner Web site at http://backoffice.microsoft.com/securitypartners/. This Web site also keeps track of the latest security technologies, describes how Microsoft products use secure communications in each of their products, and contains up-to-the-minute news in the world of Internet security. The site is an excellent source of information about Internet security.

Before deciding on a specific certificate authority, there are a few considerations to take into account:

▼ Will the certification authority be able to issue you a certificate that is compatible with all browsers used to access your server?

■ Is the certification authority a recognized and trusted entity?

■ How will the certification authority provide verification of your identity?

■ Does the authority have a system for receiving online certificate requests, such as requests generated by the Web Server Certificate Wizard?

■ How much will the certificate cost initially and for renewal or other services?

▲ Is the certification authority familiar with your organization or company's business interests?

Once you have a server certificate, the Secure Communications section can be configured using the Edit button. You also can peruse the information assigned to the certificate by clicking the View Certificate button. Applying the certificate to the IIS Web site allows access to the full range of SSL security (described earlier in this section).

## HTTP Headers Property Sheet

Similar to the footers described previously in this section, the Web site can be configured to include (HTTP) headers. These headers are a bit different in that they generally are information that is embedded into the actual code of the Web page; hidden from the connected user's view. This property sheet, shown in Figure 4-10, allows you to configure and manage the HTTP header content. The property sheet has four distinct sections: Enable Content Expiration, Custom HTTP Headers, Content Rating, and MIME Map.

### Enable Content Expiration

By selecting Enable Content Expiration, you cause information on the Web page to seemingly disappear at a certain date and time. This is particularly convenient when content on the Web page pertains to

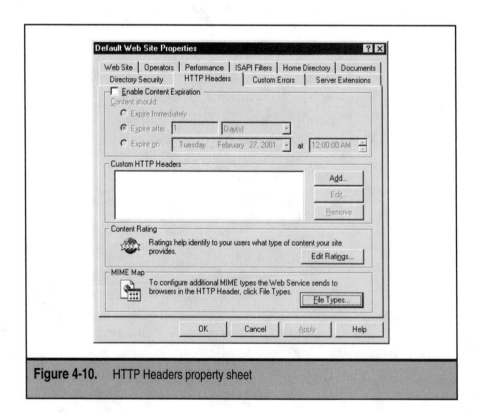

**Figure 4-10.**   HTTP Headers property sheet

sales offers that expire on a certain date, or event announcements whose time has passed. The available options are *Expire immediately*, meaning the content will be set to disappear when the setting is applied; *Expire after* a given minute, hour, or day; and *Expire on* a specific date and time selected on a calendar.

## Custom HTTP Headers

Employing this section, you can send custom HTTP headers to the connected Internet browser. To use this section, you need to have at least minimal experience coding using HTML (Hypertext Markup Language). For each added Custom HTTP Header, you must specify a header name and the header value (code). You insert a new HTTP Custom Header by clicking the Add button, modify any listed items by clicking the Edit button, and delete an item from the list by clicking the Remove button.

To get a preview of HTML code, the following example identifies the connected user. If it is the first time that the user has visited the Web site, he or she is routed to a registration page. If it is identified that the individual has visited before, a Welcome Back message is displayed. Take special notice of the format (the indentation) of the code.

```
<HTML>
  <BODY>
    .

    .
  <%
    If Request("CustomerStatus") = "" Then
      Response.Clear
      Server.Transfer("/CustomerInfo/Register.asp")
    Else
      Response.Write "Welcome back " & Request("FirstName") & "!"

          .

          .

    End If
  %>
  </BODY>
</HTML>
```

## Content Rating

You might already be familiar with Web site ratings. When you surf the Web, you see that many Web sites have ratings based on the content provided throughout the site. The Recreational Software Advisory Council (RSAC) has put together a set of standards for specific types of content that might be present on a Web page. There are four types of media content that are rated: violence, sex, nudity, and language. The standards are based on the work of Dr. Donald F. Roberts of Stanford University, who spent nearly 20 years of his life studying the effects of the media on the public.

Internet browsers have a ratings mechanism built into them that allow users to establish what type and how much of each of the four types of media content is tolerable to them while surfing the Internet. These built-in ratings systems actually read ratings information built into the header of each page that is opened in the Internet browser. IIS 5.0 includes the capacity to place custom rating header information into the Web site's pages, allowing the Internet browser to read this information and restrict or allow certain media content to display in the browser window. The interaction between the Web site's ratings header information and the Internet browser ratings mechanism keeps surfers safe from viewing offensive Web page content.

When you click the Edit Ratings button in the Content Rating section, a property sheet appears and gives you more information about the RSAC, allows you to visit its Web site (http://www.rsac. org/ratingsv01.html), or allows you to take an online quiz to help you decide which rating you should give the content represented on your Web site. In addition, the RSAC can be queried to rate the Web site for you.

The second tab on the configuration sheet for the content ratings, the Ratings tab, is where you construct the ratings for the Web site. Once ratings are enabled by clicking the Enable Ratings for this resource check box, the four media content types are available to set the rating using the sliding bar. Each media content type has five levels of ratings, shown in Table 4-1.

| Category | Level | Description |
|---|---|---|
| Violence | 0 | No violence |
| | 1 | Fighting |
| | 2 | Killing |
| | 3 | Killing with blood and gore |
| | 4 | Wanton and gratuitous violence |
| Sex | 0 | None |
| | 1 | Passionate kissing |
| | 2 | Clothed sexual touching |
| | 3 | Non-explicit sexual touching |
| | 4 | Explicit sexual activity |
| Nudity | 0 | None |
| | 1 | Revealing attire |
| | 2 | Partial nudity |
| | 3 | Frontal nudity |
| | 4 | Provocative frontal nudity |
| Language | 0 | Inoffensive slang |
| | 1 | Mild expletives |
| | 2 | Moderate expletives |
| | 3 | Obscene gestures |
| | 4 | Explicit or crude language |

**Table 4-1.**    Ratings Levels for the Four Media Content Types

In addition to providing the media content rating for the Web site, you can enter the e-mail address of the person that performed the ratings configuration. This is a courtesy action allowing the visiting user to have a point of reference should the ratings of the page not meet the individual's expectations.

As content is added, modified, and deleted from the dynamic Web site, it makes sense to put an expiration date on the initial media content rating. This throws up a red flag to remind the user that the Web site ratings should be reviewed periodically to identify any changes in the ratings levels for the Web site. Any time the content ratings are modified, the date is time stamped at the bottom of the Ratings tab for quick review. This provides a point of reference and helps control the different individuals who have administrator rights to the Web site.

**NOTE:**   One of the most common issues with the Content Advisor is when the user forgets the password tied to the ratings mechanism in the Internet browser. If a user needs support for a missing password, there is a utility available that can reset the ratings password in Microsoft Internet Explorer back to a blank value. You can download this utility from http://www.swynk. com/trent/articles/contentadvisor.asp.

## MIME Map

Multipurpose Internet Mail Extensions (MIME) mapping is a way of configuring Internet browsers to view files that are in multiple formats. MIME is an extension of the Internet mail protocol that enables sending any 8-bit–based e-mail messages. These are used to support extended character sets, Internet e-mail, voice mail, and facsimile images. Depending on what services the Web site provides, you can associate specific files with specific file extensions to work in the MIME format.

Setting these file types is similar to how the Windows operating system works with file type associations. For example, when you attempt to open a text file that is located in the computer's file system, the text file is automatically opened inside Notepad. This is because a file with a .txt file extension is associated with Notepad. By clicking the File Types button, you can associate specific file types with the MIME standard.

## Custom Errors Property Sheet

When a user surfs the Internet and a visited Web site has an unknown error, making it unavailable, a specific error message is displayed in the Internet browser window. One familiar and common error message is the |404 – Not found|. This basically means that the Web page the user is attempting to access is not available. The |404 – Not found| error message actually is a message from the Web server itself. There is a set of common HTTP error numbers that are associated with common server error events. The result, as in the cryptic 404 messages, is not necessarily a welcome sight to the visiting user and the lack of information about why the error occurred serves only to confuse the visitor.

Using the Custom Errors property sheet (see Figure 4-11) for IIS 5.0, you can customize these common error messages. Each common HTTP error number is assigned a type and an alternative Web page in the Web site that displays when the event occurs. You can create a custom error page that better describes the actual event to the user, which would keep the visitor from possibly thinking that the Web site no longer exists, and then assign the new Web page to the HTTP error number.

In IIS 5.0 there are two types assigned to the HTTP error number: File and Default. File means that when the error event occurs, the custom Web page is displayed. Default indicates that when the error event takes place, the default HTTP error message is displayed to the visitor. The most common HTTP error numbers can be modified using the Edit Properties button, and you can quickly select the server's communicated message by clicking the Set to Default button.

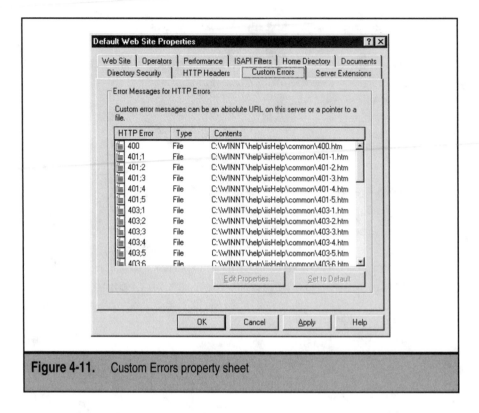

**Figure 4-11.** Custom Errors property sheet

## Server Extensions Property Sheet

The FrontPage server extensions are a group of files installed on the Web server to provide special Microsoft FrontPage functionality. Microsoft FrontPage is an application that provides a graphical interface for creating and modifying pages within the Web site. With FrontPage server extensions, administrators can view and manage a Web site in the graphical interface. Also, authors can create, edit, and post Web pages to the IIS server from a remote location. This property sheet applies specifically to the FrontPage server extensions and has three sections to learn for proper configuration for Microsoft FrontPage access. The Server Extensions property sheet (see Figure 4-12) provides for the installation, upgrade, and management of the FrontPage server extensions.

### Enable Authoring Section

This section allows authors to use FrontPage to access and modify the content of the selected Web site. Clear the Enable Authoring

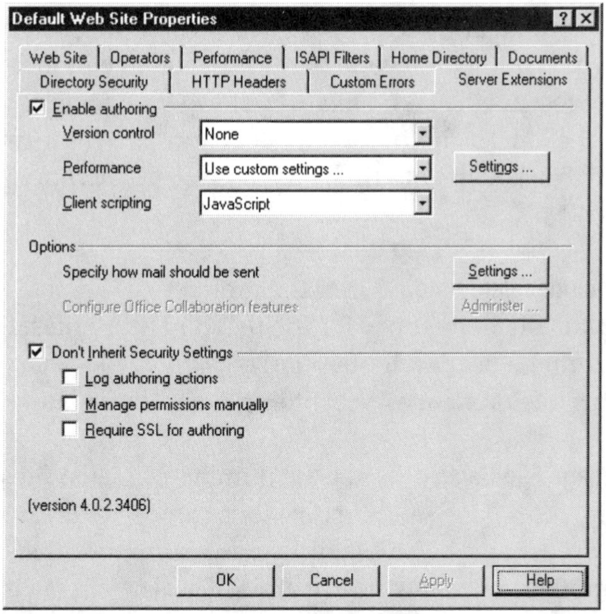

**Figure 4-12.**    Server Extensions property sheet

check box to prevent anyone from entering and altering the selected Web site. There are three options in this section for adjusting the authoring levels allowed for the Web site: version control, performance, and client scripting.

**Version Control**    Click the source control method you want to use to keep track of who is modifying Web content, identify any changes, and prevent one author's changes from erasing another's. You can choose either the built-in source control or an external program such as Microsoft Visual SourceSafe, which supplies more source-control features.

**Performance**    Click the page range that's closest to the actual number of pages in the selected Web site. The FrontPage server extensions will set aside a certain amount of cache, based on the page range you select. You also can choose a custom setting that displays a Performance window for manually configuring the performance options. It helps to understand the different caching settings if you want to perform manual tuning.

**In-Memory Document Cache**    Enter the maximum number of documents whose properties information, such as link maps and Web parameters, you want to keep active in memory. This number represents the last *number you specify* documents you worked with. For example, if you specify 4096, property information about the 4097th document will be released from memory. The default setting is 4096.

**Include File Cache**    Enter the number of files that you want to keep available in memory for inclusion in other files. For example, there might be header, footer, and copyright files that you want to include in some or all of a Web site's pages. The default setting is 16.

**Image File Cache**    Enter the number of image files in memory that the FrontPage server extensions can use to create layered pictures in Web pages. For example, one file might consist of a background; another of a navigation button. The server extensions can compose a picture by adding the background to a Web page and then overlaying the navigation button image. The picture can be composed faster if the component files are in a cache. The default setting is 16.

**Full-Text Search Index Size**    Enter the maximum amount of disk space (in megabytes) that can be allotted for storing a full-text search index. After this amount is reached, no other pages on the Web site can be indexed (unless you increase this number). The default setting is 1.

**Max Cached Document Size**    Enter the maximum size of a document (in kilobytes) that can be stored in memory. This size limit applies to all files, image files, and other files that might be stored in a cache. The default setting is 256.

**Client Scripting**    Select the scripting language, either JScript (JavaScript from Sun) or VBScript (Visual Basic Script from Microsoft) that should be generated in pages automatically by the FrontPage server extensions.

## Options Section

The Options section displays features that are specific to the FrontPage server extensions.

**Specify How Mail Should be Sent**    Clicking this item's Settings button displays the E-mail Settings dialog box, where you can specify how e-mail-based Web features, such as e-mail form handlers, are dealt with, and send e-mail to Web site visitors. You can use the dialog box to specify the Web server's e-mail address, contact e-mail address, mail server, mail-encoding scheme, and character set.

**Configure Office Collaboration Features**    Microsoft Office Web Server (OWS) must be installed on the IIS server for this feature to be available. Once it is installed, clicking the Administer button displays the Office Server Extensions administration Web pages, from which you can administer Office collaboration features such as workgroup discussions. For more information on the Office Server Extensions, see the Microsoft Office Resource Kit home page at http://www. microsoft.com/office/ork/default.htm.

## Don't Inherit Security Section

By default, each root web inherits the global security settings of the Web server. To override these settings for the selected Web site (and all its sub-pages), select this check box. Clear this check box if you want the selected root web to inherit its security settings from the global Web server settings. This section provides even more configuration options for the FrontPage server extensions security settings.

**Log Authoring Actions**    Checking this box enables the system to record the time an author's action was performed, the author's user name, the Web name, the remote host, and per-operation data and store this information in a log file in the _vti_log/Author.log file in the Web directory.

**Manage Permissions Manually**    Enabling this option disables the security setting functions of FrontPage server extensions administrative tools (such as the FrontPage MMC snap-in), so that those tools cannot be used to modify the security settings of the selected Web site. Leave this check box clear if you want to allow the security settings to be changed by using the FrontPage server extensions administrative tools.

**Require Secure Sockets Layer (SSL) for Authoring**  Selecting this option makes it possible for you to use SSL to authenticate prospective Web authors. This is recommended if you are currently using only basic authentication, which only lightly encrypts information (such as an author's user name and password) transmitted across the Web.

## Allow Authors to Upload Executables

This option permits authors to upload Common Gateway Interface (CGI) scripts or Active Server Pages (ASP) to the selected Web. Clear this check box if you want to prevent executables from being uploaded to the Web and avoid the risks associated with a possibly buggy script or a virus that's uploaded to the Web server.

**NOTE:**  If the FrontPage server extensions are not installed correctly or are out of date, the Server Extensions property sheet will tell you so. You can install, check, reset, remove, and upgrade the server extensions by right-clicking the Web site's name in the Internet Information Services MMC snap-in, choosing All Tasks in the pop-up menu, and choosing one of the FrontPage options from the list.

# CHAPTER 5

## SMTP Service Reference

The Simple Mail Transfer Protocol is a TCP/IP protocol for sending messages from one computer to another on a network. This protocol is used on the Internet to route e-mail. The SMTP Service has six property sheets to help configure the Internet e-mail service: General, Access, Messages, Delivery, LDAP Routing, and Security—each are discussed in this chapter.

**NOTE:** You can view the SMTP product documentation by typing **file:\\%systemroot%\help\mail.chm** in the Internet browser address box on the IIS 5.0 server.

## GENERAL PROPERTY SHEET

The General property sheet, shown in Figure 5-1, contains the common setup information for the SMTP service. This tabbed screen allows you to configure the general settings and includes the name of the server, the IP address, connection information, and log file settings.

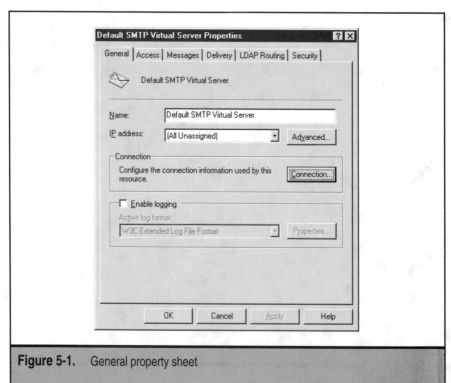

**Figure 5-1.**    General property sheet

# Name

This field can accept any name you like to identify the SMTP server. This name is for identification and organizational purposes and is the SMTP server name that appears in the tree view of the IIS snap-in.

# IP Address

Any IP addresses that have been defined for use in the network properties of the server will be available for selection. Selecting an IP address from the drop-down menu will assign that selection to the default SMTP site. This IP address will be used for connection to the server. The Advanced button enables you to configure the IP address and TCP port for each SMTP site on the server. In the Advanced configuration window you can add, remove, and edit any of the SMTP identities on the IIS server.

# Connection Section

Clicking the Connection button on the General tab enables you to manually configure incoming and outgoing connections to the SMTP server. For incoming connections you can limit the number of connections as well as establish the time-out period (in minutes) for each connection. For outgoing connections you can restrict the overall number of connections, control the time-out period (in minutes) for each connection, and limit the number of connections per specific domain and TCP port.

# Enable Logging Section

The Enable Logging section determines whether logging for the SMTP service is available and what type of logging file format is used. The active log formats available are as follows:

## Microsoft IIS Log Format

The Microsoft IIS Log Format is a file that uses standard ASCII text. These files can be opened in any file editor that can read text files such as Notepad and WordPad, which are included with Windows 2000. While the Microsoft IIS Log Format is selected in the drop-down box, click the Properties button to customize the log file options. These options include how often the log file should be cleared and the location and name of the log file. The Microsoft IIS Log Format file is not as customizable as the W3C Extended Format. For most organizations this log format will suffice for the amount of information that is stored.

### NCSA Common Log Format

NCSA Common Log Format is a fixed (non-customizable) ASCII format. It records basic information about user requests such as remote host name, user name, date, time, request type, HTTP status code, and the number of bytes received by the server. Items are separated by spaces; time is recorded as local time.

### ODBC Logging

ODBC logging is available only with Windows 2000 Server. This log file format is a fixed layout that is logged to a database, such as Microsoft SQL Server. The property sheet of this log file format offers the manual configuration of the specific database properties. These properties are crucial for successful connectivity to an external database.

### W3C Extended Log File Format (Default)

The W3C Extended Log File Format is similar to the Microsoft IIS Log Format file in that the format is ASCII text, but it is highly customizable in the amount of information that can be logged. With this log format selected in the drop-down box, the Properties button displays the standard General property tab for setting a new log creation period and log file location; it also includes an additional properties sheet called *Extended Properties*. This extended logging allows retrieval of numerous items that are not available with the Microsoft IIS Log Format File.

# ACCESS PROPERTY SHEET

The Access property sheet (see Figure 5-2) is used to configure client access to the SMTP server and to establish transmission security. It has four sections: Access Control, Secure Communication, Connection Control, and Relay Restrictions. These sections are described next.

## Access Control Section

In the Access Control section, you can configure the SMTP service to allow anonymous access or to prompt users for their user name and password. Clicking the Authentication button enables you to choose one or more of the following authentication methods:

▼ **Anonymous Access**   When this method is selected, no user name or password is required to gain access to the SMTP services.

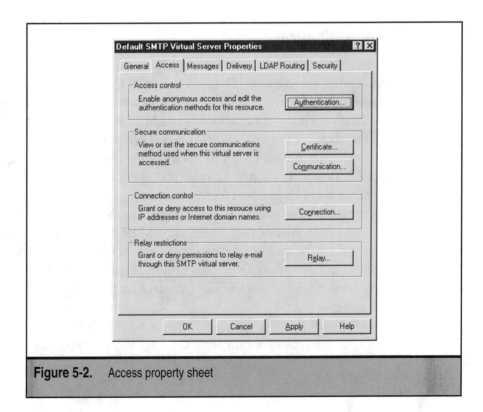

**Figure 5-2.**   Access property sheet

- **Basic Authentication**   With Basic Authentication enabled, the password will be sent over the network in clear text using standard commands. If this option is selected you must specify a Windows 2000 domain name, which is appended to the account name for authentication. This method also includes an option to enable Transport Layer Security (TLS). This encrypts incoming messages.

▲ **Windows Security Package**   Enabling the Windows Security Package method causes the client and server to negotiate the Windows Security Support Provider Interface. This security feature makes it possible for businesses to provide secure logon services for their customers. To use this approach, an e-mail client that supports the Windows security package must be used. Microsoft Outlook Express is one mail client that does support this authentication method.

## Secure Communication Section

The Secure Communication section allows you to assign a secure server certificate to the SMTP service. Part of the Windows 2000 Server services, a server certificate is an encrypted file containing Server identification information, which is used to verify the identity. Clicking the Certificate button initiates the wizard process.

The Communication button displays the communication security window. This feature ensures that data is encrypted and that the client uses the TLS method for connection to the SMTP server. Utilize the Web Server Certificate Wizard to install a valid server certificate; then you can configure the SMTP server to require that access take place on a secure channel by selecting the Require Secure Channel option. Once this option is enabled, you can strengthen security even further by selecting the Require 128-bit Encryption option.

The default key strength is 40-bit encryption. The larger the number of bits, the more difficult the key is to decrypt. Keep in mind that if the SMTP client can communicate only at 40-bit encryption, and the server is configured for 128-bit, the client will be refused connection. Also, due to export restrictions, 128-bit encryption is available only in the United States and Canada.

## Connection Control Section

The Connection Control section allows you to grant or deny use of the SMTP server to specific users or groups. By default, the SMTP server is accessible to all IP addresses, but you limit the allowable connections by IP address, groups of IP addresses (subnets), and Internet domain names.

## Relay Restrictions Section

The SMTP server can be used to relay e-mail messages, but this feature is not enabled by default. Relaying messages means that the SMTP service receives incoming messages and then forwards them based on information from the sender. An excellent example of e-mail relaying is when you receive unwanted spam e-mail in your inbox. If the SMTP server is on the Internet, you will want to leave this feature at its default or the server could end up propagating unsolicited commercial e-mail (or worse).

Using this feature, you can grant relaying to all computers and then make exceptions by denying access to specific computers, or you can disallow relay access to all computers and then bestow relay access to specific computers.

# MESSAGES PROPERTY SHEET

The Messages property sheet (see Figure 5-3) empowers you to determine transmission requirements and limits for the SMTP server. There are specific limits that you can place on the incoming messages; they are discussed next.

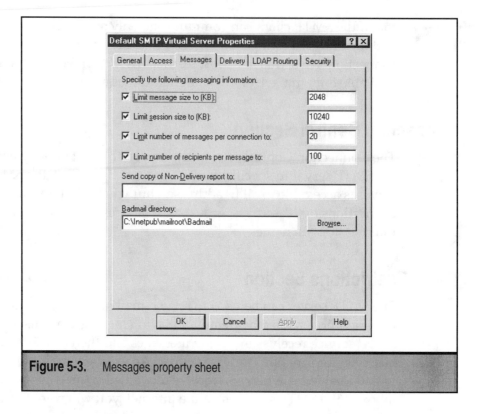

**Figure 5-3.** Messages property sheet

## Limit Message Size to (KB)

Using this option, you can limit the maximum size of an e-mail message permitted through the SMTP server. If an e-mail exceeds this maximum number, the user will receive an error message. The default value is 2,048 kilobytes.

## Limit Session Size to (KB)

When a user connects to the SMTP server to send e-mail, this option restricts the total size of data that can be transmitted during one session. The default value is 10,240 kilobytes. You should make sure to keep this value greater than or equal to the value entered for the Limit message size to (KB) option.

## Limit Number of Messages Per Connection To

Enabling this option controls the total message count that can be transmitted during a session. The default value is 20.

## Limit Number of Recipients Per Message To

Some e-mails contain multiple addressees, allowing a single message to be distributed to many different individuals. This option limits the number of addressees that can be input to receive the message. The default value is 100.

The last two items on the Messages properties sheet, Send Copy of Non-Delivery Report To and Badmail Directory, make it possible for you to proactively monitor the SMTP server. The Send Copy of Non-Delivery Report To option allows you to enter a specific SMTP mailbox that receives reports on messages that cannot be delivered for one reason or another. When a message is undeliverable, it is returned to the sender with a non-deliver report (NDR).

Entering an SMTP mailbox here causes the SMTP service to send a copy of the same NDR to the designation so it can be reviewed for possible delivery problems. When the NDR cannot be returned to the sender after a specified retry limit, the e-mail is marked as bad. When you designate a Badmail Directory, and the retry limit on the NDR has been reached, a copy of it will be placed in the location specified by this field.

**NOTE:** Check the Badmail Directory constantly and resolve any issue found in the NDRs. A full Badmail Directory can adversely affect the SMTP server performance.

# DELIVERY PROPERTY SHEET

The Delivery property sheet, shown in Figure 5-4, enables you to configure the delivery and routing settings for the SMTP server's

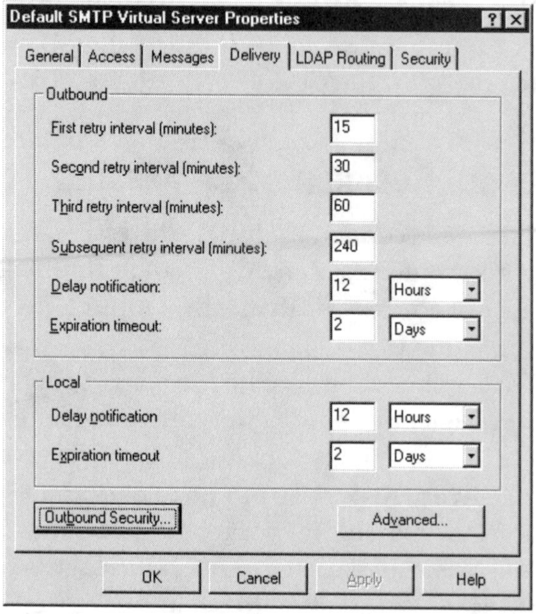

**Figure 5-4.** Delivery property sheet

outbound e-mail. The Outbound and Local sections, and the Security
and Advanced settings can be configured on this page.

## Outbound Section

The Outbound section contains several configuration options for the
SMTP service that affect the performance of the outbound e-mail.

### First Retry Interval (Minutes)

This option tells the SMTP service the number of minutes that it
must wait before issuing the first delivery status notification. The
default value is 15 minutes, but it can be modified to any number
from 1–9999.

### Second Retry Interval (Minutes)

Once the first retry value has been reached, the number of minutes listed in this field indicates how long the SMTP service will wait before issuing the second delivery status notification. The default value is 30 minutes; it accepts any value from 1–9999.

### Third Retry Interval (Minutes)

The interval listed in this field indicates how long the SMTP service will wait before issuing the third delivery status notification. The default value is 60 minutes; it accepts any value from 1–9999.

### Subsequent Retry Interval (Minutes)

After the third delivery status notification has been issued, the outbound e-mail will retry a fourth and final time. The default for this field is 240 minutes but it accepts 1–9999 as a valid range.

### Delay Notification

Setting a delay period for the notification allows you to compensate for any local and remote delivery delays due to network congestion. This field can be set in minutes, hours, or days. The default is 12 hours; it can be set to a minimum of 1 minute and a maximum of 9999 days.

### Expiration Timeout

Configuring this value tells the SMTP service when to give up after all outbound retry intervals have passed. The default value is 2 days; it can be set as low as 1 minute and as high as 9999 days.

## Outbound Security

Clicking the Outbound Security button displays the options for configuring the security account information for outbound e-mail.

## Anonymous Access

When this method is selected, authentication for outbound transmissions is disabled. This option is the default.

## Basic Authentication

With Basic Authentication enabled, the password will be sent over the network in clear text using standard commands. When this option is selected, you must specify a Windows 2000 domain account and password that will be utilized with this method.

## Windows Security Package

Enabling the Windows Security Package method causes the client and server to negotiate the Windows security support provider interface. This security feature makes it possible for businesses to provide secure logon services for their customers. To use this method, an e-mail client that supports Windows Security Package must be used. Microsoft Outlook Express is one mail client that does support this authentication method.

## TLS Encryption

Selecting this method forces all outgoing messages to use transport layer security (TLS) encryption.

## Advanced

When the Advanced button is clicked, the Advanced Delivery options for outbound mail is displayed. These options configure the routing settings for the SMTP service.

## Maximum Hop Count

When a message is delivered, it might traverse several servers before it reaches its final destination. Each server that the message passes through is referred to as a *hop count*. Using this field, you can limit the number of servers that the message is allowed to pass through. This information is attached to the message header and read by the servers. If the maximum hop count is exceeded, a non-delivery receipt (NDR) is generated.

For every hop that a message passes through, several seconds are added to the overall route time. If speedy e-mail delivery is your goal, you'll want to minimize the number of hops the message can travel.

## Masquerade Domain

The Masquerade Domain option allows you to configure an alternative domain name that is registered in the Mail From line in the e-mail message.

## Fully-Qualified Domain Name

There are two records that can be used to identify and verify a computer in a TCP/IP network. The mail exchanger (MX) record identifies the host and domain names associated with the computer. It uses the fully-qualified domain name (FQDN) for the name. The address (A) record identifies the IP address for the computer. When both records are used, name resolution occurs faster.

## Smart Host

You can route all outgoing messages for remote domains through a smart host instead of sending them directly to the domain. This allows you to route messages over a connection that might be more direct or less costly than other routes, because the host can negotiate the shortest path for you. If you set up a smart host, you can still designate a different route for a remote domain. The route domain setting overrides the smart host setting. Type an FQDN or an IP address to identify the smart host.

## Attempt Direct Delivery Before Sending to a Smart Host

When the Smart Host option is selected, the SMTP service seeks to deliver remote messages before forwarding them to the Smart Host server. It's possible that enabling this option will improve message delivery time due to the extra time a Smart Host takes to calculate the most direct message path.

## Perform Reverse DNS Lookup on Incoming Messages

Reverse Domain Naming System (DNS) lookup causes the SMTP service to attempt verification of the client's submitted IP address

with the client's host/domain information. When this option is
enabled, all incoming messages are verified, which could cause
SMTP service performance problems.

# LDAP ROUTING PROPERTY SHEET

Lightweight Directory Access Protocol (LDAP) is a network protocol
designed to work on TCP/IP stacks to extract information from a
hierarchical directory. This gives users a single tool with which to
search through data in order to find a particular piece of information
such as a user name, e-mail address, security certificate, or other
contact information. Enabling LDAP routing on the property sheet
makes the fields on this page available for configuration. The LDAP
Routing property sheet, shown in Figure 5-5, enables you to rework
LDAP for the SMTP service.

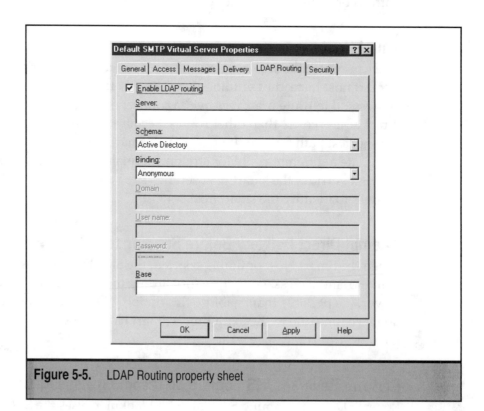

**Figure 5-5.**    LDAP Routing property sheet

# Server

In this field, enter the name of a server that is running the LDAP directory service. If the exchange LDAP service is selected in the schema type on this properties page, this field is not applicable.

# Schema

The Schema field enables you to select the specific LDAP directory service that is being used. The options are Active Directory when Windows 2000 is providing the LDAP service, Site Server Membership Directory when the Microsoft Commercial Internet System provides the service, and Exchange LDAP Service when Microsoft Site Server 3.0 or higher furnishes the LDAP directory.

# Binding

The Binding type determines how the SMTP server is authenticated by the directory service. The available options are Anonymous, for no user name and password transmission; Plain Text, for when the information is passed to the server without encryption; Windows SSPI, for Windows encryption services; and Service Accounts for allowing the SMTP service to provide the authentication.

# Domain

This option is available if you select either the Plain Text or Windows SSPI binding types. This entry is the domain where the service user account resides.

# User Name

The User Name option applies if you select either the Plain Text or Windows SSPI binding types, and must be entered as part of the domain entry. Enter the user account that will be used to authenticate with the LDAP directory. Because LDAP uses distinguished names (DN) for connection, you must enter the user name in that format.

DNs employ a hierarchal path designation for identifying locations and sublocations for the connection, much like the drive and directory location of a file in the file system. To understand locations and sublocations, picture the city you live in as the location, and the personal residences on your street as the sublocations. Like a tree, the path reads from the bottom to the top, with a progression of Container, Organizational Unit, and then Organization; for example, *cn=user1.ou=users.o=company*.

## Password

When either Plain Text or Windows SSPI binding type is selected, this option becomes available. Enter the password of the user name that was entered in the previous field.

## Base

Assigning an entry to this field instructs the SMTP service to begin looking in a specific container of the directory to find the LDAP services. Once the starting point is set, the container and all of its subcontainers are searched for the LDAP provider.

# SECURITY PROPERTY SHEET

The Security property sheet, shown in Figure 5-6, allows you to grant administrative access to specific groups or users in the Windows 2000 Active Directory. This administrative access gives limited privileges on the specific SMTP server.

Clicking the Add button inserts new Web site operators; highlighting a listed account and clicking the Remove button revokes the rights. By default, the Administrators group that is local to the IIS server is granted the Operator right.

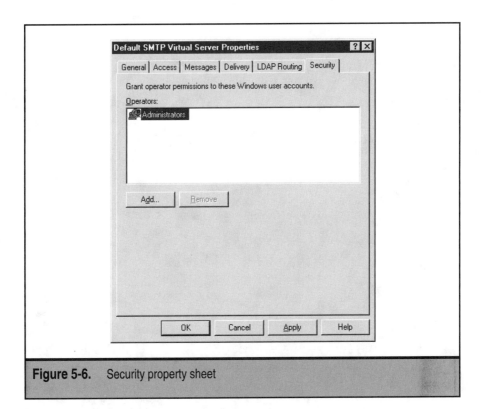

**Figure 5-6.**    Security property sheet

# CHAPTER 6

## NNTP Service Reference

The NNTP service provides a robust set of tools to make full-featured news groups available to the IIS 5.0 server. Users can connect to the server using their favorite news reader client software and read messages already posted online, submit new messages to initiate a discussion thread, search the listings for a specific word or phrase, or download messages to read later.

Microsoft Outlook Express includes a very high-quality news reader (and an e-mail client), but some people prefer to use a news reader that has more features and additional functionality. One popular news reader is Forte Inc.'s Free Agent. This free and powerful news reader can be downloaded from Forte Inc.'s Web site: http://www.forteinc.com/ agent/freagent.htm.

## GENERAL PROPERTY SHEET

The General property sheet, shown in Figure 6-1, contains the common setup information for the NNTP service. Like the General tab for the SMTP service, the NNTP configuration includes the name of the server, the IP address, connection information, and log file settings.

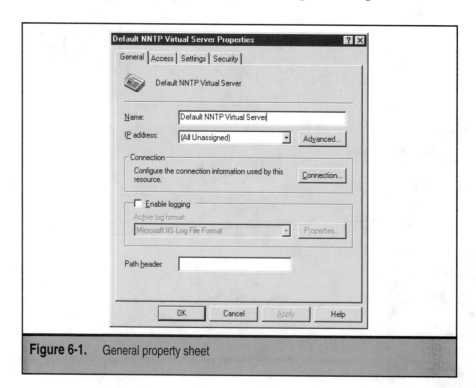

**Figure 6-1.** General property sheet

# Name

This field can accept any name you want to identify the NNTP server. This name is for identification and organizational purposes and is the NNTP server name that appears in the tree view of the IIS snap-in.

# IP Address

Any IP addresses that have been defined for use in the network properties of the server will be available for selection. Selecting an IP address from the drop-down menu will assign that selection to the default NNTP site. This IP address will be used for connection to the server. The Advanced button enables you to configure the IP address and TCP port for each NNTP site on the server. In the Advanced configuration window you can add, remove, and edit any of the NNTP identities on the IIS server.

# Connection Section

Clicking the Connection button in this section allows you to manually configure incoming and outgoing connections to the NNTP server. For incoming connections, you can limit the number of connections and set the timeout period (in minutes) for each connection. For outgoing connections you can limit the overall number of connections, set the time-out period (in minutes) for each connection, and restrict the number of connections per specific domain and TCP port.

# Enable Logging Section

The Enable Logging section configures whether logging for the NNTP service is available and what type of logging file format is used. The active log formats available are as follows:

## Microsoft IIS Log Format

The Microsoft IIS Log Format is a file that uses standard ASCII text. These files can be opened in any file editor that can read text files, such as Notepad and WordPad, which are included with

Windows 2000. While the Microsoft IIS Log Format is selected in the drop-down box, you click the Properties button to customize the log file options. These include how often the log file should be cleared and the location and name of the log file. The Microsoft IIS Log Format file is not as customizable as the W3C Extended format. For most organizations, this log format will suffice for the amount of information that is stored.

### NCSA Common Log Format

NCSA Common Log Format is a fixed (non-customizable) ASCII format. It records basic information about user requests such as remote host name, user name, date, time, request type, HTTP status code, and the number of bytes received by the server. Items are separated by spaces; time is recorded as local time.

### ODBC Logging

ODBC logging is only available with Windows 2000 Server. This log file format is a fixed layout that is logged to a database, such as Microsoft SQL Server. The property sheet of this log file format allows the manual configuration of the specific database properties. These properties are crucial for successful connectivity to an external database.

### W3C Extended Log File Format (Default)

The W3C Extended Log File Format is similar to the Microsoft IIS Log Format file in that the format is ASCII text, but it is highly customizable in the amount of information that can be logged. With this log format selected in the drop-down box, the Properties button displays the standard General properties tab for setting a new log creation period and log file location; it also includes an additional properties sheet called *Extended Properties*. This extended logging allows retrieval of numerous items that are not available with the Microsoft IIS log file format.

# ACCESS PROPERTY SHEET

The Access property sheet (see Figure 6-2) is used to configure client access to the NNTP server and to establish transmission security. It has three sections: Access Control, Secure Communication, and Connection Control, which are discussed next.

## Access Control Section

In the Access Control section you can configure the NNTP service to allow anonymous access or to prompt users for their user name and password. Clicking the Authentication button allows you to choose fone or more of the following authentication methods.

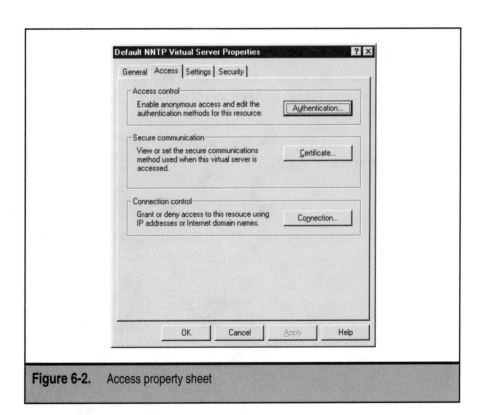

**Figure 6-2.** Access property sheet

## Anonymous Access

When this method is selected, no user name or password is required to gain access to the NNTP services.

## Basic Authentication

With Basic Authentication enabled, the password will be sent over the network in clear text using standard commands. If this option is selected you must specify a Windows 2000 domain name, which is appended to the account name for authentication.

## Windows Security Package

Enabling the Windows Security Package method causes the client and server to negotiate the Windows Security Support Provider Interface. This security feature makes it possible for businesses to provide secure logon services for their customers. To use this method, an e-mail client that supports Windows security package must be used. Microsoft Outlook Express is one news client that does support this authentication method.

## Enable SSL Client Authentication (Requires Server Certificate)

This option enables Secure Sockets Layer (SSL) for authentication to the NNTP server. SSL is a protocol that supplies secure data communication through data encryption and decryption. With this option enabled, the Require SSL Client Authentication and Enable Client Certificate Mapping to Windows User Accounts become available.

## Require SSL Client Authentication

Enabling the Require SSL Client Authentication option forces any client connection that wants to use the NNTP service to have SSL installed and running on its computer before access is granted.

## Enable Client Certificate Mapping to Windows User Accounts

If the connecting client computer has a user certificate installed, this option allows you to map (or tie) the certificate to the individuals'

Windows 2000 user account. This provides a seamless authentication method for the user because the authorization for access to the NNTP server will be provided by their Windows 2000 login information. This option requires that a SSL certificate be version 3.0 or later. When the selection is chosen, the Client Mappings button becomes available.

## Mapping Client Certificates to User Accounts

Mapping a client certificate to a user account allows you to provide seamless integration between the Web services (not just NNTP) and the user's Windows 2000 network information. There are two commonly known ways to map certificates: one-to-one and many-to-one. The newest method of certificate mapping is Directory Service (DS) mapping.

**One-to-One**   One-to-one mapping maps individual client certificates to accounts. The server compares the copy of the client certificate it holds with the client certificate sent by the browser. The two must be absolutely identical for the mapping to proceed. If a client gets another certificate containing all of the same user information, it must be mapped again.

**Many-to-One**   Many-to-one mapping uses *wildcard* matching rules, which verify whether a client certificate contains specific information, such as issuer or subject. This mapping does not compare the actual client certificate; rather it accepts all client certificates fulfilling the precise criteria. If a client gets another certificate containing all of the same user information, the existing mapping will work.

**Directory Service Mapping**   Directory Service (DS) mapping is a new feature of Windows 2000 and the Active Directory (AD) service. DS certificate mapping uses native Windows 2000 Active Directory features to authenticate users with client certificates. DS mapping grants the client certificate the capability to be shared across many servers when they participate in the Windows 2000 domain.

Because DS mapping is new, wildcard matching is not as advanced as it is in the IIS 5.0 mapping function. DS mapping is accomplished in the Windows 2000 operating system; if applied, it disables the use of one-to-one and many-to-one mapping for the entire Web site. The IIS 5.0 server must be part of the Windows 2000 Active Directory for this option to be available. For more information about DS mapping, see the Windows 2000 documentation.

### Determining Which Mapping Method to Use

If you decide to use client certificate mapping you must first determine which client mapping method is the best solution for the IIS 5.0 server. If the IIS 5.0 server is on a large network, choosing many-to-one or DS mapping will allow the administrator to create one or more matching rules to map certificates to one or more Windows 2000 user accounts. For an IIS 5.0 server that resides on a small network (small number of users), one-to-one mapping provides greater control for certificate usage and revoking certificates. However, many-to-one mapping facilitates easier administration of the certificate-to-user settings.

If you just require additional security measures for the Web site (on a small or large network), one-to-one mapping is the best choice because it enables the administrator to affirm that only specific certificates are being used to access the site. This also allows for easier management when certificates need to be revoked.

If the IIS 5.0 server sits on the Internet, the many-to-one method permits you to accept a wider range of certificates and then map them all to a certain account with the proper rights to the site. If you are accepting certificates that have been issued by a particular certification authority, the many-to-one mapping allows you to define a matching rule to automatically map a certificate issued by the organization to a user account.

## Secure Communication Section

The Secure Communication section enables you to assign a secure server certificate to the NNTP service. The Communication button displays the communication security window. This feature ensures that data is encrypted and that the client uses the Transmission Layer Security (TLS) method for connection to the NNTP server. Once a valid server certificate has been installed using the Web Server Certificate Wizard, you can configure the NNTP server to require that access take place on a secure channel by selecting the Require Secure Channel option. Once this option is enabled, you can strengthen security even further by selecting the Require 128-bit Encryption option. The default key strength is 40-bit encryption. The larger the number of bits, the more difficult the key is to decrypt. Keep in mind that if the NNTP client can communicate only at 40-bit, and the server is configured for 128-bit, the client will be refused connection. Also, due to export restrictions, 128-bit encryption is available only in the United States and Canada.

## Connection Control Section

The Connection Control section allows you to grant or deny use of the NNTP server to specific users or groups. By default, the NNTP server is accessible to all IP addresses, but you limit the allowable connections by IP address, groups of IP addresses (subnets), and Internet domain names.

# SETTINGS PROPERTY SHEET

The Settings property sheet, shown in Figure 6-3, allows you to control how messages are posted to the news server and how the posts are managed. Using this property sheet you can place restrictions on how a client posts, the size of messages that can be posted, choose who can moderate the news lists, and assign a new administrators. These configuration settings are covered in the following sections.

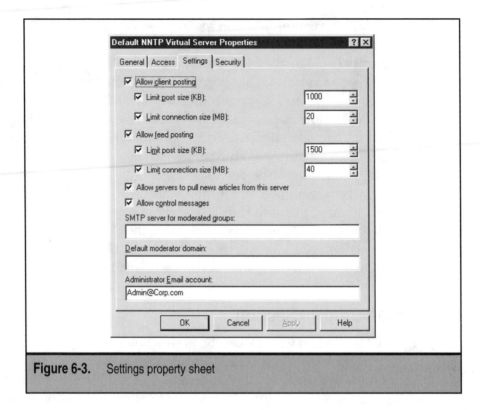

**Figure 6-3.**    Settings property sheet

## Allow Client Posting

Selecting this option gives the new client the ability to post messages
to the news server. Using the sub-options in this section, you can
restrict the size of the postings. Limiting both client postings and feed
postings helps minimize the amount of disk space that is required for
the NNTP service and the messages that are stored on the server.

### Limit Post Size (KB)

By choosing to constrain the post size, you can control how large a
single posted message can be. The default is 1,000 kilobytes.

### Limit Connection Size (MB)

Limiting the connection size restricts the entire group of message
postings for a single news client during a single session. The default

setting is 20 megabytes, but you will want to consider decreasing this number to 5 or 10 megabytes.

## Allow Feed Posting

IIS's NNTP service can be configured to retrieve messages from external news services. This is particularly useful for creating a local copy of the external source in order to make access to the news groups convenient and faster. Selecting this option enables the NNTP service to synchronize these news-feed services. By using the two other options in this section, you can limit the volume of messages that are retrieved for local use.

### Limit Post Size (KB)

This option restricts the size (in kilobytes) of a single message that can be delivered from the news feed service. The default value is 1,500 kilobytes.

### Limit Connection Size (MB)

The Limit connection size (MB) option allows you to limit the total size of all messages that are obtained from the news feed service during a single session. The default setting is 40 megabytes.

## Allow Servers to Pull News Articles From This Server

Because there might be other NNTP servers in the organization or other news servers on the Internet, you might want to allow the original content available on your NNTP server to be accessible for retrieval by other locations. This makes your content obtainable in multiple places and helps the performance of your NNTP server by permitting connecting users to get the content from other locations.

## Allow Control Messages

Enabling this option causes the NNTP service to process control messages automatically and log the information in the transaction log.

### SMTP Server for Moderated Groups

This option specifies the SMTP mail server where all postings to moderated groups are forwarded. A moderated group is a news group that is "watched" by an individual or group of individuals, usually to manage appropriate content and to act as a referee for those suspect news group posters that go against the news group policies. This value must be either a valid computer name (with a valid IP address), or a directory path. A directory path is used only for moderated messages that are sent to a designated directory location.

### Default Moderator Domain

Using this option assigns a default domain where all moderated postings are sent. Articles posted to moderated newsgroups that do not have a specified moderator are sent to the default moderator domain account, which generally uses the *news_ group_ name@default_ moderator_domain* format.

### Administrator E-mail Account

As with the SMTP service, NNTP creates non-delivery reports (NDR) for the messages that cannot be delivered to the news server. This field should contain the valid e-mail account of the individual who should receive a copy of these NDRs.

## SECURITY PROPERTY SHEET

The Security property sheet (see Figure 6-4) allows you to authorize administrative access to specific groups or users in the Windows 2000 Active Directory. This administrative access provides limited privileges on the specific NNTP server. Clicking the Add button inserts new Web site operators; highlighting a listed account and clicking the Remove button revokes the rights. By default, the Administrators group that is local to the IIS server is granted the Operator right.

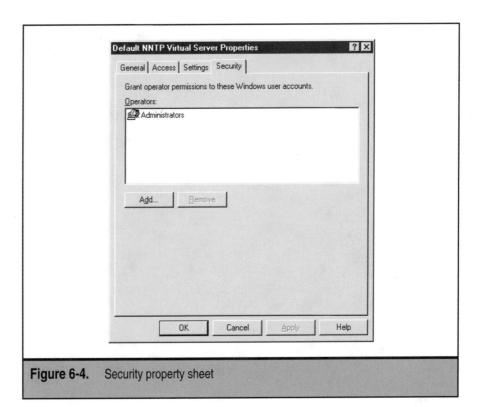

**Figure 6-4.**    Security property sheet

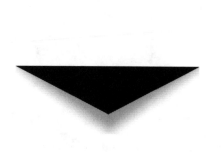

# CHAPTER 7

## Server Properties Reference

Along with including configuration settings for each service, IIS provides a general set of properties for modifying and tuning the IIS server itself. These settings are accessed by right-clicking the specific IIS server's name in the Internet Services Manager, and then choosing Properties from the context menu. The specifics for configuring the IIS server are covered in this chapter. By understanding what is available and how the modifications can increase the IIS server's capabilities, you can better control how IIS operates.

# INTERNET INFORMATION SERVICES PROPERTY SHEET

The initial property sheet that displays when accessing the IIS server configuration settings is the Internet Information Services tab (shown in Figure 7-1). This tab allows you to configure the WWW and FTP services for the entire server, enable or disable bandwidth throttling, and modify the way the IIS displays different file types to the client's browser. These settings are described in the following sections.

## Master Properties Section

The Master Properties section enables you to set default global WWW or FTP values for the entire site. These are the same options as when configuring the properties of each service individually. Select the type of service—either WWW or FTP—from the drop-down list. To set the default values used by current or new Web sites, click the Edit button. If you have already changed the properties value for an individual Web site, you are prompted to determine whether the new master properties settings should overwrite the current settings.

## Enable Bandwidth Throttling Section

Bandwidth throttling enables you to minimize the impact that the Web services have on the server's network connection. Select this option to limit the bandwidth used by Web and FTP services on your

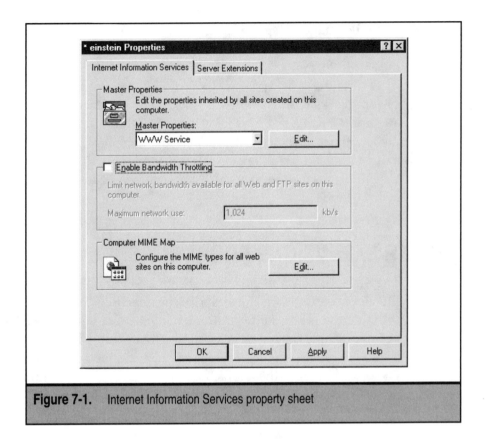

**Figure 7-1.**   Internet Information Services property sheet

computer. Limiting the bandwidth is especially useful if your
network card has multiple purposes such as e-mail and remote
logons. Bandwidth throttling limits only the bandwidth used
by static HTML files.

## Computer MIME Map Section

Multipurpose Internet Mail Extensions (MIME) mapping is a way
of configuring Internet browsers to view files that are in multiple
formats. MIME is an extension of the Internet mail protocol that
enables sending any 8-bit-based e-mail messages. These are used
to support extended character sets, Internet e-mail, voice mail, and

facsimile images. Depending on what services the Web site provides, you can associate specific files with specific file extensions to work in the MIME format.

Setting these file types is similar to how the Windows operating system works with File Type Associations. For example, when you attempt to open a text file that is located in the computer's file system, the text file is automatically opened inside Notepad. This is because a file with a .txt file extension is associated with Notepad. By clicking the File Types button, you can associate specific file types with the MIME standard.

# SERVER EXTENSIONS PROPERTY SHEET

The Server Extensions property sheet (see Figure 7-2) configures the global settings for the webs on the specific IIS 5.0 server. By utilizing the many configuration changes here, you can increase performance of the IIS server, set the global mail encoding options, modify the global security information, and shape the way the entire IIS server manages the log file output. Making global modifications affects every service that is installed on the IIS server. If a setting is changed here, it will be propagated to every component running on the server.

## General Section

The General section regulates the global common settings for the server extensions. It has two options: Performance and Client Scripting. The Performance option has a second-level menu that contains many options for improving the Web server's capability to service client and server requests.

### Performance

Click the page range that's closest to the actual number of pages in the selected web. The FrontPage server extensions will set aside a

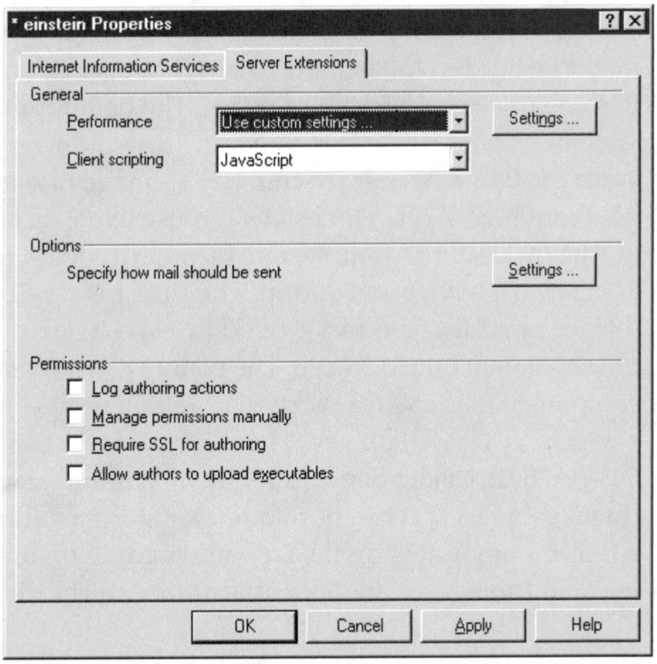

**Figure 7-2.**    Server Extensions property sheet

certain amount of cache, based on the page range you select. You can also choose a custom setting that displays a Performance window for manually configuring the performance options. It helps to understand the different caching settings if you want to perform manual tuning.

**In-Memory Document Cache**    Enter the maximum number of documents whose properties information, such as link maps and Web parameters, you want to keep active in memory. This number represents the last *<number you specify>* documents you worked with. For example, if you specify 4096, properties information about the 4097th document will be released from memory. The default setting is 4,096.

**Include File Cache**   Enter the number of files that you want to keep available in memory for inclusion in other files. For example, there might be header, footer, and copyright files that you want to include in some or all of a Web site's pages. The default setting is 16.

**Image File Cache**   Enter the number of image files in memory that the FrontPage server extensions can use to create layered pictures in Web pages. For example, one file might consist of a background; another of a navigation button. The server extensions can compose a picture by adding the background to a Web page and then overlaying the navigation button image. The picture can be composed faster if the component files are in a cache. The default setting is 16.

**Full-Text Search Index Size**   Enter the maximum amount of disk space (in megabytes) that can be allotted for storing a full-text search index. After this amount is reached, no other pages on the Web site can be indexed (unless you increase this number). The default setting is 1.

**Max Cached Document Size**   Enter the maximum size of a document (in kilobytes) that can be stored in memory. This size limit applies to all files, image files, and other files that might be stored in a cache. The default setting is 256.

### Client Scripting

Select the scripting language, either JScript (JavaScript from Sun) or VBScript (Visual Basic from Microsoft) that should be generated in pages automatically by the FrontPage server extensions.

## Options Section

The Options section displays features of the global setting for how mail will be sent through the Web sites on the server using the FrontPage server extensions.

## Specify How Mail Should be Sent

Clicking this item's Settings button displays the E-mail Settings dialog box, in which you can direct how e-mail-based Web features (such as e-mail form handlers) will send e-mail to Web site visitors. You can use the dialog box to specify the Web server's e-mail address, contact e-mail address, mail server, mail-encoding scheme, and character set.

**Mail Encoding**   The default e-mail encoding scheme for the FrontPage server extensions is 8-bit. This is a non-communicated Internet standard for e-mail, but some e-mail servers might receive different ones. You can change from one scheme to another if you know that an e-mail recipient uses a different encoding scheme. If the schemes do not match, the recipient will not be able to read the message; it will look garbled. The FrontPage server extensions offer the following e-mail encoding schemes: 8-bit, 7-bit, binary, quoted-printable, base64, ietf-token, and x-token. For more information on e-mail encoding, use the Webopedia for research on the various encoding schemes: http://www.pcwebopedia.com/.

**Character Set**   If your site interacts with locations worldwide, you need to provide the capability to support multiple languages for e-mail messages. Because different languages use different characters for communicating in writing, standards must be used to make sure that an e-mail message can be converted and read by anyone that receives it. Character sets supply this functionality.

The FrontPage server extensions include support for the current list of character-set standards. Each item available for selection represents a different language. The ISO-8859, included in the list of options, is a full series of 10 standardized multilingual single-byte coded (8-bit) graphic character sets for writing in alphabetic languages. As of today, there are only 10 ISO-8859 standards; however, this character-set standard is constantly growing, and there are current proposals for new ones on the horizon. The options available through the FrontPage server extensions are listed in Table 7-1.

| Character Set | Supported Languages |
|---|---|
| US-ASCII (default) | United States English |
| ISO-8859-1; Latin1, West European | French (fr), Spanish (es), Catalan (ca), Basque (eu), Portuguese (pt), Italian (it), Albanian (sq), Rhaeto-Romanic (rm), Dutch (nl), German (de), Danish (da), Swedish (sv), Norwegian (no), Finnish (fi), Faroese (fo), Icelandic (is), Irish (ga), Scottish (gd), and English (en); incidentally also Afrikaans (af) and Swahili (sw) |
| ISO-8859-2; Latin2, East European | Czech (cs), Hungarian (hu), Polish (pl), Romanian (ro), Croatian (hr), Slovak (sk), Slovenian (sl), and Sorbian |
| ISO-8859-3; Latin3, South European | Esperanto (eo) and Maltese (mt) |
| ISO-8859-4; Latin4, North European | Estonian (et), the Baltic languages Latvian (lv, Lettish) and Lithuanian (lt), Greenlandic (kl) and Lappish |
| ISO-8859-5; Cyrillic | Bulgarian (bg), Byelorussian (be), Macedonian (mk), Russian (ru), Serbian (sr) and pre-1990 (no ghe with upturn) Ukrainian (uk) |
| ISO-8859-6; Arabic | Arabic (ar) language only |
| ISO-8859-7; Greek | Modern monotonic Greek (el) |
| ISO-8859-8; Hebrew | Hebrew (iw) and Yiddish (ji) |
| ISO-8859-9; Latin5, Turkish | Latin5 replaces the rarely needed Icelandic letters ðýþ in Latin1 with the Turkish ones |

**Table 7-1.**  FrontPage Server Extensions Character Sets

| Character Set | Supported Languages |
|---|---|
| ISO-8859-10; Latin6, Nordic | Introduced in 1992, Latin6 rearranged the Latin4 characters, dropped some symbols and the Latvian &rcedil, added the last missing Inuit (Greenlandic Eskimo) and non-Skolt Sami (Lappish) letters and reintroduced the Icelandic ðýþ to cover the entire Nordic area |

**Table 7-1.**    FrontPage Server Extensions Character Sets *(continued)*

# Permissions Section

The Permissions section of the Server Extensions properties page establishes the global security settings of the Web server. All webs in the site inherit these settings, but the settings can be overridden through the configuration pages on the specific subweb. This section provides even further configuration options for the global FrontPage Server Extensions security settings.

## Log Authoring Actions

Checking this box enables the system to record the time an author's action was performed, the author's user name, the Web name, the remote host, and per-operation data; and to store this information in a log file in the _vti_log/Author.log file in the Web directory.

## Manage Permissions Manually

Enabling this option disables the security setting functions of FrontPage server extensions administrative tools (such as the FrontPage MMC snap-in), so that those tools cannot be used to modify the security settings of the selected Web site. Leave this check box clear if you want to allow the security settings to be changed by using the FrontPage server extensions administrative tools.

### Require Secure Sockets Layer (SSL) for Authoring

Selecting this option makes it possible for you to use SSL to authenticate prospective Web authors. This is recommended if you are currently using only basic authentication, which just lightly encrypts information (such as an author's user name and password) transmitted across the Web.

### Allow Authors to Upload Executables

This option permits authors to upload Common Gateway Interface (CGI) scripts or Active Server pages to the selected Web. Clear this check box if you want to prevent executables from being uploaded to the Web and avoid the risks associated with a possibly buggy script or a virus that's uploaded to the Web server.

# CHAPTER 8

## MMC Utilities Reference

Some administration tools to make your job of managing the IIS 5.0 server easier are available on the right-click menus of the Internet Information Services MMC snap-in. The particularly useful features are listed in this chapter. These tools are also available on the MMC file menu, but by making them available as a right-click of the mouse button allows quick and easy access. You should take the time to read carefully through the information presented in this chapter because these tools are critical to proper operation of your IIS server. Included from the right-click menu are the Restart IIS, Permissions Wizard, and Backup and Restore utilities.

# RESTART IIS

When you right-click an IIS 5.0 server name in the MMC, you see an option to restart IIS. This feature allows you to quickly recycle the IIS 5.0 server and all the installed services with one click. In previous versions of IIS, the only way to successfully recycle the services was to reboot the entire server. By providing this feature, IIS 5.0 eliminates the need to take the server completely offline while it restarts.

**NOTE:** You might notice that the Windows 2000 Services MMC snap-in includes a feature to recycle services on the server. Do not use this Windows 2000 feature for the IIS 5.0 site. The restart IIS utility was developed specifically for IIS 5.0. Using the Windows 2000 version will not allow the IIS services to start up in the correct order.

**TIP:** In addition to being able to recycle the IIS services for a specific server from the MMC snap-in, Microsoft includes a command-line utility for recycling the Web site. IISRESET.exe, located in the C:\WINNT\SYSTEM32 directory on the server, uses command-line switches to provide additional functionality for recycling the IIS services. A command-line utility has certain benefits, such as being able to schedule restarts of the IIS services or allowing IIS service interoperability with any applications you want to develop. See the following for the IISRESET.exe options:

```
Usage:
iisreset [computername]
```

| | |
|---|---|
| /RESTART | Stop and then restart all Internet services. |
| /START | Start all Internet services. |
| /STOP | Stop all Internet services. |
| /REBOOT | Reboot the computer. |
| /REBOOTONERROR | Reboot the computer if errors occur when starting, stopping, or restarting Internet services. |
| /NOFORCE | Do not forcefully terminate Internet services if attempting to stop them gracefully fails. |
| /TIMEOUT:val | Specify the timeout value ( in seconds ) to wait for a successful stop of Internet services. On expiration of this timeout the computer can be rebooted if the /REBOOTONERROR parameter is specified. The default value is 20s for restart, 60s for stop, and 0s for reboot. |
| /STATUS | Display the status of all Internet services. |
| /ENABLE | Enable restarting of Internet Services on the local system. |
| /DISABLE | Disable restarting of Internet Services on the local system. |

# PERMISSIONS WIZARD

For the FTP and WWW services, when you right-click and then navigate to All Tasks on the pop-up menu, the Permissions Wizard becomes available for access. The Permissions Wizard walks you, step-by-step, through configuring security on publishing points for the selected service. When you initiate the Permissions Wizard, you are presented with the startup screen, shown in Figure 8-1. From this screen, you can Cancel the wizard or click the Next button to continue.

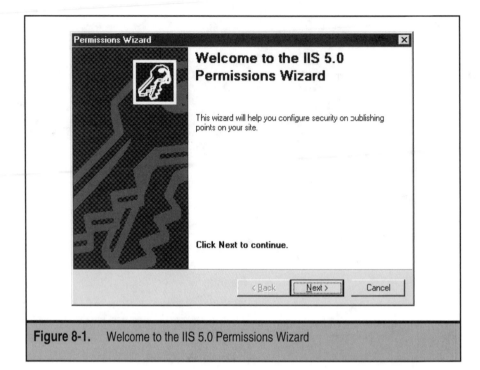

**Figure 8-1.** Welcome to the IIS 5.0 Permissions Wizard

As shown in Figure 8-2, the next step in the wizard process is to decide whether you want to use security settings for an existing parent site or directory or import new security settings from an existing template.

If you prefer to use the template method, a Site Scenario screen (shown in Figure 8-3) displays that lets you select a security scenario template.

When you have selected the scenario template, or if you chose to use the security settings of a parent site or directory, the Windows Directory and File Permissions window, shown in Figure 8-4, is

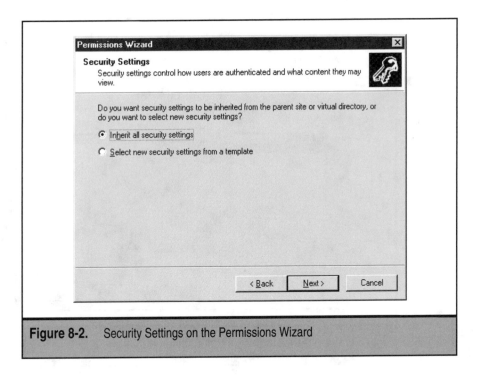

**Figure 8-2.**   Security Settings on the Permissions Wizard

displayed. This step in the wizard process allows you to decide if you want to replace all directory and file permissions, leave the current directory and file permissions intact and then add the selected permissions, or to just keep the current directory and file permissions and discard the selections you have made.

When you click the Next button after making your choice, the Permissions Wizard completes the process by acting on the modifications you have specified.

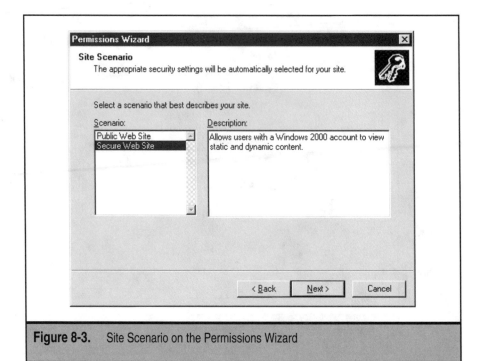

**Figure 8-3.**    Site Scenario on the Permissions Wizard

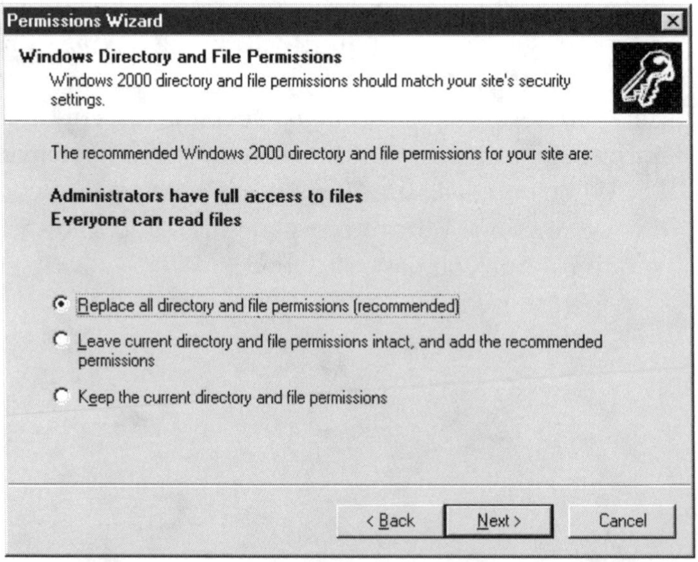

**Figure 8-4.**    Windows Directory and File Permissions on the Permissions Wizard

# BACKUP AND RESTORE CONFIGURATION

In earlier versions of IIS, the computer's registry stored the IIS configuration settings. If the computer's registry became corrupted the entire IIS site would be lost unless you performed painstaking measures to back up the IIS registry entries. Backing up and then restoring these registry settings was such a difficult task that most site administrators never took the time to properly save the IIS settings in the event of a disaster.

IIS 5.0 uses a Metabase for storing the IIS configuration settings. The Metabase is a thin database structure for storing the IIS configuration settings. The Metabase performs some of the same functions as the system registry but uses less disk space. In addition, the Metabase is stored in the file system, so it can easily be saved using any backup method you desire.

By right-clicking any IIS server name in the MMC snap-in, the Backup/Restore Configuration option becomes available for selection. Selecting this option displays the screen in Figure 8-5.

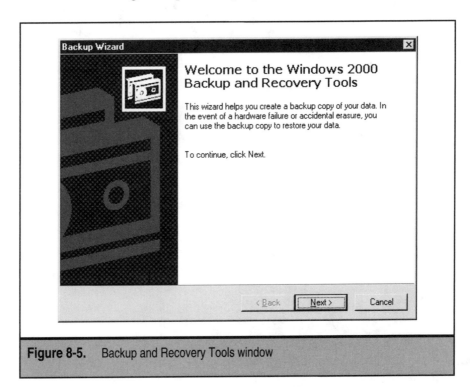

**Figure 8-5.**   Backup and Recovery Tools window

Working with the Backup/Restore Configuration utility is relatively simple. Click the Create Backup button to give your new IIS configuration backup a name; backup is generated within a few seconds. To restore one of the backups listed in the Backups window, just highlight it and click the Restore button. To remove a backup from the list, highlight it and click the Delete button. When you opt to restore a backup, the restoration procedure takes a lot longer than creation of the backup did because the IIS services must be recycled during the process.

**NOTE:** While you can back up the IIS configuration using the Internet Services Manager (HTML), it can be restored only using the Internet Information Services MMC snap-in.

To back up the Metabase to tape, make sure to include, in your backup program, the C:\WINNT\SYTEM32\INETSRV\METABACK directory on the IIS server. This is the location where the configuration backups are stored. They are stored with an .MD# file extension. For example, the first backup's file extension is: .MD0. The second backup is .MD1, and so on.

# CHAPTER 9

## Active Server Pages

A s you surf the Internet, identify those pages that you visit most often. Why do you keep going back to the same sites? Of course, one important factor is that those Web sites exhibit material that is personal to you—data that you need to do your job, fulfill a hobby, or gather information that helps you in day-to-day life. But, there is another factor that makes Web sites popular and keeps the Web site information from going stale.

When you look at the Web pages you access every day or every week, take notice of how they are organized and how they display data. The heavily populated Web sites attract and keep visitors by making data interactive and ever changing. These Web pages have been automated to provide access to data in a way that keeps the interest of its visitors. Using Active Server Pages (ASP), you can also create Web sites that keep folks coming back.

This chapter covers ASP and outlines how you can use them to increase the potential that a whole Web community makes your Web site a mainstay, or the entire corporate employee-base sees your intranet site as a business value. Before going too deeply into ASP, it helps to understand the underlying technology—HTML.

## HTML PRIMER

There are a millions of pages of data on the Internet. Surfing through the World Wide Web, you can pick any topic and usually find enough information to satisfy your current urge for knowledge. Much of this information has been in the same spot, unmodified, for years—so you could be taking in a lot of stale, outdated facts. You can easily spot these static Web pages. Every piece (text, images, hyperlinks, and so forth) of the Web page is always the same, no matter when you visit. The content is uneventful, and when you look at the address line of your Internet browser, you see that the file extension of the page is either HTML or HTM. Web pages that are saved with the HTML or HTM extension generally are used for display or presentation purposes only, and are rarely updated.

## Creating a Simple HTML Web Page

Creating static Web pages is simple. Either by using your favorite Web page editor (like Microsoft's FrontPage application) or by using Hypertext Markup Language (HTML) with a basic text editor (Notepad or Write), a static Web page can be produced in a few minutes. I generated the Web page in Figure 9-1 by typing HTML text into Notepad and saving with an .HTML file extension.

**Figure 9-1.**    A simple Web page created using Notepad

The HTML text was uncomplicated to construct. In fact, as you can see in the following example, the code took no more than eleven lines:

```
<HTML>
<HEAD><TITLE>Welcome to my website</TITLE></HEAD>
<BODY>
      <H1>Welcome to my website</H1>
      This is my first website! Thanks for stopping by.
      <BR><BR>
      Leave me an
      <A HREF="mailto:myemail@myemail.com">email</A>
      to let me know you like it!
</BODY>
</HTML>
```

To better understand how the HTML on this Web page works, let's break it down into manageable components:

▼ **<HTML>**   The initial line of the code tells the Internet browser that indeed this is an HTML Web page.

**NOTE:**   If you look at the bottom of the code, you will see HTML's relative: </HTML>. Every beginning statement must have an ending statement. Throughout the listed script you'll see references to certain components; each has a code "brother" to finish the statement.

■ **<HEAD><TITLE>**   The Head - Title line instructs the Web browser to display the information contained in the code as the title of the browser's window.

■ **<BODY>**   The BODY reference notifies the browser that the actual Web page is starting.

■ **<H1>**   The beginning and ending H1 statements encompass the main heading of the Web page and direct the browser to display the data using the HEADING 1 font. An H2 would display the text in a HEADING 2 font, H3 displays HEADING 3, and so on.

■  **Text**   In a few sections of the HTML code you notice lines that only have free text, such as: "This is my first website! Thanks for stopping by." This free open text is displayed, as written, in the Web browser.

■  **<BR><BR>**   The Line Break command is similar to pressing the ENTER key on the keyboard, creating a hard return. In this case, two hard returns are communicated to the Web browser.

▲  **<A HREF>**   This line in the code informs the Web browser that a hyperlink should be displayed. In the listed code, the word "e-mail" is designated to routinely link to an e-mail address. Clicking on this link initiates an e-mail message with the e-mail address automatically inserted in the To: line. When you look at the picture of the Web page (shown in Figure 9-1), the e-mail address is not visible; you can see only the underlined "e-mail."

*TIP:*  If you are interested in learning more about HTML and creating Web pages using HTML, visit Web Reference's HTML site: http://webreference.com/html/.

## Creating a HTML Web Page Using Microsoft FrontPage

Microsoft FrontPage is a graphical tool for designing and editing Web pages. Although the underlying technology is HTML, FrontPage enables you to create Web pages quickly using an interface that is comfortable and easy to work with. If you are familiar with using Microsoft Office products (Word, Excel, PowerPoint, Outlook, and so forth), you can rapidly master FrontPage.

When you open FrontPage you are immediately presented with an application interface similar to Microsoft Outlook, as shown in sFigure 9-2. In addition, the program's File Menu and toolbars are exactly like those you are accustomed to in Microsoft Word.

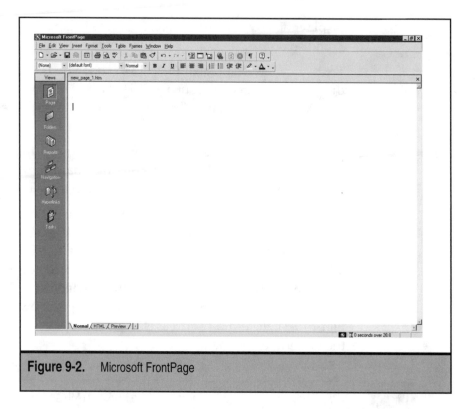

**Figure 9-2.** Microsoft FrontPage

If you are a diehard HTML fan, FrontPage still allows you to enter your code by clicking on the HTML tab located at the bottom of the program's window. However, the real value of FrontPage is the ability to construct static HTML Web pages without entering a line of code.

FrontPage opens on the Normal tab. This tab displays a blank page like you see when you choose to start a new document in Microsoft Word. To create the Web page, just start typing. Use the same formatting you would use in Microsoft Word. To provide the same HTML Web page as seen in the previous section, no code is entered—just typing and formatting text. The HTML code is still available when you click the HTML tab; it's generated for you automatically, because Web browsers still need the HTML code to know how to properly display Web pages. When you're finished typing and formatting text, clicking the Preview tab at the bottom of FrontPage's window enables you to view your Web page. This enables you to test the Web page before permanently placing it on a Web site.

Microsoft FrontPage offers a host of features that make it a very useful tool beyond creating only static Web pages. If you want to learn more about Microsoft FrontPage and the features it offers for creating rich, full-featured Web sites, visit the Microsoft FrontPage Web site: http://www.microsoft.com/frontpage/, or invest in *Microsoft FrontPage 2000: The Complete Reference* (Osborne/McGraw-Hill, ISBN: 007211939X).

## How a HTML Page Is Viewed

To help expand on how simple it is to create a viewable HTML Web page, it helps to understand how the visitor's Web browser is capable of locating and displaying the HTML page. Later, you'll learn how the Web browser interacts with Active Server Pages and you'll see that there is a very small but critical difference.

After the Web page is crafted and placed on a Web site, the user types the Web page location in the browser's Address line. The browser places a request to the remote Web server. The Web server locates the specified Web page (usually index.htm, index.html, home.htm, or home.html) and sends instructions on displaying it back to the Web browser. The Web browser then processes the HTML code and opens the Web page.

# ACTIVE SERVER PAGES (ASP)

For companies that need to exhibit a professional presence to potential clients, or for internal organizations that require more than stale information, the static HTML Web pages are a serious disadvantage. When a person surfs the Internet, the Web sites that are flashy, easy to navigate, engaging, and beneficial, are the pages that they go back to visit again and again.

In 1996, to combat stale Web pages, Microsoft released ASP 1.0. ASP is more than just typing and formatting text on a Web page. ASP is a technology that helps produce Web applications and dynamic

Web pages. When ASP was released, it really advanced much of the way that the Internet works almost overnight. Using ASP, you can create simple forms for the visitor to enter data or you can completely customize the visitor's Web site experience.

Since ASP 1.0, there have been two more version releases; each bundled as part of Internet Information Server. The latest release, ASP version 3.0, is included with IIS 5.0. IIS 5.0 is able to completely process ASP code and serve Web applications to the client's Web browser. ASP is what is called a *server-side technology,* meaning that the processing for the Web applications is handled completely by the Web server.

ASP is always evolving. Recent additions to the ASP technology allow Web pages to use common scripting programs such as Microsoft's VBScript and JavaScript for producing complex applications. Microsoft's VBScript will be covered in more detail later in the book.

If you have in-depth questions about ASP that are not covered in this book, the following Web sites offer some valuable resources:

▼ **15 Seconds (http://www.15seconds.com)**   This site presents some very well-informed technical articles and how-to's. The site is separated into easy to navigate sections: .NET | IIS 5.0 | IIS 4.0 | Data Access | Beginning | Troubleshooting | Security | Performance | Component Building | ADSI | ISAPI | Site Server | FTP | Upload | State | Email | Scripting | XML.

■ **4GuysFromRolla.com (http://www.4guysfromrolla.com)**   This site offers technical articles, how-to's, an ASP FAQ, and an online ASP Chat forum. This Web site is more of the next step after you become familiar with ASP, due to its more advanced documentation.

■ **LearnASP (http://www.learnasp.com)**   Formerly ActiveServerPages.com, this site offers step-by-step tutorials for getting up-to-speed on ASP programming. This site has plenty of ASP code to download and work with and a very comprehensive search engine for locating a specific ASP coding subject.

▲ **ASPWatch.com (http://www.aspwatch.com)**   This impressive
site provides ASP articles, with a strong emphasis on using
ASP to connect to databases. It also has an online ASP book,
which is a work in progress. New chapters are added to the
book continually.

# Methods for Creating Active Server Pages

As with HTML, there are some different options for producing
ASP scripts. The process of creating ASP scripts is very similar to
constructing the static HTML pages. In fact, ASP and HTML must
cooperate together to complete the Web site application. ASP is
different from HTML because the ASP code is recognized only by
a server that can process ASP scripts.

## Microsoft FrontPage

Microsoft FrontPage is one of the most popular Web page editing
tools. As described earlier in this chapter, FrontPage allows you to
quickly create HTML pages without entering code. FrontPage also
supports the formulation of ASP code with little or no knowledge
of the ASP language. FrontPage includes some ASP-type components
that are available as part of the application's installation. These
components require no programming skills. You select the
component you want to use and place it on the blank document.

For example, you can easily compose a user-input form that
automatically stores the entered data into a new Web page that is
created on the fly. While FrontPage includes several automated
ASP-type components, you also can add third-party components.
One particular company called Webs Unlimited makes J-Bots. J-Bots
is a collection of remarkable add-ons that extend the capabilities of
FrontPage. For more information on Webs Unlimited and J-Bots,
visit http://websunlimited.com.

## Microsoft Visual InterDev 6.0

Microsoft Visual InterDev 6.0 is part of Microsoft's Visual Studio—a
suite of programming tools that includes Visual Basic and Visual C++. Visual

InterDev serves as an ASP development tool. In addition to being a powerful ASP developing environment, Visual InterDev also provides strong ties to SQL server. This makes Visual InterDev the most powerful tool available for developing Web applications that store data and retrieve information from Microsoft's dominant database server application. For more information on Visual InterDev, visit Microsoft's Visual InterDev home page at http://msdn.microsoft.com/vinterde/default.asp.

### Notepad

Because ASP is an extension of the HTML language, you can use Notepad to create the ASP code. As demonstrated earlier in this chapter, when the simple HTML page was created, both HTML and ASP code can be entered into a standard text file and then saved with either an .HTM, .HTML, or .ASP filename extension.

### Other Notable Editors

All the offerings listed previously in this section are Microsoft solutions for editing and creating ASP coded Web pages; however, there are other Web site authoring applications that you will definitely want to take a look at. Some are listed here:

▼ **SoftQuad's Hotmetal Pro**   http://www.hotmetalpro.com/

■ **Adobe's Web Collection**   http://www.adobe.com/ products/ webcoll/main.html

▲ **Sausage Software's HotDog**   http://www.sausagetools.com/

## How an ASP Page Is Viewed

As discussed previously, the Web server can fulfill any client request for a Web page. However, when a Web application is being used, how does the Web browser know how to process ASP code? It doesn't. Read through the following and see if you can identify the differences between a common HTML request and an ASP request.

After the HTML is created and placed in an instruction file on a Web site, the user types the Web page location in the browser's address line. The browser places a request to the remote Web server. The remote Web server locates the instruction file; reads and processes the ASP code contained within the file; then sends instructions, in HTML code, for how to display the Web page back to the Web browser. The Web browser then processes the HTML code and displays the Web page.

As you noticed in the preceding paragraph, the Web server does the processing of the ASP code. The user's Web browser still reads HTML code and displays the Web page as it normally would. Internet browsers are like dumb terminals because they display only what they are told to display. Because ASP is dynamic, the Web page does not even really exist until after the user's Web browser makes the request. Because the Web server performs the actual processing for the client, it is crucial to have a powerful, robust Web server installed such as IIS 5.0.

## Creating a Simple ASP Web Page

After understanding how ASP functions, how HTML and ASP code work together, and how the user's Web browser views Web pages created with ASP technology, the next step is to design your first ASP document.

Without going too deeply into ASP code, let's create a simple Web page that displays the correct server time. Instead of using one of the fancy graphical editors, just produce the page in Windows Notepad. Typing the code into Notepad, instead of a program such as FrontPage, will help you to understand how the ASP code is structured, to observe how it fits in with standard HTML, and will enable you to troubleshoot code if a graphical editor is not available.

*CAUTION:*   Before attempting to create the ASP page, make sure you have a live IIS 5.0 server installed with the FrontPage extensions. Whereas HTML pages can be viewed from anywhere on the computer as if they were any other file in the file system, ASP pages must have an IIS server available to interpret and process the code.

To start, enter the standard HTML information that is needed for any Web page:

```
<HTML>
<HEAD><TITLE>This is my first ASP Web Page</TITLE></HEAD>
<BODY>
      <H1>Time Page</H1>
      Thanks for stopping by. The current date and time is:
</BODY>
</HTML>
```

Now, after typing the HTML code into Notepad, let's add the ASP component. The specific ASP component that we want to add is the VBScript Time command. ASP commands, specified to run on the server, generally are preceded by percent signs (%). Additionally, like HTML, there must be a pointer to start the statement and an ending pointer to identify where the ASP code concludes.

**NOTE:** VBScript is covered in more detail in Chapter 11.

So, in the Notepad code, at the end of the free text line "Thanks for stopping by. The current time is:" append the following VBScript command:

```
<% = FormatDateTime(Now) %>
```

The complete script now should look like the example in Figure 9-3.

After the VBScript command is placed in the HTML code, save the Notepad file by choosing File | Save As. Find the *Inetpub\wwwroot* directory on the IIS 5.0 server. In Notepad's Save As Type selection, select the All Files option; then name your first ASP page: **TimePage.asp** and click the Save button. For a clarification on saving the Notepad file, see Figure 9-4.

To test the new page, open the Web browser and type the address to the TimePage.asp file. Do this by using the standard convention of http://<servername>/TimePage.asp. When the Internet browser opens the Web page, you should see something similar to the example in Figure 9-5.

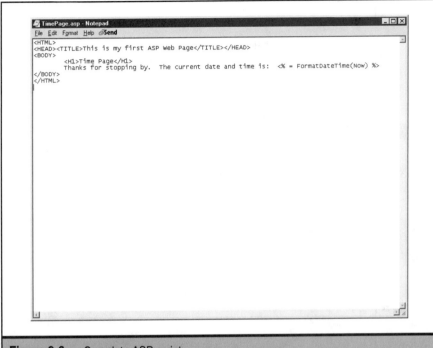

**Figure 9-3.** Complete ASP script

**Figure 9-4.** Saving the ASP script created in Notepad

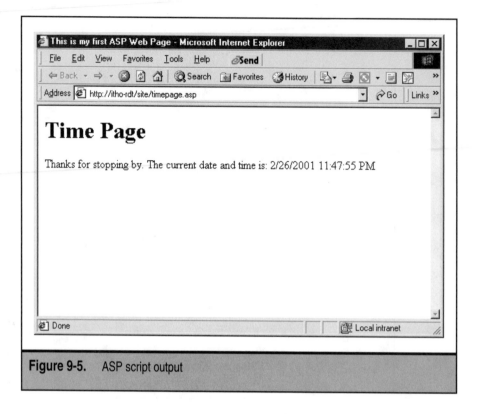

**Figure 9-5.**    ASP script output

Because the Date and Time commands are being processed as a server-side application, each time TimePage.asp is refreshed in the Web browser, the time changes. If the time happens to be 11:59:59 P.M., the date also will change with the refresh of the Web browser window. The IIS 5.0 server takes the Web browser's request for the page, identifies that it must process the FormatDateTime (NOW) command, and then sends the updated information to the Web browser. Although most of the information on the Web page is static HTML, the one ASP component makes this Web page dynamic. Additionally, each time the page is refreshed, the client makes another request of the server that gets processed and fulfilled.

Luckily, IIS 5.0 happens to be the most powerful Web server on the market. For large Internet sites, you can imagine the amount of processing power necessary for the Web server to accommodate thousands (sometimes millions) of requests per hour. For large corporations accessing company data, robust Web server software is essential to provide for the multitude of server requests.

## How IIS Processes the TimeDate.asp

We've created an ASP script and watched how the technology automates functions and generates dynamic components—but how exactly does IIS process the Web browser requests?

When IIS receives a request for a Web page, it identifies the file extension of the document. If the file extension is .HTM or .HTML the Web page is sent directly to the Internet browser that requested it. If the file extension is .ASP, IIS passes the code to the asp.dll file on the Web server. Asp.dll is a Dynamic Link Library (DLL) file developed specifically for IIS. The DLL file pushes any scripting commands contained in the ASP page to the proper scripting engine on the Web server. Asp.dll acts as a traffic cop, pushing VBScripts to the VBScript engine and JavaScripts to the JScript engine for processing. While the respective script engine is processing the ASP script component, asp.dll keeps tabs on the progression. When the script has completed, asp.dll retrieves the scripting engine's output and passes it back to the IIS server, which in turn transmits it immediately to the Web browser.

## SUMMARY

Anyone can post a Web site and can generally create a Web page using any of the Web page formatting tools available for download from various vendor Web sites. You've probably used an Internet search engine to locate Web locations based on a particular subject you are interested in. How many times have you found some interesting information, book marked the Web page, and then gone back a few times to find that the data is always the same? How many times do you return to those Web sites? It's just as easy to copy the information off of the never-changing Web page and place it into a document on your computer for later access. There's no need to visit the Web page more than once, but if you create a Web page that is interactive and changes constantly, Web surfers will visit regularly just to keep up.

Creating a popular Web site is hard to do, but it can be done by first understanding the technologies that work behind the scenes. Combining HTML and ASP, you can put together a presence on the Internet or within the enterprise that is both pleasing to the eye and interactive enough to keep people coming back.

# CHAPTER 10

## Database Connectivity

Information is key to running a business. Organizations hoard mounds of data because it provides a business edge and makes processes simpler. In the past, before data could be stored electronically, it was kept in hard copy format and filed in large vaults. Manual processes were created for tagging and organizing the data so that the information could be obtained when it was needed. Depending on the needs of the organization, people were hired specifically for retrieving the records from the data storage area.

When database application servers such as Microsoft SQL Server were introduced, companies raced to import their hard copy data into electronic form. Now they can easily attain data by using a database front end to search and recover the needed information. And, instead of having access limited to a 9-to-5 schedule, the data can be utilized any time. Salaries to employ data retrievers are no longer necessary.

However, unless the company had a skilled team of developers in-house, they had to pay a substantial amount of money to have a custom front-end application built to suit their needs. Sure, the data was easy to retrieve—unless the front-end application failed or new data types needed to be added to the database, in which cases the company was wedged into waiting for the developer to "get around" to supporting the application.

The Internet is everywhere. Applications that used to have a "clunky" look and feel have adopted a web-type interface that streamlines usability and makes the application experience more pleasant. As time passes, companies increasingly used the Internet for researching and browsing data from sources all over the world. The Web browser has become the most commonly used application. It's easy to understand and makes data quickly accessible.

Who knows where it all started, but somewhere along the line some CEO sparked an idea that all of a company's resources should be migrated to the Web. People everywhere know how to use a Web browser. If employees are as comfortable as possible retrieving data, productivity goes up. New hires don't have to go through as much technology training because they have already trained at home without knowing it. When new applications or upgrades are made available, as long as the interface stays the same, seasoned employees do not need retraining. More important, using Web technology to power the company's applications allows access to the data from anywhere. Employees can log on to the company's resources by using a dial-up modem or high-speed Internet connection, and perform the same job at home or in a hotel as they can from an office.

For larger corporations with offices in virtually every area of the United States, being able to consolidate all of the company's information into data storehouses means saving money by not purchasing a server for each office. And, as more companies push for business globalization, the centralized data feeds information to the world, at any time of the day or night. The data is not bound by geographic region, so the company doesn't need to be, either.

As companies increasingly port applications to Web interfaces to provide better business integrity, the capability to easily bridge a connection between the Web and database servers becomes a critical aspect of employment. IIS 5.0, Windows 2000, and ASP make this task possible. Using this combination of technologies, you can streamline company processes by centralizing the data and the administration of the data.

# CREATING YOUR FIRST ASP DATABASE CONNECTION

Using standard tools (and some defined procedures), you can quickly create a connection to any Microsoft SQL database for IIS. IIS reads the detailed connection information from the HTML's Active Server

Page (ASP) code. This connection string specifies the name of the SQL server that contains the information that is being sought, the user account and password that have rights to connect to the data, and the explicit types of data that are required to be displayed on the dynamic Web page.

Because IIS, ASP, and SQL Server are all Microsoft technologies, there is a multitude of ways to create an active Web page for data retrieval. When you are more comfortable and familiar with creating database connections, it is fun to mess around with programming code such as VBScript and JavaScript. These powerful scripting languages can make your Web pages perform an endless supply of tricks. But before delving into writing actual code, you need to understand how the connection works and how IIS performs the data retrieval process.

In the previous chapter on ASP, you experienced typing code into an HTML document to produce a dynamic ASP component. However, there are a number of tools for which code does not need to be entered. The best way to succeed at building your first ASP data Web pages is to use the simplest tools available: Microsoft FrontPage and Microsoft SQL Server.

## Using Microsoft FrontPage

As well as providing common Web authoring components such as click buttons and data fields, and quick HTML solutions, Microsoft FrontPage includes a Database Connection Wizard. This wizard enables you to create an association to different types of databases:

▼ Microsoft Excel spreadsheet

■ Microsoft Access database

▲ Microsoft SQL Server database

By enabling users to publish Excel spreadsheets and Access databases, Microsoft made FrontPage a tool that can be used by small to medium companies that want to make data readily available through a Web interface, without the need for a high-end Enterprise database server such as SQL Server. Additionally, for those companies that continue to grow and use Access databases for publishing data, it's easy to upgrade to SQL Server using Access's database Upsizing Wizard. For those SQL Server gurus, there is an import component in the SQL Enterprise Manager (covered in the next section) that can convert the Access database to a SQL format.

## First Steps

For this exercise you'll concentrate on the connection to a SQL server database. The database we will connect to in the example is a database created by Microsoft Systems Management Server (SMS); however, you can use any database that is available to you. SMS is an Enterprise-class systems management service. It automatically inventories the hardware and software of a computer system, distributes software, and provides remote management and software license management services. SMS retrieves information from the computer's hardware such as manufacturer and serial number and retrieves software information such as name and version. When SMS inventories the computer, the data is automatically distributed to a centralized SQL Server database where it can be accessed for management and reporting. Because SMS uses a SQL database, Microsoft FrontPage has no trouble creating a data connection for the IIS 5.0 server.

*TIP:* For more information on Microsoft Systems Management Server visit the following Web sites:

▼ http://www.myITforum.com

▲ http://www.microsoft.com/smsmgmt/default.asp

or check out the following books:

▼ *Admin911: SMS* (ISBN: 0072130229)

▲ *Microsoft SMS Installer* (ISBN: 0072124474)

Before creating your first SQL database connection using Microsoft FrontPage, you must make sure a few things are available:

▼ Microsoft FrontPage (of course)

■ SQL Server

■ SQL connection account with appropriate rights to the database

■ IIS 5.0 site with the FrontPage extensions installed and running (see Chapter 2 for more information on this procedure)

▲ Author rights to the IIS 5.0 site (reference Chapter 2 for information on how to modify rights on the IIS server)

## Creating the SQL Connection Account

The SQL Connection account is a specific name and password used by the IIS server to connect to the SQL database. When SQL server is first installed a system administrator (sa) account is created. This account has god-like powers over the SQL server and all the databases contained there. Although you can use the sa account for the IIS database connection, you want to avoid using it because of the security repercussions of utilizing a critical account.

If you are familiar with the Windows 2000 Domain Administrator account, the scenario is very similar. The Domain Administrator account has the same god-like powers over the entire network. Instead of using this account, you would create your own domain user account but give it only the rights needed to manage the network. Thus, instead of using the sa account to connect to the SQL database, you create a specific user account with access to the particular database. A vivid analogy is the reason you use a check card instead of carrying your entire savings in your pocket. If the check card gets lost or stolen, you cancel it and get another one. Meanwhile, your money sits safely tucked away, protected in your bank account.

Some organizations have a special team that cares for all of the company's SQL Servers and databases. This team is a highly specialized group that generally has misgivings about someone messing around with SQL Server. They are usually very protective of SQL to ensure that the proper security is maintained (and, of course, keep their jobs). If this is the case in your company, have one of the SQL team to create the connection account for you. If not, the following instructions will guide you through creating the account yourself.

To create a SQL Connection user account and password, follow these steps:

1. Open SQL Enterprise Manager. SQL Enterprise Manager is a MMC snap-in that gives administrative access to the SQL server properties.

2. As shown in Figure 10-1, expand the SQL server tree down to the database properties level; then right-click the Users property and choose New Database User.

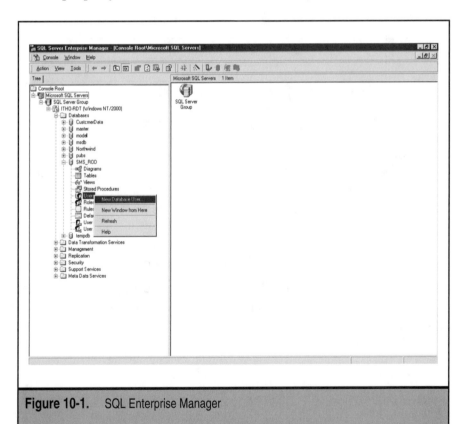

**Figure 10-1.**   SQL Enterprise Manager

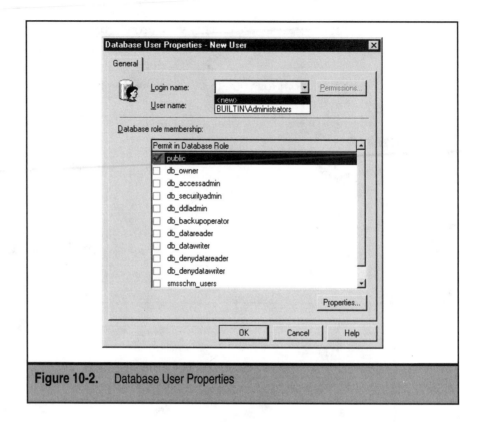

**Figure 10-2.** Database User Properties

**NOTE:** The version of SQL Enterprise Manager in this example is Microsoft SQL 2000. Earlier versions of SQL Server look a little different from the figures displayed, but the functions are the same.

3. When the Database User Properties box displays (see Figure 10-2), in the Login Name drop-down list, choose New.

4. When the SQL Server Login Properties window displays (see Figure 10-3), enter the name of the new database user account

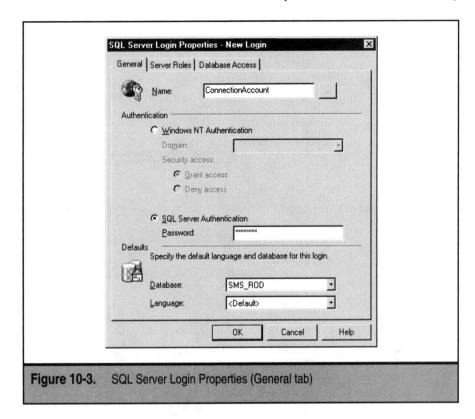

**Figure 10-3.** SQL Server Login Properties (General tab)

(ConnectionAccount in this example). Select SQL Server Authentication, create a password, and select the specific database in the drop-down list for default database. For this example, SMS_ROD has been chosen because it is the actual name of the SMS database that is being accessed.

5. Click the Database Access tab. As shown in Figure 10-4, put a check mark beside the specific database to which the connection account needs access, and make sure the only Database Role selected is Public.

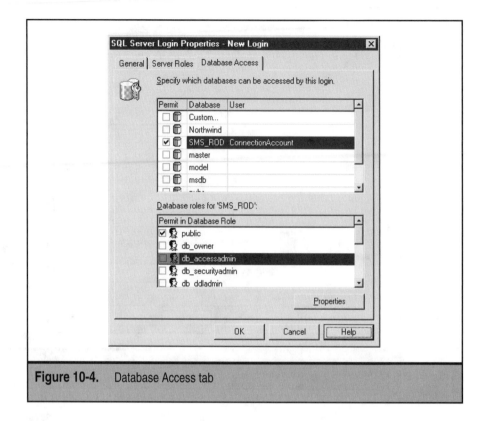

**Figure 10-4.**    Database Access tab

*NOTE:*    The IIS server does not need any special access rights beyond the Public database role for retrieving and displaying data. This helps retain SQL Server's strict security properties.

## Creating the Database Results Web Page

Once the SQL Server connection account has been configured (either by your own hands or through a SQL server guru), you can create the data access Web page. Make sure to have the account name and password ready and then complete the following steps:

1.   Open Microsoft FrontPage and connect to the IIS server by choosing File | Open Web and then typing the Web address of the IIS server in the Folder Name field. When the IIS Web opens, a new Web page is automatically started in the right-hand pane.

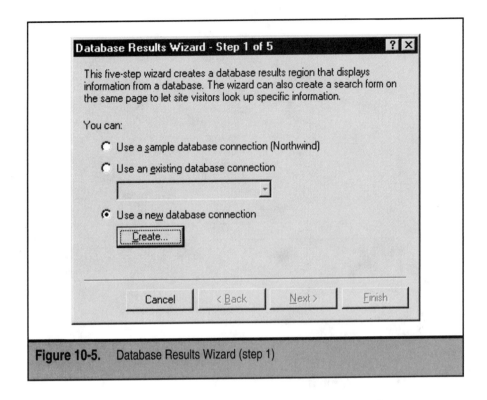

**Figure 10-5.** Database Results Wizard (step 1)

2. On the FrontPage file menu, choose Insert | Database | Results.

3. When the Database Results Wizard starts (see Figure 10-5), select the option to Use a New Database Connection and click the Create button.

**NOTE:** You'll need to create a new database connection only once. FrontPage will save this for later use and you will be able to choose it from the drop-down list for the Use an Existing Database Connection option.

4. The Web Settings property window will display and the Database tab is automatically given focus. Click the Add

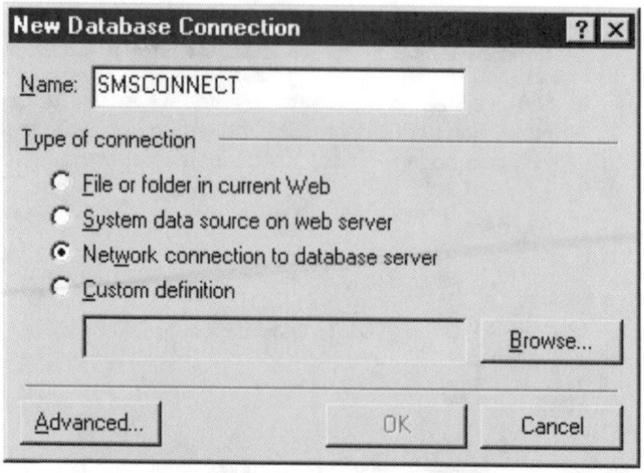

**New Database Connection**  ? ✕

Name: SMSCONNECT

Type of connection

- ○ File or folder in current Web
- ○ System data source on web server
- ● Network connection to database server
- ○ Custom definition

[                    ]  Browse...

Advanced...          OK          Cancel

**Figure 10-6.**  New Database Connection window

button to display the New Database Connection window (shown in Figure 10-6).

5. Give the database connection a name by entering it in the Name field.

**TIP:**  Make the database connection name something that helps define the specific database to which the Web page will be connecting. Because the connection could be used in the future and for multiple Web pages, or different databases will be used for different pages, giving it a detailed name will help in selecting the correct one. Because the example connects to the SMS SQL database, the database connection name is SMSCONNECT.

6. In the Type of Connection section, select Network Connection to Database Server; then click the Advanced button.

*TIP:*  Alternatively, you could select one of the other options available if it fits your situation. The other available options are

▼ **File or Folder in Current Web**   If you are creating a connection to a file or folder in the currently selected Web, choose this option. Clicking the Browse button with this option selected displays the files and folders housed in the Web site you are editing.

■ **System Data Source on Web Server**   When a system data source exists on the Web server itself, select this option. Clicking the Browse button with this option selected shows the Microsoft Access and SQL Server connections already defined in the Web site.

▲ **Custom Definition**   This option creates a connection to a File Data Source name (File DSN) or Universal Data Link (UDL) file in the current Web. If a given database driver requires parameters that you can't set using Microsoft FrontPage, you can create a custom database connection to edit the connection string that will be passed to the database driver.

7. When the Advanced Connection Properties window displays (shown in Figure 10-7), enter the SQL Connection Account and password that was created previously and click OK.

8. Once back at the New Database Connection window, click the Browse button to display the configuration screen shown in Figure 10-8. This property window allows you to select the actual type of database server that IIS will be accessing; type in the server's computer name, and enter the specific database that will be accessed. Make sure SQL Server is selected as the database driver.

9. Click OK until you are back at the Database tab of the Web Settings window. Click the Verify button. Before the Verify

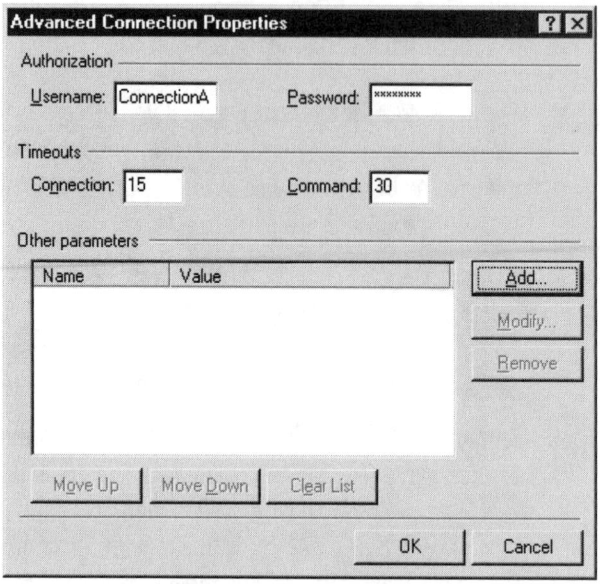

**Figure 10-7.** Advanced Connection Properties dialog box

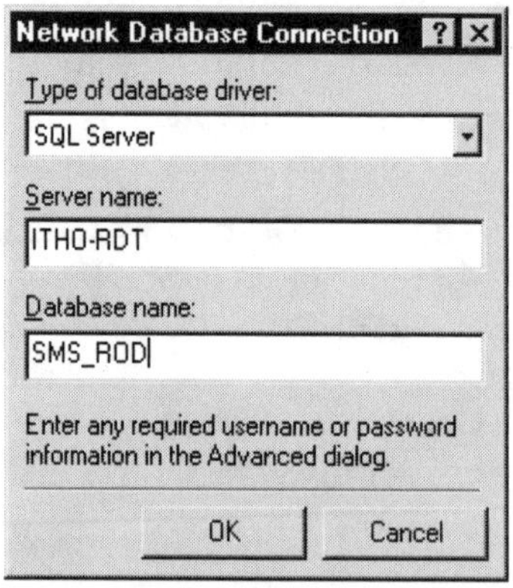

**Figure 10-8.** SQL connection properties

button is clicked, the new connection is displayed with a question mark (?) beside it. Verifying the connection ensures that the SQL server exists and the connection account name and password you entered are correct. When the connection tests successfully, the new connection displays with a check mark beside it (see Figure 10-9). If the connection does not pass the verification test, make sure you have entered all the information correctly and have been given the correct information.

10. When the connection is successful, clicking the OK button takes you back to the Database Results Wizard step 1 window. The newly created database connection is selected for you automatically. Click the Next button.

11. On the step 2 screen of the Database Results Wizard, choose the specific data (SQL table) that you want the Web page to display by selecting it from the Record Source drop-down list, as shown in Figure 10-10.

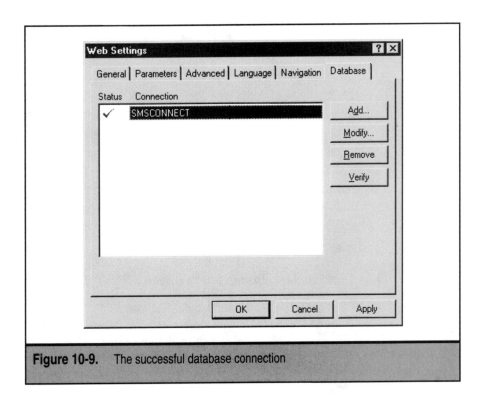

**Figure 10-9.** The successful database connection

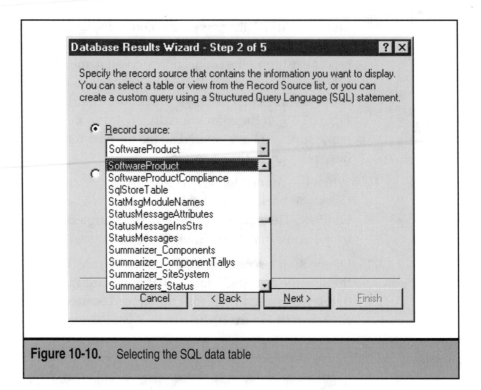

Figure 10-10.    Selecting the SQL data table

**NOTE:**   After you familiarize yourself with SQL Server, you can create your own queries to retrieve specific information by choosing the Custom Query option. SQL Server has its own query language that is very close to being a programming language. If you are interested in learning more about the SQL Server query language, visit the SQL section of SWYNK.com: http://www. swynk.com/sysapps/sql.asp. This site offers abundant information on SQL Server including sample queries that you can download and play with. When you use the Custom Query option you can enter the detailed SQL query to retrieve specific data.

12. Click the Next button after you have selected the record source.

13. On the step 3 window of the Database Results Wizard, you can click the Edit List button to customize the specific fields (shown in Figure 10-11) that are shown on the dynamic Web page.

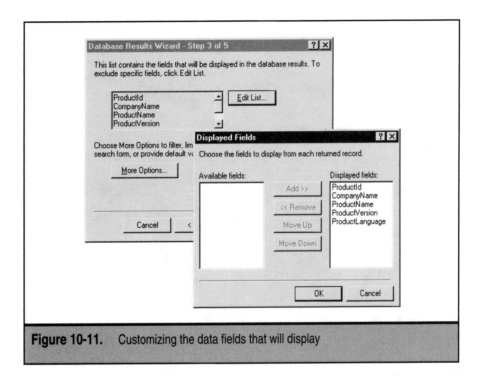

**Figure 10-11.**   Customizing the data fields that will display

Clicking the More Options button enables you choose specific criteria by which to sort the data or configure the order by which the data is displayed. Also, on the More Options configuration window, you can enter custom text that will display if the IIS connection doesn't find any data to show.

14. Once you have customized the information using the step 3 window, clicking Next takes you to the step 4 window where you can choose how the data is formatted on the Web page. For this example, I have chosen Table – One Record per Row, as shown in Figure 10-12. When you choose a main selection in the formatting drop-down list, several options are available for each. The main selections are

■ As a Table—One record per row

■ As a List—One field per item

■ As a Drop-Down List—One record per item

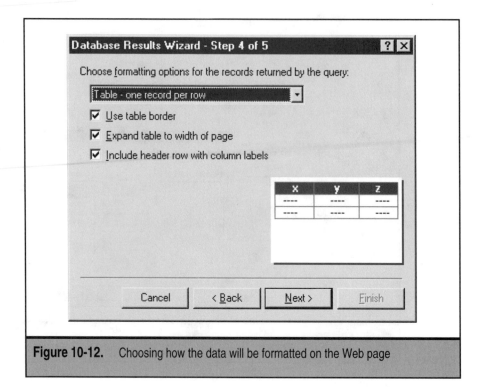

**Figure 10-12.** Choosing how the data will be formatted on the Web page

15. After you are finished configuring the Web page formatting options, click the Next button.

16. The step 5 window (see Figure 10-13) enables you to choose how many records per page are displayed at one time. The options are

   ■ Display All Records Together
   ■ Split Records into Groups

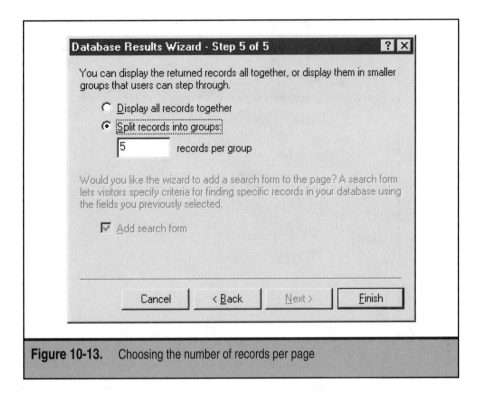

**Figure 10-13.**  Choosing the number of records per page

17. Once you decide how the records should be grouped (for this example, I chose to split the records into five records per group), click the Finish button and FrontPage creates the Web page for you.

Because the new Web page is a dynamic Web document, it cannot be viewed using the FrontPage Preview tab. The new page can be tested only by first saving the Web page; then opening it in a Web browser by typing in the address and Web page name. For example, to access the page that I saved, I typed http://itho-rdt/SoftwareInventory.asp, and the Web page in Figure 10-14 was displayed.

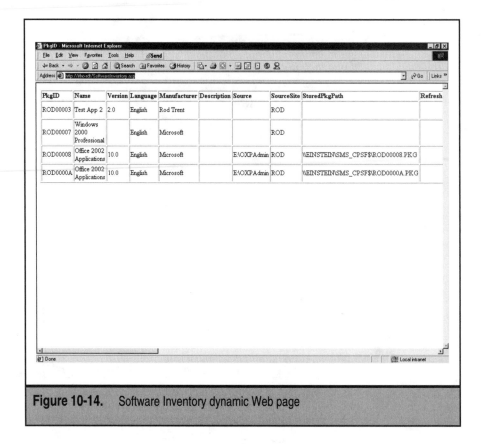

**Figure 10-14.** Software Inventory dynamic Web page

Setting up a dynamic data connection to SQL Server is pretty simple using Microsoft FrontPage. Now that you know how to accomplish this task, you can play with the different options to get the best look and the obligatory data for future Web pages.

## SUMMARY

As you can see from this chapter, utilizing IIS 5.0, Windows 2000, and ASP you can easily create a central repository for data that should be readily available to a multitude of people. Microsoft has incorporated the latest technologies into Windows 2000 and IIS 5.0, which enable you to not only provide active Web sites, but also make access to critical data timely and simple.

The more you work to simplify the way data is accessed, the more likely that Web surfers will make use of the technology you put in place. The Internet interface—the Web browser—is a vehicle that makes data easily accessible to beginners and advanced computer users alike. The Web browser is the first application to come along that takes the complexity out of using a computer and puts new and old users on equal footing. By Web-enabling the data to which you are entrusted, you allow the information to be accessed by any authorized user, not just those who have gone through long hours of training.

# CHAPTER 11

## More Web Technologies

Chapter 10 looks at giving your IIS Web site the capability to connect to external data repositories and then making it available through a Web page. This capability enriches a Web site and makes the information more valuable because it is easier to glean.

Chapter 9 lays the foundation for incorporating technologies that permit the data to be accessed in this way. Laying ASP over HTML gives your Web site the capability to create any type of interactive Web page. It automates processes that would otherwise produce a Web site that leaves the user bored after the first few visits.

But, there's so much more to creating Web pages that dazzles and captivates the audience. Web technologies are continually evolving at an extremely rapid pace. As the evolution revolves, snippets of new processes and components emerge. This chapter outlines some of the more recent technologies that can push your Web site even further on the cutting edge. Not only will you read about components that "spiff-up" your Web pages, but you'll also identify key technologies that can further automate your Web site and make even the simplest information seem to jump off the screen. Along with each Web component discussed, you'll also receive sample code to try out on your own Web pages.

## DHTML

Earlier in this book, we discussed HTML and outlined specific steps for creating your first Web page using nothing but Microsoft Notepad and a few lines of HTML code. Dynamic HTML (DHTML) is a newer technology that is like HTML on steroids. DHTML takes standard HTML objects and allows you to put in animation effects. DHTML actually is a Microsoft enhancement to HTML, which started with HTML version 4.0.

You can apply DHTML animation effects to just about anything on a page—text, paragraphs, pictures, buttons, marquees, and so forth—and tie the effect to a trigger event such as clicking a mouse, pointing a mouse, or loading a page. You can create an animation that makes text fly in from the right when the page is loaded.

DHTML offers the following advantages over standard HTML:

▼ **Document Object Model (DOM)**   Dynamic HTML provides a comprehensive object model for HTML. This model exposes all page elements as objects. You can easily manipulate these objects by changing their attributes or applying methods to them at any time. Dynamic HTML also provides full support for keyboard and mouse events on all page elements.

■ **Dynamic content**   Text or graphics can be added, deleted, or modified on the fly. For example, a Web page can display an updated headline without refreshing the page. The text surrounding the headline will reflow automatically.

■ **Dynamic styles**   Internet Explorer 4.0 and above fully supports Cascading Style Sheets (CSS). As such, any CSS attribute, including color and font, can be updated without a server round trip. For instance, text can change color or size when a mouse pointer passes over it. Multimedia filters and transition effects can be applied to HTML elements simply by adding the filter CSS attribute.

**NOTE:**   Introduced in HTML version 3.0, Cascading Style Sheets (files with a .css extension) are enhancements that improve control over design elements. They also add wider accessibility support to Web pages. CSS version 1.0 introduced the concept of Cascading Style Sheets to store design information that could be applied to entire Web sites. CSS version 2.0 introduced effects such as position boxes and the ability to layer page elements on top of or behind one another. In essence, you create a specific template for how the Web site should look; then apply it so that it is automatically generated for each new Web page you construct. This gives you complete control over the uniformity of the Web site. When visitors access a different page in your site, they immediately know they are still within the same Web location and have not been magically transported across the World Wide Web.

■ **Absolute positioning**   CSS positioning coordinates for existing page content can be updated at any time to create animated effects without reloading the page.

■ **Data Binding**   Data-driven application front ends can be built that present, manipulate for example, sort, filter, and update data on the client without numerous round trips to the server.

▲ **Scriptlets**    A scriptlet is a Web page written using Dynamic HTML, which content providers can use as a component in their Web applications. With scriptlets, content providers can create subject matter once; then easily reuse the material in other Web pages or applications. A familiar example of a DHTML scriptlet is a Web application written using JavaScript.

**NOTE:**   It's important to understand that DHTML is a technology for providing active Web content; not necessarily a programming language. Any programming language that can be used to automate components for use on the Internet falls under the DHTML umbrella. However, some Web browsers don't support DHTML, so pages containing DHTML might not be displayed properly or might contain errors when viewed by some site visitors.

## DHTML Support

Microsoft FrontPage enables you to target your Web for compatibility with specific browsers and technologies. If you enable or disable DHTML, or if you target a Web for compatibility with a browser that doesn't support DHTML, the commands that utilize DHTML will be unavailable (that is, they will appear dimmed) on menus in FrontPage at authoring time. Table 11-1 illustrates the different Web browser versions and whether DHTML is supported.

| Browser | Browser Version | DHTML |
|---------|-----------------|-------|
| Internet Explorer | 4.0 and later | Enabled |
| Internet Explorer | 3.0 and earlier | Disabled |
| Netscape Navigator | 4.0 and later | Enabled |
| Netscape Navigator | 3.0 and earlier | Disabled |
| Microsoft WebTV | N/A | Disabled |

**Table 11-1.**   DHTML Support by Web Browser and Version

# Microsoft FrontPage and DHTML

Microsoft FrontPage provides some very useful DHTML tools that enable you to quickly convert standard HTML items into dynamic Web page components. Using FrontPage, you can enable the following dynamic content:

▼ **Page transitions**   You can create special effects that are displayed when a site visitor enters or leaves your site, or browses to or from a specific page. By applying transition effects consistently and judiciously throughout your Web, you can create slide-show-style presentations with professional-looking transitions between pages.

■ **Banner advertisements**   A banner ad is like a rotating billboard on a Web page. It displays a timed sequence of pictures using a transition effect between pictures. Authors typically use these banners to place advertising on pages. You can create a hyperlink from the banner ad to the Web site or page for the company, product, or service featured in the ad.

■ **Hover buttons**   Creating a hover button is an easy way to add animation to your Web without any scripting. Like any other button, a hover button contains a hyperlink to another page or file. However, when a site visitor clicks or points to a hover button, the button can also glow, display a custom picture, or play a sound effect. You also can use a picture for a hover button or for the hover effect on a hover button.

■ **Marquees**   A marquee displays a scrolling text message. You can customize a marquee to achieve exactly the effects you want.

▲ **Sound effects**   Sounds and sound effects add another dimension to your Web. If your company has a musical or audio "logo," jingle, or theme, you can play it when a site visitor surfs to your home page from another site on the World Wide Web. You also can add sound effects to a hover button. When a site visitor browsing your page clicks or points to the hover button, the sound effect is played.

To use Microsoft FrontPage to create DHTML effects, you must be running an IIS server with the FrontPage extensions installed and applied; and Dynamic HTML must be enabled for the particular FrontPage Web. To enable DHTML for the Web, follow these steps:

1. Open Microsoft FrontPage and open the specific Web site.

2. Click Tools | Page Options and then click the Compatibility tab.

3. Click the check box (shown in Figure 11-1) to enable Dynamic HTML.

## HTML and DHTML Differences

To better understand the differences between HTML and DHTML it is useful to identify the additional "behind-the-scenes" code differences. A Web page that includes DHTML components actually embellishes on the HTML code already present. It simply adds to the existing script.

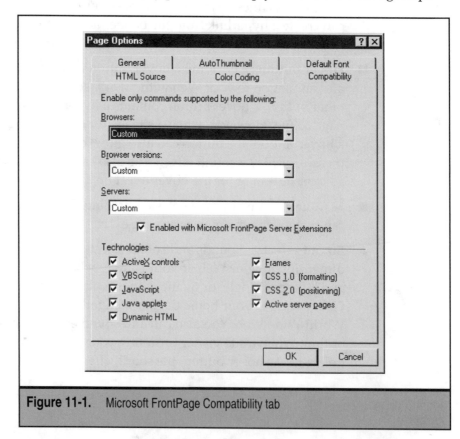

**Figure 11-1.** Microsoft FrontPage Compatibility tab

The best way to identify the differences between the two scripting techniques is to view the differences between the two codes. Listed in the following is the HTML code from the book's previous example for creating your first Web page (from Chapter 9).

```
<HTML>
<HEAD><TITLE>Welcome to my Website</TITLE></HEAD>
<BODY>
     <H1>Welcome to my Website</H1>
     This is my first Website! Thanks for stopping by.
     <BR><BR>
     Leave me an
     <A HREF="mailto:myemail@myemail.com">email</A>
     to let me know you like it!
</BODY>
</HTML>
```

Using the HTML code as a reference, you can easily identify the differences between it and the DHTML code listed next. The following code causes the title: "Welcome to my Website" to increase its font size when the surfer's mouse moves over it. The font size returns to normal when the mouse is moved away from the title text.

```
<HTML>
<HEAD><TITLE>Welcome to my Website</TITLE><script language=
"JavaScript" fptype="dynamicanimation">
<!--
function dynAnimation() {}
function clickSwapImg() {}
//-->
</script>
<script language="JavaScript1.2" fptype="dynamicanimation"
src="file:///C:/Program%20Files/Microsoft%20Office/Office/
fpclass/animate.js">
</script>
</HEAD>
<BODY onload="dynAnimation()" language="Javascript1.2">
     <H1 dynamicanimation="fpAnimformatRolloverFP1"
     fprolloverstyle=
```

```
"font-size: 36pt; font-weight: bold" onmouseover="rollIn(this)"
onmouseout="rollOut(this)" language="Javascript1.2">Welcome to my
Website</H1>
        This is my first Website! Thanks for stopping by.
        <BR><BR>
        Leave me an
        <A HREF="mailto:myemail@myemail.com">email</A>
        to let me know you like it!
</BODY>
</HTML>
```

If you look carefully at the DHTML code, you see that a JavaScript component, animate.js, was added to the HTML and specific instructions were given to the component for it to perform. If you really want to delve into learning JavaScript, it is a very useful Web programming language to learn, as you can create solutions that will run on just about any platform, or any Web server. JavaScript is covered in more detail later in this chapter.

If learning JavaScript is not something you think you will ever be tasked with, there are easier ways to create similar JavaScript components without ever learning a line of code. One example, using Microsoft FrontPage, is described in the next section.

## Working with DHTML in Microsoft FrontPage

Now that you know that DHTML components are created simply by adding key scripting elements into standard HTML, it's time to create one of your own. The easiest way to rapidly develop a Web page that contains DHTML components is to use Microsoft FrontPage. Using FrontPage as your DHTML generator, there are only three actual steps involved to animate an object on the page:

1. Select an event.

2. Set the action.

3. Configure the settings for the action.

In the previous section, you saw a DHTML script that increased the font size of the Web page's title when the mouse cursor was placed over the text. This dynamic title can be produced in Microsoft FrontPage in just a few steps. To create the DHTML code in FrontPage, follow these directions:

1. Run FrontPage and then open a Web that resides on the IIS 5.0 Web server.

2. Enable viewing of the DHTML Effects toolbar. The toolbar is not loaded by default. To open it, choose View | Toolbars and then select the DHTML Effects option.

3. Open the simple HTML Web page that you created in Chapter 9.

4. Select and highlight the entire title text: "Welcome to my Website."

5. Click the Choose an Event drop-down list on the DHTML Effects toolbar, shown in Figure 11-2, and select Mouse Over.

6. Select Formatting from the Choose an Effect drop-down list. Note that this option only becomes available after an event is chosen.

7. Select Choose Font from the drop-down list next to the Formatting option.

8. When the Choose Font option has been selected, you are presented with a Font dialog box. In the Font Style, choose Bold. In the Font Size, choose 36pt and click OK.

You will see the Web page's title framed within a cyan-colored box. FrontPage uses this color framing convention so you can quickly identify dynamic components on the page, and separate them from the plain HTML text. To test the new DHTML element, click FrontPage's Preview tab and run the mouse cursor over the title text.

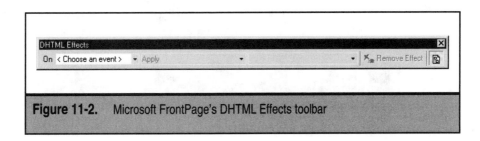

**Figure 11-2.**   Microsoft FrontPage's DHTML Effects toolbar

Creating this animated effect was a simple process because Microsoft FrontPage writes the script for you in the background. You need to select only the options you want for a text or graphic component; FrontPage does the rest. As you've experienced in this chapter and previous chapters, Microsoft FrontPage is a powerful tool to help get you up and running with your own IIS 5.0 Web site.

To better understand the DHTML effects that FrontPage has to offer, review Table 11-2.

| Event | Action | Settings |
|---|---|---|
| Click | Fly-out | To Left, To Top, To Bottom-Left, To Bottom-Right, To Top-Right, To Top-Left, To Top-Right by Word, To Bottom-Right by Word |
| | Formatting | Choose Font, Choose Border |
| Double-Click | Fly-out | To Left, To Top, To Bottom-Left, To Bottom-Right, To Top-Right, To Top-Left, To Top-Right by Word, To Bottom-Right by Word |
| | Formatting | Choose Font \| Choose Border |
| Mouse Over | Formatting | Choose Font \| Choose Border |
| Page Load | Drop in by word | N/A |
| | Elastic | From right, From bottom |
| | Fly-in | To Left, To Top, To Bottom-Left, To Bottom-Right, To Top-Right, To Top-Left, To Top-Right by Word, To Bottom-Right by Word |

**Table 11-2.**   DHTML Events Available in Microsoft FrontPage

| Event | Action | Settings |
|-------|--------|----------|
|       | Hop    | N/A      |
|       | Spiral | N/A      |
|       | Wave   | N/A      |
|       | Wipe   | Left-to-Right, Top-to-Bottom, From Middle |
|       | Zoom   | In, Out  |

**Table 11-2.**  DHTML Events Available in Microsoft FrontPage *(continued)*

## Additional Information on DTHML

DHTML has become a popular aspect of many Web sites. If you want your IIS Web site to dazzle the audience, DHTML is a simple device that produces impressive results. For more information on DHTML, become a regular visitor to the following Web sites:

▼ **DHTML Zone**   http://www.dhtml-zone.com/ default1.asp?Area=DHTML

■ **DHTML Tutorial**   http://www.1001tutorials.com/

■ dhtml/index.shtml

▲ **Taylor's Dynamic HTML Tutorial**   http:// hotwired.lycos.com/Webmonkey/ authoring/ dynamic_html/tutorials/tutorial1.html

# JAVASCRIPT

Java, developed by Sun MicroSystems (http://www.sun.com), is a scripting language that runs on multiple platforms. Released in the mid-1990s, it enables developers to write applications that can run on any type of computer without it being written specifically for that computer's operating system. JavaScript, a subset of Java, is a compact, object-based scripting language for developing client and server Internet applications.

JavaScript Web components suffer in performance because each JavaScript application on the Web page must be downloaded to the computer accessing it before it is run. This extra step causes the actual execution of the JavaScript component to take longer than a DHTML or VBScript (described later in this chapter).

Despite the performance issues, JavaScript is a powerful Web language that is enjoyable to use, as you will see in the next code sample section. The best way to learn more about JavaScript is to download and use code that is freely available on the Internet. The following Web sites are updated frequently with news, information, and JavaScript code:

▼ **JavaScript.com**   http://www.javascript.com

■ **JavaScript Resource**   http://javascript.internet.com/

▲ **Java Boutique**   http://javaboutique.internet.com/

If you want to learn JavaScript offline, you'll want to invest in a good book that you can read anywhere (although I suggest you do it in front of a computer because you'll be dying to try out the examples). *Beginning JavaScript,* from Wrox Press, Inc. is a recommended purchase (ISBN: 1861004060).

## Code Samples

The examples in this section should give you something to have fun with. Just place the JavaScript code into the body of your HTML page (using the HTML view). This means that the code listed in the following sections needs to be placed between the <Body> and </Body> lines in the HTML code.

### Listing the Season and Year on the Web Page

While not a critical aspect of a Web page, making the season and year information available for display is a fun way to catch the visitor's eye. The following script reads the system's clock and then calculates and displays the actual season and year on the Web page:

```
<SCRIPT LANGUAGE="JavaScript">
var now = new Date();
var month = now.getMonth() + 1;
var date = now.getDate();
var year = now.getYear();
var season;
if (month > 1 && month <= 3) season = "Winter";
if (month == 3 && date > 19) season = "Spring";
if (month > 3 && month <= 6) season = "Spring";
if (month == 6 && date > 20) season = "Summer";
if (month > 6 && month <= 9) season = "Summer";
if (month == 9 && date > 21) season = "Fall";
if (month > 9 && month <= 12) season = "Fall";
if (month == 12 && date > 20) season = "Winter";
//Y2K Fix
if (year < 2000) year = year + 1900;
//Winter Season Fix
if (season == "Winter") year = year - 1;
document.write(season + " " + year);
// End -->
</script>
```

## A Simple Pop-Up Window

The following pop-up window code places a button on the Web page, which, when clicked, displays an alert window (as shown in Figure 11-3).

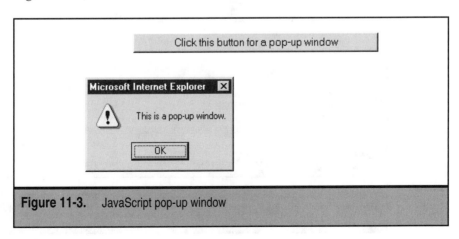

**Figure 11-3.**   JavaScript pop-up window

```
<CENTER>
<FORM>
<INPUT TYPE="button" VALUE="Click this button for a pop-up
window"
onClick='alert("This is a pop-up window.")'>
</FORM>
</CENTER>
```

## Sending an E-mail with a Predefined Subject

Surfing around the Internet, you've probably stumbled across Web
pages that offer a button to click that will automatically generate an
e-mail for you. The following script performs this function. It places a
button on the Web page, and once clicked, creates an e-mail with the
appropriate address and subject, as shown in Figure 11-4.

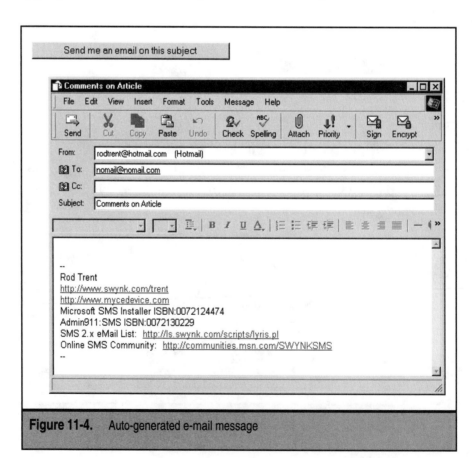

**Figure 11-4.**   Auto-generated e-mail message

```
<FORM>
<INPUT TYPE="button" VALUE="Send me an email on this subject"
onClick="parent.location='mailto:nomail@nomail.com?subject=Comments
on Article'">
</FORM>
```

## Displaying Files and Folders

You can use JavaScript to display files and folders on the local computer with a few simple lines of code. The following script displays a button to click that has the words: C:\ Drive, on it. When the button is clicked, the files and folders for the computer's C: drive are displayed in the browser window.

```
<center>
<form action="file:///c|/"><input type="submit" value="c:\
 drive"></form>
<p>
```

## Printing from a Web Page

If you want Web site visitors to be able to easily print your Web page you can add the following JavaScript. It places a "Print This Page." button on the page and when the user clicks it, the printer dialog box displays:

```
<p><input type="submit" name="B1" value="Print This Page..."
onclick="window.print()"></p>
```

# Additional Information on JavaScript

JavaScript is a great technology to immediately enrich the user's experience when they visit your Web site. Using this Web language can make a boring Web page jump with life. For more information on JavaScript and to download some freely reusable scripts, visit the following Web sites:

▼ **http://www.javascriptit.com/home/start.asp**   JavaScript It! is a shareware program that enables Web developers to easily add advanced JavaScript and DHTML code to their Web pages. JavaScript It! also equips Web developers with Java applets to their Web pages.

■ **http://www.jsworld.com/** JavaScript World offers several very nice features. The site is very well done and provides JavaScript tutorials, news, and downloadable scripts.

▲ **http://www.javascripts.com** JavaScripts.com is touted as the largest JavaScripts repository online. Thousands of scripts are freely available for download.

## VBSCRIPT

Microsoft Visual Basic Scripting (VBScript), a subset of the Microsoft Visual Basic programming language, is a fast, portable, lightweight interpreter for use in Web pages and other applications that use Microsoft ActiveX Controls, Automation servers, and Java applets. VBScript is automatically available with Internet Explorer and IIS. It also can be downloaded separately from Microsoft's Scripting Engines download site: http://www.microsoft.com/msdownload/vbscript/scripting.asp.

VBScript is particularly easy to learn if you have any programming experience with Microsoft's Visual Basic programming language. Over the last couple years, Microsoft has pushed VBScript into clear view with the release of Windows 2000. Windows 2000 fully supports VBScript as a solution to manage and administer the Windows 2000 operating system as well as the Active Directory structure. Whereas JavaScript is a useful tool for creating quick Web page components, VBScript is positioned as more of a full-featured Web application builder. Delving deep into VBScript is highly recommended, as it will only continue to proliferate the computer industry and Internet world.

Although it is important to understand that VBScript code can be embedded for automating your HTML documents, VBScripts (identified by a .VBS file extension) also can be utilized outside of the Web server environment. When the Microsoft Scripting Engines are installed, two separate executables are set up:

▼ **Cscript.exe**   Cscript is the command-line version of the VB Scripting engine. It provides the ability to run .VBS files within an MS-DOS window and allows the use of command-line switches. Example: Cscript MyFile.vbs /switch.

▲ **Wscript.exe**   Wscript is the Windows version of the VB Scripting engine. VBS files written to run only within the Windows *graphical user interface* (GUI) make use of this engine.

In fact, when IIS is installed, several Administration VBScripts are inserted into specific directories on the Web server. Microsoft provided these scriptlets to help in IIS administration and to give you a head start in realizing the power and usefulness of VBScript. The different scripts, their locations on the server, a description of their functions, and the syntaxes are identified in Table 11-3.

| Script Name | Location | Description |
|---|---|---|
| Adsutil.vbs | \Intepub\AdminScripts | Uses the Active Directory Services Interface (ADSI) to administrate the IIS server. |
| | | Syntax: |
| | | Cscript Adsutil.vbs |

**Table 11-3.**   IIS Administration VBScripts

| Script Name | Location | Description |
|---|---|---|
| Chaccess.vbs | \Intepub\AdminScripts | Enables modification of the Web site's access permissions.<br><br>Syntax:<br><br>Cscript chaccess.vbs <--ADSPath \| -a DSPATH><br>[--computer \| -c COMPUTER1 [,COMPUTER2...]]<br>[+read \| -read]<br>[+write \| -write]<br>[+script \| -script]<br>[+execute \| -execute]<br>[+browse \| -browse]<br>[--verbose \| -v]<br>[--help \| -?] |
| Contftp.vbs | \Intepub\AdminScripts | Releases a FTP server that has been paused.<br><br>Syntax:<br><br>Cscript contftp.vbs <--ADSPath \| -a server1[,server2, server3...]><br>[--computer \| -c COMPUTER1 [,COMPUTER2...]]<br>[--verbose \| -v]<br>[--help \| -?] |

**Table 11-3.**    IIS Administration VBScripts *(continued)*

| Script Name | Location | Description |
|---|---|---|
| Contsrv.vbs | \Intepub\AdminScripts | Releases a Web site where the services have been paused. |
| | | Syntax: |
| | | Cscript contsrv.vbs <--ADSPath I -a server1[,server2, server3...]> |
| | | [--help I -?] |
| ContWeb.vbs | \Intepub\AdminScripts | Releases the Web server where all services have been paused. |
| | | Syntax: |
| | | Cscript contWeb.vbs <--ADSPath I -a server1[,server2, server3...]> |
| | | [--computer I -c COMPUTER1 [,COMPUTER2...]] |
| | | [--verbose I -v] |
| | | [--help I -?] |

**Table 11-3.**    IIS Administration VBScripts *(continued)*

| Script Name | Location | Description |
|---|---|---|
| Dispnode.vbs | \Intepub\AdminScripts | Displays the properties of the specified node. Different properties are displayed depending on the class of the node.<br><br>Syntax:<br><br>Cscript dispnode.vbs <br><--ADSPath \| -a ADS PATH OF NODE><br><br>[--help \| -h] |
| Disptree.vbs | \Intepub\AdminScripts | Prints the tree of administration objects starting either at the specified node or the root node of the local machine.<br><br>Syntax:<br><br>Cscript disptree.vbs [--ADSPath \| -a ROOT NODE]<br><br>[--NoRecurse \| -n]<br><br>[--help \| -?] |

**Table 11-3.** IIS Administration VBScripts *(continued)*

| Script Name | Location | Description |
|---|---|---|
| FindWeb.vbs | \Intepub\AdminScripts | Searches a computer for a specified Web site and displays information about the site. |
| | | Syntax: |
| | | Cscript findWeb.vbs [--computer \| -c COMPUTER] |
| | | <--Website \| -w WEBSITE> |
| | | [--help \| -?] |
| Logenum.vbs | \Inetpub\iissamples\ sdk\admin | Allows you to configure logging services for IIS. |
| | | Syntax: |
| | | Cscript logenum.vbs [<adspath>] |
| Metaback.vbs | \Inetpub\iissamples\ sdk\admin | Allows you to create a backup of your Metabase. |
| | | Syntax: |
| | | Cscript metaback.vbs |
| Metabackrest. vbs | \Inetpub\iissamples\ sdk\admin | Allows you to restore backups of your Metabase. |
| | | Syntax: |
| | | Cscript metabackrest.vbs |

**Table 11-3.**   IIS Administration VBScripts *(continued)*

| Script Name | Location | Description |
|---|---|---|
| Mkw3site.vbs | \Intepub\AdminScripts | Creates a new virtual Web server.<br><br>Syntax:<br><br>Cscript mkw3site.exe<br><--RootDirectory I<br>-r ROOT<br>DIRECTORY><br><br><--Comment I -t<br>SERVER COMMENT><br><br>[--computer I -c<br>COMPUTER1<br>[,COMPUTER2...]]<br><br>[--HostName I -h<br>HOST NAME]<br><br>[--port I -o PORT<br>NUM]<br><br>[--IPAddress I -i IP<br>ADDRESS]<br><br>[--SiteNumber I -n<br>SITENUMBER]<br><br>[--Don'tStart]<br><br>[--verbose I -v]<br><br>[--help I -?] |

**Table 11-3.**    IIS Administration VBScripts *(continued)*

| Script Name | Location | Description |
|---|---|---|
| MkWebdir.vbs | \Intepub\AdminScripts | Creates a virtual Web directory on the specified Web site and with the specified path. |
| | | Syntax: |
| | | Cscript mkWebdir.vbs [--computer \| -c COMPUTER1, COMPUTER2, COMPUTER3] |
| | | <--Website \| -w WEBSITE> |
| | | <--virtualdir \| -v NAME1,PATH1, NAME2,PATH2,...> |
| | | [--help \| -?] |
| MkWebsrv.vbs | \Inetpub\iissamples\ sdk\admin | This sample admin script allows you to create a Web server. |
| | | Syntax: |
| | | Cscript mkWebsrv.vbs <rootdir> [-n <instancenum>][-c <comment>][-p <portnum>][-X (don't start)] |

**Table 11-3.**   IIS Administration VBScripts *(continued)*

| Script Name | Location | Description |
|---|---|---|
| Pauseftp.vbs | \Intepub\AdminScripts | Pauses a FTP site. Syntax: Cscript pauseftp.vbs <--ADSPath \| -a server1[,server2, server3...]> [--computer \| -c COMPUTER1 [,COMPUTER2...]] [--verbose \| -v] [--help \| -?] |
| Pausesrv.vbs | \Intepub\AdminScripts | Pauses a specific Web site. Syntax: Cscript pausesrv.vbs <--ADSPath \| -a server1[,server2, server3...]> [--help \| -?] |
| PauseWeb.vbs | \Intepub\AdminScripts | Pauses the Web services on a server. Syntax: Cscript pauseWeb.vbs <--ADSPath \| -a server1[,server2, server3...]> [--computer \| -c COMPUTER1 [,COMPUTER2...]] [--verbose \| -v] [--help \| -?] |

**Table 11-3.**    IIS Administration VBScripts *(continued)*

| Script Name | Location | Description |
|---|---|---|
| Startftp.vbs | \Intepub\AdminScripts | Starts the FTP site.<br>Syntax:<br>Cscript startftp.vbs <--ADSPath \| -a server1[,server2, server3...]><br>[—computer \| -c COMPUTER1[,COMPUTER2...]]<br>[--verbose \| -v]<br>[--help \| -?] |
| Startsrv.vbs | \Intepub\AdminScripts | Starts a specific Web site.<br>Syntax:<br>Cscript startsrv.vbs <--ADSPath \| -a server1[,server2, server3...]><br>[--help \| -?] |
| StartWeb.vbs | \Intepub\AdminScripts | Starts the Web service for a specific server.<br>Syntax:<br>Cscript startWeb.vbs <--ADSPath \| -a server1[,server2, server3...]><br>[--computer \| -c COMPUTER1 [,COMPUTER2...]]<br>[--verbose \| -v]<br>[--help \| -?] |

**Table 11-3.**    IIS Administration VBScripts *(continued)*

| Script Name | Location | Description |
|---|---|---|
| Stopftp.vbs | \Intepub\AdminScripts | Completely stops the FTP site.<br><br>Syntax:<br><br>Cscript stopftp.vbs <--ADSPath I -a server1[,server2, server3...]><br><br>[--computer I -c COMPUTER1 [,COMPUTER2...]]<br><br>[--verbose I -v]<br><br>[--help I -?] |
| Stopsrv.vbs | \Intepub\AdminScripts | Stops a specified Web site.<br><br>Syntax:<br><br>Cscript stopsrv.vbs <--ADSPath I -a server1[,server2, server3...]><br><br>[--help I -?] |
| StopWeb.vbs | \Intepub\AdminScripts | Stops the Web services for a specific server.<br><br>Syntax:<br><br>Cscript stopWeb.vbs <--ADSPath I -a server1[,server2, server3...]><br><br>[--computer I -c COMPUTER1 [,COMPUTER2...]]<br><br>[--verbose I -v]<br><br>[--help I -?] |

**Table 11-3.** IIS Administration VBScripts *(continued)*

| Script Name | Location | Description |
|---|---|---|
| Synciwam.vbs (see the following Tip) | \Intepub\AdminScripts | Synchronizes the IWAM accounts<br><br>Syntax:<br>Cscript synciwam.vbs [-v \| -h]<br><br>-v verbose: print a trace of the scripts activity<br><br>-h help: print script usage |

**Table 11-3.** IIS Administration VBScripts *(continued)*

**TIP:** *Synciwam.vbs*—There are certain operations that can cause the IWAM account, which is the identity under which out of process IIS applications run, to become out of sync between the COM+ data store and IIS or the SAM. On IIS startup the account information stored in the IIS Metabase is synchronized with the local SAM; however, the COM+ applications will not automatically be updated. The result of this is that requests to process applications will fail.

When this happens, the following events are written to the system event log:

▼ 10004 Source:   DCOM got error "Logon failure: unknown user name or bad password. "and was unable to logon .\IWAM_MYSERVER in order to run the server: {1FD7A201-0823-479C-9A4B-2C6128585168}.

▲ Event ID: 36 Source: W3SVC   The server failed to load application '/LM/W3SVC/1/Root/op'. The error was 'The server process could not be started because the configured identity is incorrect. Check the username and password.

Running this utility will update the COM+ applications with the correct identity.

VBScript uses different methods for operation within the HTML code. The VBScript code generally is placed within the HTML Head section (between the <Head> and </Head> markers) instead of the Body as with JavaScript; however, it can be placed in the Body, depending on how you want the script to run. There are two rules to follow for your VBScript placement in the HTML code:

▼ **Scripts in the Head section**   Scripts should be placed in the Head section to be executed when they are called or when an event is triggered. When you place a script in the head section, it guarantees that the script is loaded before anyone uses it.

▲ **Scripts in the Body section**   Scripts should be placed in the Body section to be executed when the page loads. When you place a script in the Body section it generates the content of the page.

For official support of VBScript, visit Microsoft's support site: http://msdn.microsoft.com/scripting/default.htm?/scripting/vbscript/. This site includes several valuable resources for documenting the scripting language and provides answers for frequently asked questions (FAQs).

## Code Samples

VBScript is a powerful technology. Microsoft has incorporated this scripting language into Windows 2000 and makes it available for use with IIS 5.0. VBScript is actually in its infant stages, but has already garnered a strong community. For these reasons it's almost imperative that you get experience with VBScript rather quickly. To help get you on your way, the VBScript code samples in this section can be placed into your HTML code to give you an illustration of the power of VBScripting.

## Determining the Time of Day

The VBScript listed in this section determines the time of day (morning, afternoon, and evening) and displays it on the Web page:

```
<HTML>
<HEAD><TITLE>Dynamic Greeting Sample</TITLE>
<SCRIPT LANGUAGE="VBScript">
<!-- OPTION EXPLICIT
If Hour(time) < 6 then
document.write "<b>Good grief!</b>"
ElseIf Hour(time) < 12 then
document.write "<b>Good morning!</b>"
ElseIf Hour(time) < 17 then
document.write "<b>Good afternoon!</b>"
Else document.write "<b>Good evening!</b>"
End If
-->
</SCRIPT>
</HEAD><BODY>
<p>This is a sample document</p>
</BODY></HTML>
```

## Countdown to the Year 3000

The following VBScript solution is a fun little tidbit to add to the Web page. It gets the current time and date of the computer and then displays the various countdown information in the following format:

```
Countdown to year 3000:
It is 11986 months to year 3000!
It is 364803 days to year 3000!
It is 8755257 hours to year 3000!
It is 525315409 minutes to year 3000!
It is 31518924508 seconds to year 3000!
<p>Countdown to year 3000:</p>
<p>
<script language="VBScript">
millennium=cdate("1/1/3000 00:00:00")
```

```
document.write("It is " & DateDiff("m", Now(), millennium) &
" months to year 3000!<br>")
document.write("It is " & DateDiff("d", Now(), millennium) &
" days to year 3000!<br>")
document.write("It is " & DateDiff("h", Now(), millennium) &
" hours to year 3000!<br>")
document.write("It is " & DateDiff("n", Now(), millennium)
& " minutes to year 3000!<br>")
document.write("It is " & DateDiff("s", Now(), millennium)
& " seconds to year 3000!<br>")
</script>
```

## Turning CAPSLOCK On

The following script, placed into the Body of the HTML document, will force the computer's CAPSLOCK key on when the individual visits the Web page. This is a useful script when your Web page has input fields and you expect the user's contribution to be case sensitive.

```
<script language="VBScript">
set WshShell = CreateObject("WScript.Shell")
WshShell.SendKeys "{CAPSLOCK}"
</Script>
```

**NOTE:** This script uses the Wscript.Shell command. This command will work with *only* those computers that have the latest Microsoft Scripting Engines installed. To get these engines, visit http://www.microsoft.com/msdownload/vbscript/scripting.asp.

## Turning NUMLOCK On

Similarly, you might want to make sure the visitor's NUMLOCK key is turned on. Embed the following script in your HTML body to provide that function.

```
<script language="VBScript">
set WshShell = CreateObject("WScript.Shell")
WshShell.SendKeys "{NUMLOCK}"
</Script>
```

**NOTE:**   This script uses the Wscript.Shell command. This command only works with computers that have the latest Microsoft Scripting Engines installed (http://www.microsoft.com/msdownload/vbscript/scripting.asp).

## Running Local Applications

When the VBScripting engines are installed on the computer that is accessing the Web page, you can cause literally amazing things to happen. The following script, placed in the Body of the HTML document, causes the computer's Control Panel to open when the page is opened in the Internet browser. You can replace the "c:\winnt\system32\control.exe" information with any existing path and program on the computer and the script will run it.

```
<Script Language="VBScript">
Set Shell = CreateObject("WScript.Shell")
Shell.Run "c:\winnt\system32\control.exe"
</Script>
```

**NOTE:**   This script uses the Wscript.Shell command. This command will work only with those computers that have the latest Microsoft Scripting Engines installed (http://www.microsoft.com/msdownload/vbscript/scripting.asp).

## Creating a File

Using the script listed in this section you can use VBScript to create a file on the visitor's computer. This example creates a text file named MyFile.txt on the C: drive. This method is very similar to what you experience when a *cookie* is placed on your computer by various Web sites. Cookies generally are used to automate logging onto a particular Web site by storing user-specific information in the file. This information is read from the cookie when the individual returns to the Web site.

```
<Script Language="VBScript">
Set FSO = CreateObject("Scripting.FileSystemObject")
```

```
FSO.CreateTextFile "c:\MyFile.TXT"
</Script>
```

## Getting Free Hard Disk Space

The script example provided in the following code queries the visitor's
hard drive and returns a dialog box—shown in Figure 11-5—that
lists the amount of free hard disk space. Should you use your Web
site to install actual applications on the visiting computer, this can
determine whether there is enough hard disk space available and
curb user frustration if the installation fails because of inadequate
resources.

```
<Script Language="VBScript">
ON ERROR RESUME NEXT
 dim dfs, mb, fso, sh
Set fso = CreateObject("Scripting.FileSystemObject")
Set sh = WScript.CreateObject("WScript.Shell")
 Set dfs = fso.getdrive("C:\")
 mb = dfs.freespace
 mb = mb \ 1024 \ 1024
  MsgBox "C drive has " & mb & " megabytes free.", 64, "DRIVE INFO"
</Script>
```

## An Interactive Web Page

Shown in Figures 11-6 and 11-7, the VBScript example in this section
prompts the user for input using a dialog box, and then displays a
second dialog box that verifies the text that was entered. Using a
similar interactive method on your Web page can help confirm the
user's input before it is recorded.

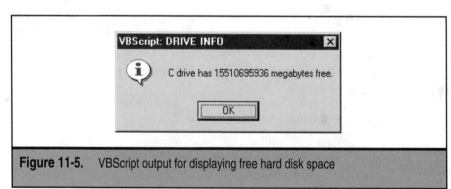

**Figure 11-5.** VBScript output for displaying free hard disk space

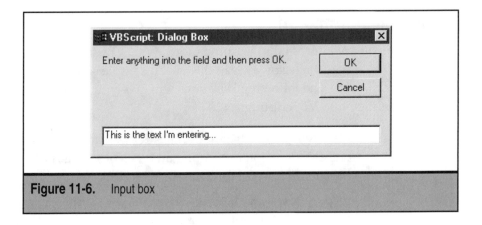

**Figure 11-6.**    Input box

```
<Script Language="VBScript">
dim response
response = inputbox("Enter anything into the field and then
press OK.", "Dialog Box")
  if response <> "" then
   msgbox "You entered " & response & ".", 64, "Thank you for
your entry!"
 end if
 </Script>
```

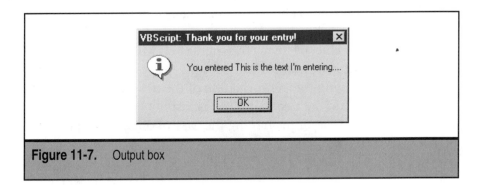

**Figure 11-7.**    Output box

## Additional Information

If you are interested in learning more about VBScript—and you should be—the best way is to download sample scripts and work with them. The following Web sites will give you a start on your journey into VBScripting:

▼ **http://www.scriptsearch.com/**   ScriptSearch.com is a one-stop location for finding all types of scripts, but is particularly useful for locating VBScripts.

■ **http://www.swynk.com/winscript**   SWYNK.com is a BackOffice Administrator's dream, offering weekly articles and support. The WinScript section is continually growing and offers a wide range of administrative VBScripts.

▲ **http://www.mm-inet.com/vb/**   VisualBasicScript.com stores many downloadable VBScripts in a wide range of subjects and links to other VBScript Web sites.

# XML

Extensible Markup Language (XML) is a set of rules, guidelines, and conventions for the design of text formats for data, in a way that produces files that are easy to generate and read. Development of XML started in 1996 and has been a W3C (http://www.w3c.org) standard since February 1998. Like HTML, XML makes use of tags (words bracketed by '<' and '>') and attributes (of the form name="value"). However, whereas HTML specifies what each tag and attribute means, XML uses the tags only to define pieces of data, leaving the interpretation of the data completely up to the application that reads it. XML is just now receiving wide acceptance as a solution for promoting the ease of data presentation in Web pages.

## Additional Information on XML

XML effectively is a new Web technology but it has already gained support from a number of Web sites. The following XML-related Web sites offer various resources for learning how to use this new technology:

▼ **http://www.xml.com/**    Part of the O'Reilly network, XML.com is the most comprehensive XML site on the Internet. It offers extensive information on what it is, how to use it, and provides an updated news service.

▲ **http://msdn.microsoft.com/xml/default.asp**    Microsoft's own XML site has plenty to offer. Learn how Microsoft is positioning XML as the standard Web technology across its many software applications and server releases. Of course, Microsoft has implemented its own technologies into standard XML to further extend the Web language.

# SUMMARY

So many technologies have been developed around the Internet that it seems as if it's actually "alive." Each new technology, or each revision, further solidifies the future of the Web. This makes it critical for anyone approaching a career on the Web, or just using Web technologies, to gather as much information on the components that make up the Web experience.

The Internet is constantly evolving; through this evolution new elements are born. If you will be working with Internet technologies, you need to keep informed on the tools available to make your job easier. Understanding these technologies will ultimately make you a better value to an employer and also allow you to produce Web content that is appealing to a large audience.

# CHAPTER 12

## Upgrading from IIS 4.0

For those already familiar with IIS 4.0, this chapter is for you. Because the majority of the world's networks run on a Microsoft operating system, IIS 4.0 is a popular Internet server. Companies world-wide deployed IIS 4.0 because it was a free add-on for Windows NT 4.0 through the downloadable option pack. For these organizations, upgrading to IIS 5.0 will be part of the Windows 2000 rollout—and there are several things to know for the upgrade process to be a success.

There are several methods for upgrading IIS 4.0, but it boils down to two distinct categories: the *in-place* upgrade and the *parallel* (or *migration*) technique. These methods are explained in the following sections.

# IN-PLACE UPGRADE

The in-place upgrade of IIS 4.0 to IIS 5.0 basically consists of taking your existing IIS production Web server offline, and then upgrading the Windows NT server to Windows 2000 Server with IIS 5.0 by using the Setup Wizard (normally accomplished by starting the Windows 2000 setup from CD).

This method of upgrading means that you can use the existing hardware of the current server, and don't have to worry about purchasing extra equipment. If you have a newer server, are comfortable with the current hardware, or don't have budget money to purchase new equipment, this method will allow you to move your Web site to the latest version.

When upgrading any Web server that is critical and requires high availability, this method of upgrade should be considered carefully. Upgrading a production Web server is extremely risky. First, the server must be taken offline for a period of time while the upgrade completes. Second, because Murphy's Law seems to strike at the most inopportune times, an unwanted scenario could occur. For example, because equipment generally has to run 24 hours a day, it's possible not to know that a hardware problem exists until the server is shut down for maintenance and then certain components fail to respond when powered back up.

If the upgrade of the existing equipment fails, the Web site could be down longer than anticipated. When upgrading any software, it is crucial to test the old settings and data with the new version. By performing an in-place upgrade on a production server, you are forced to perform this testing and debugging after the fact, which could lead to serious problems with no option to cancel. This leaves very little room for error. If you use the in-place method, be very sure you have a trustworthy backup.

The parallel upgrade methods (described next) actually are the preferred approaches to upgrade an existing IIS 4.0 site. If you have the budget for new equipment or an extra server available, you certainly should elect against the in-place upgrade.

# PARALLEL UPGRADE (IIS 4.0 TO IIS 5.0 MIGRATION)

Using some sort of parallel migration technique is the ideal way to upgrade from IIS 4.0 to IIS 5.0. If you have access to extra equipment, the benefits of this method can make you feel more comfortable about the upgrade. For these types of upgrades, Microsoft has developed the IIS Migration Wizard. The Windows 2000 Resource Kit CD includes the IIS Migration Wizard, which automatically transfers most configuration settings from IIS 4.0 to IIS 5.0 and IIS 5.0 to IIS 5.0 (thus, it can be used later to move your IIS 5.0 Web site to new equipment). It also provides migration steps for the following additional servers:

▼ **Netscape Enterprise Server 3.5 (Windows version)**   You can find the wizard to migrate from Netscape Enterprise Server 2.x and 3.x to IIS 4.0 in the Microsoft Internet Information Server 4.0 Resource Kit.

▲ **Apache HTTP Server 1.3 (UNIX version)**   You might want to note that although the Migration Wizard is a very useful tool for performing a parallel upgrade, Microsoft does not support it. Therefore, if you happen to need assistance when using the utility, you might have trouble obtaining it. To find it on the Windows 2000 Resource Kit CD, look in the Migration Wizard folder. The utility must be installed before it can be used.

During the installation of the Migration Wizard, there is one setup screen of which you should be aware. As shown in Figure 12-1, for the installation to proceed, you must determine what type of components should be installed on the server where the installation is being run. When the wizard setup is launched, it sets up a virtual Web directory on the server so that the source and target components can be installed from a remote location through the Web browser. This portion of the installation only makes the migration Web site available. It is best to install both components to one server; then allow the wizard Web site to control which components are installed to the source data server and the target data server.

After the IIS Migration Wizard components have been installed, the Migration tool can be accessed by opening http://*servername*/iismu/ welcome.htm in the Web browser. The wizard is completely Web-based and walks you through choosing the components on the source server that should be marked for backup, and then through selecting the target server where the data will be transferred.

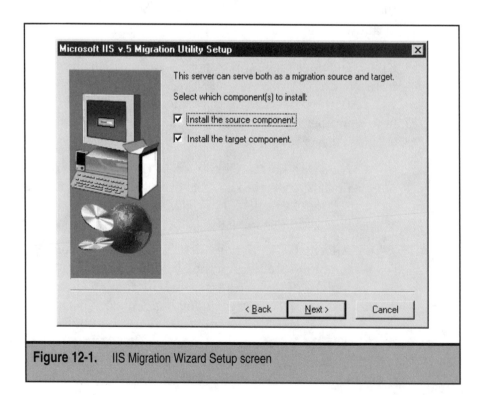

**Figure 12-1.** IIS Migration Wizard Setup screen

This backup continues to be available in the \WINNT\System32\ Inetsrv\IISmu directory on the server, even after the migration procedure is complete. This backup enables you to retain the old site information as long as you need it. The Migration Wizard collects all of the site settings, configurations, and data into a *servername*.CAB file, which can be saved to any type of appropriate-sized backup media. Thus, the Migration Wizard not only provides services for migrating a Web server, it also offers a convenient tool for safeguarding the entire Web site. Once installed, the Migration tool can be used at any time. Using the IIS Migration Wizard, you can perform the parallel migration methods outlined in the next two sections.

## Parallel Migration Method One: Clean Installation

The first method for performing a parallel upgrade is to migrate the IIS 4.0 Web site to a clean installation. Basically, you perform a clean installation of Windows 2000 Server and IIS 5.0 on new hardware, and then migrate the settings, content, and applications to the new server using the IIS Migration Wizard. This enables you to thoroughly test and debug the migrated server before deploying it. Once the new IIS server checks out, you can take the original production Web server offline.

By using this method, you avoid taking your production Web server offline for a potentially extended time period while you upgrade and test it. Following deployment, if problems arise with the new server that didn't appear during testing, the original server is available as a backup. It also enables you to upgrade the server hardware at the same time the IIS version is upgraded.

When using this method the only concern is if you have a large number of Web sites, the IIS Migration Wizard could fail in its process. The Migration Wizard is limited in the number of sites it can migrate at one time. This limitation is entirely based on the server resources available to the Migration Wizard, such as RAM and disk space, and really is intended to transfer only a minimal number of Web sites. The wizard was developed on the assumption that most organizations use one Web server to host a negligible amount of sites.

## Parallel Migration Method Two: Install, Migrate, Upgrade

Method two is an upgrade of a duplicate of the IIS server. On a second computer, you install the same version of Windows NT Server and IIS as exists on the current production server and then replicate content and applications. Once the data has been transferred, upgrade the new server to Windows 2000 Server with IIS 5.0 by performing the Windows 2000 Server setup and installing IIS 5.0 during the setup. This approach enables you to thoroughly test and debug the migrated server before it is deployed and the original Web server is available as a backup if the new server fails. Once the process has been marked a success, the old server can be taken offline. This technique also is a practical choice if you want to perform the upgrade of the operating system, IIS, and server hardware at the same time.

# AFTER THE UPGRADE: SUBTLE DIFFERENCES BETWEEN IIS 4.0 AND IIS 5.0

There are several key features that are new to IIS 5.0 (outlined in Chapter 1). Attributes such as performance and stability improvements are important to know; however, if you are familiar with IIS 4.0, it is beneficial to understand the more obscure differences between the two versions after the upgrade. These distinctions will help you understand how the new aspects work and how to get around in the rewritten application.

## Installation

With IIS 4.0, you were able to install the product in any directory on the Windows NT 4.0 server. However, when you perform a standard IIS 5.0 installation, the option to choose the destination is not available. The primary reason for this change is that since IIS 4.0's initial release, developers have found that the standard Web server administrator was not necessarily the top security person in the organization. Thus, installing the application wherever the administrator chose sometimes put the security of the Web site at risk; then Microsoft ended up with the blame for an insecure Web server application. To better protect the public and the identity of its Web server, Microsoft developed IIS 5.0 around the integrated Windows 2000 file and directory security.

Nevertheless, you can use an unattended installation method for changing the FTP and Web services locations. You can use one of two methods to accomplish this:

▼   An unattended installation of the Windows 2000 Server operating system

▲   A customized Windows 2000 component installation

## Unattended Windows 2000 Server Installation

An unattended installation of Windows 2000 Server requires the creation of an unattend.txt answer file for the entire operating system. This text file contains all the information for installing Windows 2000 Server automatically. In the \SUPPORT\TOOLS directory on the Windows 2000 Server CD is a DEPLOY.CAB file. Inside this extractable file is the SetupMgr.exe utility that works as a wizard to walk through the creation of the unattended answer file for Windows 2000. You can open the DEPLOY.CAB file, view its contents, and extract all the files contained within using a recent version of WinZip (http://www.winzip.com).

As part of the automated operating system installation, you can define the specific paths for the IIS 5.0 files installation when Windows 2000 is set up. Because this book concentrates more on the IIS 5.0 portion, you should reference the Deployment Guide that is also included in the DEPLOY.CAB file for the Windows 2000 server automated setup.

## Unattended Windows 2000 Component Installation

If you've already installed IIS 5.0 and want to change its location, you will have to uninstall it and start from scratch using a similar customizable installation method. The custom Windows 2000 component installation can be employed after the operating system is already installed, as described in the next few steps:

1. Create an Unattend.txt installation file. This file will be accessed during the unattended component installation. The answer file can be any Windows 2000 answer file, as long as the following information is included, as displayed, in the file:

```
[Components]
iis_common = on
iis_inetmgr = on
iis_www = on
iis_ftp = on
iis_htmla = on


[InternetServer]
PathFTPRoot
Value:path to FTPRoot
Value:path to WwwRoot
```

2. Use the System Stand-Alone Optional Component Manager (Sysocmgr.exe) command to start the installation of the FTP or Internet Information Services components. Assuming the answer file you created in step 1 was named Iis.txt, the command line to execute the installation would be:

```
sysocmgr /i: %windir%\inf\sysoc.inf /u:c:\iis.txt
```

**NOTE:** Sysocmgr.exe is a utility that is included in the %WINDIR%\System32 directory as part of the Windows 2000 installation, and can help you install any operating system add-on components. If you will be working with Windows 2000 at all, you should familiarize yourself with the utility; it has a horde of command-line options, as shown in Figure 12-2.

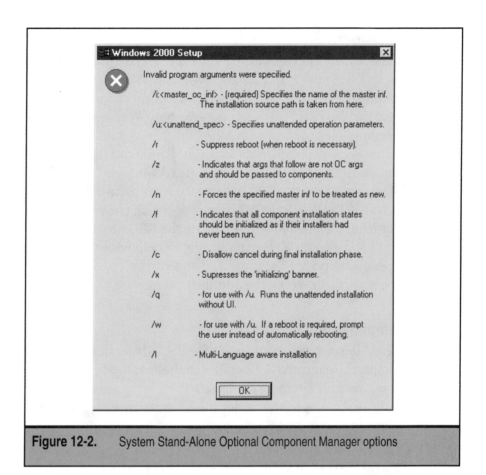

**Figure 12-2.**    System Stand-Alone Optional Component Manager options

## Files and Directories

If you were accustomed to the directory structure of IIS 4.0, there are a few changes in IIS 5.0 that you should get acquainted with. As outlined in the next few sections, some specific files and directories have changed locations. The primary reason for these changes is to provide better security. When deploying a Web site and making it readily available to those that should be granted access, security is a critical concern.

## IISHelp

In IIS 4.0, the help files were located in \%systemroot%\winnt\help\
iis. In IIS 5.0 the help files are located in \%systemroot%\winnt\
help\iishelp. Although this is not a radical change (primarily because
clicking the help link will open the help Web documents without
needing to know where to look), there is a small but critical alteration
in the security of the new location. IIS 4.0 did not share the \iis
directory; instead it shared the entire Windows NT \help directory
structure as a virtual Web directory. This permitted anyone to have
access to the Windows NT help files, which created a possible security
breach if the user were to infiltrate the NT knowledge. IIS 5.0 resolves
this issue by only Web enabling the \iishelp folder. The Windows 2000–
specific help files are protected and can be opened only by those
individuals to whom the administrator grants permission.

## Administrative Scripts

The Administrative VBScripts for IIS 5.0, mentioned in a previous
chapter, are located, by default, in the Adminscripts folder under
the \inetpub directory. In IIS 4.0, these scripts were housed in a
Adminsamples folder under the \%systemroot%\system32\inetsrv
directory.

## Default Documents

When IIS 4.0 is installed, a default document is automatically created,
which allows anyone typing in the Web address of the server to view
this initial Web page. IIS 5.0 instead installs a IISStart.asp file that
reads access requests to the server and determines their origin. If it
is a local request (from the server itself), localstart.asp (Figure 12-3)
is executed, as well as a separate browser window for the IIS Help
documentation. If the request is identified as originating remotely, an
"under construction" page is displayed. Once a default document is
created on the new Web server, IISStart.asp does not start up. This
enables you to make the IIS server available only when it is ready.

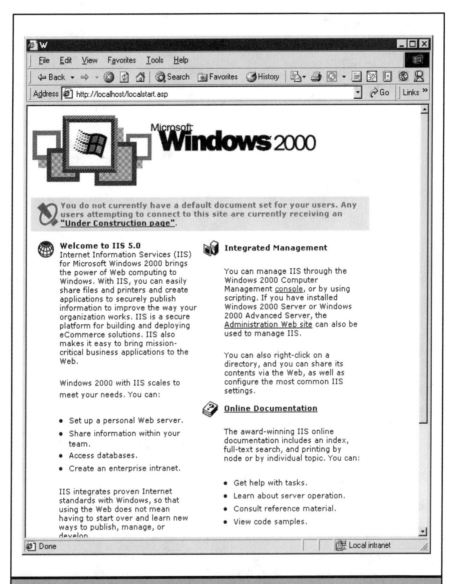

**Figure 12-3.**   Localstart.asp

## IISADMPWD

Underneath the default Web site IIS 4.0's installation includes a virtual folder called IISADMPWD. This folder contains files that authorize visiting users to change their NT password through a Web interface. This virtual directory is not displayed in IIS 5.0 unless the installation is an upgrade from IIS 4.0. Because of the potential security risk of the user's capability to change account passwords over the Internet, the IISADMPWD virtual directory is not configured by default. However, the .htr files that provided this feature are still included in the Winnt\System32\Inetsrv\Iisadmpwd directory and can be utilized by walking through the following instructions:

1. Open the Internet Services Manager Microsoft Management Console (MMC).

2. Right-click the Default Web Site, click New, and select Virtual Directory.

3. When the Virtual Directory Creation Wizard starts, follow the instructions to create the virtual directory with the alias IISADMPWD.

*NOTE:*   Make sure the path points to the Winnt\System32\Inetsrv\Iisadmpwd directory and that both Read and Execute permissions are selected.

In addition to creating the virtual directory, you also must enable the option for users to change passwords. In IIS 5.0 this is turned off by default due to issues arising from users changing passwords over the Internet. Passwords can easily be stolen when passed across an insecure connection such as an unfiltered Internet connection. On the other hand, intranet access should be a bit more secure, particularly when Windows 2000 Server is providing the network connection. To enable password changes, set the PasswordChangeFlags value in the IIS 5.0 Metabase by doing the following:

1. At a command prompt, navigate to the Inetpub\Adminscripts directory.

2. Type **adsutil.vbs** (for more information on adsutil.vbs, see Chapter 11); then press the ENTER key.

**NOTE:** If this is the first time that Adsutil.vbs has been run, you might get error messages stating that Cscript is not registered. Follow the prompts and choose Yes to register Cscript.

Type **adsutil.vbs set w3svc/1/PasswordChangeFlags [*value*].** w3svc/1 represents the Default Web site and [value] can be set to one of the following options:

▼ 0 - SSL connection required.

■ 1 - Password changing allowed on non-secure ports.

■ 2 - Password changing disabled.

■ 3 - Password changing disabled. (Undocumented)

▲ 4 - Advance notification of password expiration disabled.

## Operation

In addition to modifying the way IIS installs and changing the file and directory structures, Microsoft updated some specific operating procedures for the new version of its Internet server—outlined in the following sections. It's important to understand the changes if you've worked with previous versions. Becoming familiar with these alterations will allow you to be successful following the upgrade.

### Anonymous User Account

During the installation of both IIS 4.0 and IIS 5.0, the anonymous user account, IUSR_*servername*, is created. This account provides logging of the anonymous connections to the Web server. Because this account is widely known in the IIS world, most administrators choose to rename it, or create a brand-new account and assign it as the anonymous account. You can do this in IIS 4.0; however, in IIS 5.0, each time the server is rebooted the original account is re-created.

You can still utilize a different account in IIS 5.0 but it requires that you create a new account that does not start with IUSR. The new account must receive the Log On Locally user right and must be added to the Guest user group.

## Registry

The new IIS 5.0 Metabase was described earlier in this book. The Metabase eliminates IIS's reliance on the computer's registry for site configuration settings, and supplies easy and quick recovery if a disaster occurs because of a server failure. However, if you look in the registry you can still find the HKEY_LOCAL_MACHINE\System\CurrentControlSet\Services\Inetinfo key, which was present with IIS 4.0. IIS 5.0 does not directly use the information in this key; it is provided only as source for compatibility with the IIS 4.0 MMC snap-in. In fact, when an in-place upgrade is performed, the following registry keys are removed altogether:

▼ HKEY_LOCAL_MACHINE\Microsoft\InetMgr\InstalledBy

■ HKEY_LOCAL_MACHINE\Microsoft\InetMgr\Parameters\AddOnTools\&Key Manager

■ HKEY_LOCAL_MACHINE\Microsoft\InetMgr\Parameters\x

■ HKEY_LOCAL_MACHINE\Microsoft\InetMgr\Parameters\AddOnServices\Gopher

■ HKEY_LOCAL_MACHINE\Microsoft\InetStp\SetupID

■ HKEY_LOCAL_MACHINE\Microsoft\Windows\CurrentVersion\URL\Prefixes\ftp

■ HKEY_LOCAL_MACHINE\Microsoft\Windows\CurrentVersion\Setup\OC Manager\mts_mmc

■ HKEY_LOCAL_MACHINE\Microsoft\Windows\CurrentVersion\Setup\OC Manager\Subcomponents\iis_w3samp

- HKEY_LOCAL_MACHINE\Microsoft\Windows\ CurrentVersion\Setup\OC Manager\Subcomponents\ iis_doc_common

- HKEY_LOCAL_MACHINE\Microsoft\Windows\ CurrentVersion\Setup\OC Manager\Subcomponents\ iis_doc_ismcore

- HKEY_LOCAL_MACHINE\Microsoft\Windows\ CurrentVersion\Setup\OC Manager\Subcomponents\ iis_doc_asp

- HKEY_LOCAL_MACHINE\Microsoft\Windows\ CurrentVersion\Setup\OC Manager\Subcomponents\ iis_doc_sdk

▲ HKEY_LOCAL_MACHINE\Microsoft\Windows\ CurrentVersion\Setup\OC Manager\Subcomponents\ iis_doc_mm

It important to know which registry keys are eliminated if you have customized IIS 4.0 in any way. Additionally, because IIS 4.0 relies on the registry for configuration, any changes to IIS 4.0's properties will be reflected within these registry key structures. Before migrating or updating to IIS 5.0, you definitely should consider backing up this registry information for later reference.

Backing up a specific registry key is relatively easy. On the IIS 4.0 server, run the Registry Editor (regedt32.exe) and navigate to the registry keys previously listed. Highlight the key, click Registry-Save Key on the file menu, and save the key somewhere on the server's hard disks so it can be copied to another location (floppy, network drive, and so forth).

## Application Mapping

Application Mapping is the process in which the IIS server associates particular file types with individual programs. When a file is accessed through the Web page, the IIS processes determine which program it should be run with and executes the file using the correct application. For either IIS 4.0 or IIS 5.0, you can modify the Application Mappings configuration by opening the Properties for the Default Web Site, clicking the Configuration button on the Home Directory tab, and choosing the App Mappings tab.

If you look closely at App Mappings for both IIS versions, you see that the far right column is listed as Verbs in IIS 5.0, and Exclusions in IIS 4.0. This change means that IIS 4.0 allows new verbs by default, while IIS 5.0 disallows them. To understand verbs in IIS, correlate them to normal sentence structures. Verbs relate to actions; in IIS this is the same. Each verb that is entered causes IIS to perform that action when the file type is accessed in the Web site.

The changes made to verbs in IIS 5.0 focuses on future compatibility as new HTTP verbs are added to the Hypertext Transport Protocol. This enables you to manually add the new verb specifications without requiring an IIS update. To better understand verbs and what they provide to a Web site, see the list in Table 12-1.

| Verb | Description |
| --- | --- |
| html.addPageToGlossary | Add the current page to the glossary for the current site. |
| html.addToChangedPages | Add a page to the changed pages list. |
| html.addToGlossary | Add a page to the global glossary. |
| html.buildFromOutline | Render pages whose addresses are stored in an outline. |
| html.buildGlossary | Rebuild the glossary for a site. |
| html.buildObject | Render an object. |
| html.buildOnePage | Render one page and publish it. |
| html.buildPageTable | Collect directives and build the initial page table. |
| html.cleanForExport | Prepare text to leave the Macintosh environment. |
| html.deletePageTableAddress | Delete the page table address for the current thread. |
| html.expandURLs | Expand URLs in a given string. |

**Table 12-1.** HTML Verbs

| Verb | Description |
| --- | --- |
| html.ftpTable | Publish a table and its subtables. |
| html.getCurrentTemplateName | Get the name of the current template. |
| html.getExtraTemplates | Get the name of templates other than default to build this page with. |
| html.getFileName | Get the file name for an object. |
| html.getFileURL | Convert a file path to a file URL. |
| html.getGifHeightWidth | Get the dimensions of a GIF. |
| html.getImageData | Get data about an image, including dimensions and URL. |
| html.getJpegHeightWidth | Get the dimensions of a JPEG. |
| html.getLink | Create a link, given linetext and URL. |
| html.getOneDirective | Get one directive from a string. |
| html.getOneTagValue | Get the value of one tag from HTML text. |
| html.getOutlineHTML | Get HTML text from an outline. |
| html.getPagePref | Get a preference for a page other than the one currently being rendered. |
| html.getPageTableAddress | Get the address of the current page table. |
| html.getPath | Get the URL path from one database object to another. |
| html.getPref | Get a preference for the page currently being rendered. |
| html.getSiteFolder | Get the folder path to the root of this site. |

**Table 12-1.**    HTML Verbs *(continued)*

| Verb | Description |
|------|-------------|
| html.getWebsitesFolder | Get the path to the Websites folder in the Frontier folder. |
| html.neuterMacros | Neuter macros in a string of text, allowing only specified safe macros. |
| html.neuterTags | Neuter HTML tags in a string of text, allowing only specified tags. |
| html.normalizeName | Normalize a name according to preferences. |
| html.processMacros | Process macros embedded in HTML text. |
| html.publishBinaryObject | Publish a binary object such as an image. |
| html.refGlossary | Look up a name in the glossary. |
| html.setPageTableAddress | Set the current page table address. |
| html.traversalSkip | Determine if an object should be skipped during the rendering process. |
| html.writeFile | Write a file to disk, upload via FTP, etc. |

**Table 12-1.**    HTML Verbs *(continued)*

## IIS Resets

With IIS 4.0, companies generally had to schedule routine reboots of the Internet/intranet server because the IIS services would "hang" or even stop completely after long periods of use. This was because of memory leaks in the services themselves. Windows NT services use portions of the server's available memory to execute their functions. Services that perform poorly can increasingly grab memory until all usable memory is expended. Because a Windows NT server relies on a multitude of services to provide functions and run its devices such as hard disks and video, when a certain service "leaks" into other areas of memory, the server's critical services can cease to function. This causes the actual server to become unavailable.

Because of this potential bug in IIS 4.0, IIS 5.0 includes an IISReset.exe command. IISReset effectively recycles the IIS services. This can be automated to recycle the services periodically and when access to the site is minimal during off-hours. IISReset is installed into the \WINNT\System32 directory on the server and is run from a command line. IISReset uses the following syntax:

```
Syntax: iisreset [computername] /Option
```

and has the following options:

- ▼ **/RESTART**    Stop and then restart all Internet services.
- ■ **/START**    Start all Internet services.
- ■ **/STOP**    Stop all Internet services.
- ■ **/REBOOT**    Reboot the computer.
- ■ **/REBOOTONERROR**    Reboot the computer if an error occurs when starting, stopping, or restarting Internet services.
- ■ **/NOFORCE**    Do not forcefully terminate Internet services if attempting to stop them gracefully fails.
- ■ **/TIMEOUT:val**    Specify the timeout value (in seconds) to wait for a successful stop of Internet services. On expiration of this timeout, the computer can be rebooted if the /REBOOTONERROR parameter is specified. The default value is 20s for restart, 60s for stop, and 0s for reboot.
- ■ **/STATUS**    Display the status of all Internet services.
- ■ **/ENABLE**    Enable restarting of Internet services on the local system.
- ▲ **/DISABLE**    Disable restarting of Internet services on the local system.

To automate the recycle of the IIS services, when IIS 5.0 stops responding, you must enable it in the Windows Service Control Manager (SCM) by doing the following:

1. Right-click the My Computer icon on the Windows 2000 Server desktop and choose the Manage option.

2. Expand the Services and Applications section in the Manage Computer console; then click Services.

3. In the Services list in the right-hand pane, right-click the IIS Admin Service and choose Properties from the callout menu.

4. Click the Recovery tab and set the options as shown in Figure 12-4.

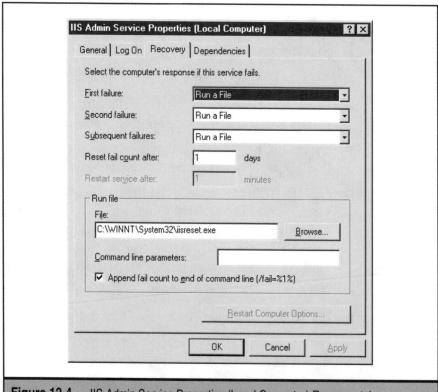

**Figure 12-4.**    IIS Admin Service Properties (Local Computer) Recovery tab

Depending on your situation, you might decide to alter some of the settings for the IIS Admin Service. You can effectively control what happens depending on the first, second, and subsequent failures of the IIS 5.0 Web services. Using the command-line options of IISReset, you also can adjust the way the reset utility performs by adding these options in the Command Line Parameters field of IIS's Recovery preferences.

Keep in mind that the VBScripts installed as part of the IIS installation also can be used to stop, pause, and restart the IIS services (see Chapter 11).

# SUMMARY

Getting up-to-speed after an upgrade from IIS 4.0 to 5.0 is important. When software upgrades are made available, getting familiar with the alterations is usually a quick process because a new release generally only introduces new features. While IIS 5.0 does offer new features and components, there are some major changes in the way it installs, where it installs to, and how it operates. All these changes were introduced to make IIS the best Internet server available. If you have worked with previous versions, take the time to understand the IIS 5.0 modifications that will allow you to quickly take advantage of a more secure and robust server.

# CHAPTER 13

## Windows 2000 Benefits for IIS 5.0

Because IIS 5.0 is included with the Windows 2000 server operating system, there are specific features of Windows 2000 that IIS takes complete advantage of. This chapter outlines those technologies and describes some reasons you should consider implementing them.

# ACTIVE DIRECTORY OVERVIEW

With the release of Windows 2000, Microsoft included Active Directory services (AD). AD is a hierarchical structure of all the resources attached to the company's network. A resource can be any number of different types of objects such as printers, computers, users, directory shares, geographical locations, and more. This new tree-like structure presents a view of the corporate network that makes administration easier to perform.

AD is a distributed system made up of a directory database. This database includes a schema, transaction logs, a directory service, and all the other provisions that make up a database. The directory *service* is the process that employs the information that is stored in the directory database.

AD provides directory services for Enterprise environments. Being an Enterprise service means that it provides functionality and availability in the following areas:

▼ **Scalability**   AD domains are security boundaries that encompass a group of objects. A domain can contain millions of objects.

■ **Extensibility**   The AD database uses a schema. This diagram contains the description of all the elements that can be created in the AD, along with their characteristics. The schema also can be modified and added to.

■ **Internet standards**   With AD, Microsoft continues to move away from proprietary protocols and methods. The name resolution, directory access, and security protocols all are basic Internet standard protocols.

- **Centralized administration**   AD administrators can manage any component in the directory from a single point in the organization.

- **Fault tolerance**   Every domain controller (DC) in the AD domain has a complete copy of the domain's directory. If one DC fails, the other DCs are still capable of fulfilling requests for AD services.

- **Security**   The access control lists (ACLs) direct who has authorization to retrieve data in the directory.

- **Interoperability**   Because Active Directory uses standard Internet operations, it is capable of interacting with other directory services that follow the same standards.

IIS 5.0 also can be a resource in the Active Directory, making use of the security model applied based on its location in the tree. For example, picture the Active Directory model with the company's corporate office as the very top branch. Below the corporate office are regions; within those regions are offices local to the city or area. When a specific IIS 5.0 server is placed within a region, it is meant as a resource for that specific region and only those with access to the region's resources would gain access to the IIS site.

# ACTIVE DIRECTORY SERVICES INTERFACE (ADSI)

One of the key technologies that enables IIS interoperability with the AD is the Active Directory Services Interface (ADSI). ADSI enables you to direct the lifecycle of abstract directory objects such as computers, printers, and user groups. With ADSI you can update user information from a Web page and distribute it automatically across the network.

When IIS 5.0 installs, a group of Admin Objects are seamlessly installed for managing the Internet server through several types of programming languages. Based on ADSI, the objects can easily be retrieved and operated by any language that supports automation, such as VBScript or JavaScript.

**NOTE:** It's important to not confuse ADSI and Active Directory. These two interact quite a bit, but they are distinct technologies.

When you install IIS 5.0, the sample IIS Admin Objects scripts are copied into the Inetpub\AdminScripts directory by default. You can use these sample scripts to configure your IIS 5.0 installation, to create virtual directories, to display information about a Web site, or to manage the status of Web sites by stopping, pausing, and starting IIS. For full information on the Admin scripts, review the VBScript section in Chapter 11.

You also can easily customize the sample scripts. Using the custom scripts, you can administer your IIS 5.0 configuration by changing the settings stored in the Metabase. The structure of the Metabase is equivalent to the structure of your IIS 5.0 installation; the property inheritance feature of the Metabase permits you to adjust IIS 5.0 configuration settings proficiently. The IIS 5.0 Metabase stores the settings for IIS 5.0. It performs some of the same functions as the system registry but uses ADSI to administer it.

# ACTIVE DIRECTORY MAPPING

A Windows 2000 Active Directory installation automatically sets up one-to-one mappings for the certificates that it issues. Any valid logon certificate should automatically be mapped to the user or server account that it represents. Many-to-one mapping can be accomplished, but you have to use the Name Mappings option in the Active Directory management tool.

## One-to-One Mapping

In one-to-one mapping, the administrator selects the client authentication certificate for mapping and enters the user name and password associated with the certificate. This is a standard client authentication certificate that is encoded using Base64 rather than binary. Base64 encoding enables older e-mail servers to handle the data easily, as many older e-mail servers cannot relay binary data.

You also can access a user's client authentication certificate from the Active Directory. A client authentication certificate is an optional UserCertificate property on the User object. The following VBScript code will open the UserCertificate object:

```
Dim oUser, vCert
Dim strName, strDN
StrName = "CN=Baggins"
StrDN = "CN=Users,DC=iis,DC=nttest,DC=microsoft,DC=com"
Set oUser = GetObject("LDAP://" & strName & "," & strDN)
vCert = oUser.userCertificate
Set oUser = Nothing
```

You can set a user's client authentication certificate by using the Directory Management administration tool. If Certificate Services is installed in the company, the certificate is automatically added to the user's list of certificates in the Active Directory, when the client requests a certificate.

To view or add a user's client authentication certificate in the Active Directory user interface, you must have Advanced Features enabled. To accomplish this, load the Directory Management administration tool, select View and check the Advanced Features option.

# AUTHENTICATED LOGIN

All users must be authenticated before they can gain access to resources in IIS 5.0. Each HTTP request from a browser runs on IIS 5.0 in the security context of a user account on the Windows operating system. IIS 5.0 executes the request in a thread that impersonates the user's security context. An application such as IIS 5.0 can have many simultaneous threads of execution internally, each acting on behalf of different users.

The operations performed during the execution of the HTTP request are limited by the capabilities granted to that user account in Windows. The user account must be created on the IIS 5.0 server or in a domain on which the server running IIS 5.0 is a member; the latter is more common in intranet applications.

IIS 5.0 supports five Web authentication models:

▼ Anonymous

■ Basic

■ Integrated Windows

■ Digest

▲ Client Certificate Mapping

**NOTE:** There also are two FTP authentication models: Anonymous and Do Not Allow Anonymous.

Digest authentication requires Windows 2000 Active Directory. Digest authentication resolves many of the security weaknesses of Basic authentication. Most notably, the password is not in clear text when you use Digest authentication. In addition, Digest authentication can work through proxy servers, unlike integrated Windows authentication.

At the time of this writing, digest authentication is not a completed standard; it is still a draft. The version of digest authentication used in IIS 5.0 follows RFC-2069, with some extensions from the IETF draft specification, which can be found at http://www.ietf.org/. Because Digest authentication is a challenge/response mechanism like integrated Windows authentication, passwords are not sent unencrypted, as in Basic authentication. For you to correctly use Digest authentication, the following must be set up on the server:

▼ Windows 2000 Server must be in a domain.

■ A file called IISUBA.DLL must be installed on the domain controller. This is copied automatically during Windows 2000 Server setup.

■ All user accounts must be configured to have the Save Password as Encrypted Clear Text option enabled. This is an option on each user object in the Active Directory. Setting this option requires the password to be reset or re-entered.

▲ IIS 5.0 must be configured to use Digest authentication.

Windows 2000 Server fully supports authenticated logon, meaning that the user must present credentials (usually a combination of user name and password) for identification. Once the user is authenticated by the operating system, a security token is attached to all applications that the user runs. All processes (applications) must have a token associated with them that identifies the user and the Windows groups to which that user belongs. The token contains the user's *security identifier* (SID) and the SIDs of all the groups to which the user belongs. A SID uniquely identifies all users and groups (of users) in the Microsoft Windows operating system.

To log on, the user must have an account in either the security account manager (SAM) database or in the Microsoft Active Directory service.

What does an SID look like? Fortunately, most administrators will never have to deal with SIDs directly. Here is a sample SID:

```
S-1-5-21-2127521184-1604012920-1887927527-1004
```

The first part, S-1-5, identifies Windows 2000 Server; the next four blocks of numbers identify the Windows domain or workgroup; the last number identifies the particular user or group. Each and every account and group in the Windows operating system has a unique SID, which also is unique to that particular domain of servers. However, some SIDs are more common than others; that is they are the same regardless of what domain you use. These SIDs are displayed in Table 13-1.

| Account | SID | Description |
|---------|-----|-------------|
| LocalSystem | S-1-5-18 | The account which most system services use. |
| Everyone | S-1-1-0 | All users; this is the Everyone group. |
| Interactive | S-1-5-4 | Users who can log on for interactive operation. |
| Network | S-1-5-2 | Users who can log on across a network. |

**Table 13-1.**    Common SIDs

Authorization is determined by using DACLs. These can be set on any Windows object; however, the most common are DACLs on files, registry nodes, and Active Directory nodes. For more information about using the Windows DACL Editor, see "Access Control" in the Distributed Systems Guide.

To demonstrate how access is determined, it is necessary to look at how DACLs are structured. As mentioned previously, a DACL is a series, or list, of ACEs; each ACE contains the SID of a user or group account and indicates whether that account has access to the object in question. For example, a DACL may contain four ACEs:

▼ Guests (no access)

■ System (full access)

■ Administrator (full access)

▲ Everyone (read access)

The deny access ACE is placed first. The order in which you place the ACEs when you set permissions on an object does not matter; for speed Windows 2000 Server will always move deny access ahead of allow access. When determining access, Windows 2000 Server looks at the DACL on the object and compares the user SID and group membership SIDs in the calling token to see if this SID is listed in the DACL. If a SID matches the SID in an ACE and if the ACE allows access, access to the object is granted; otherwise, it is denied.

# CLUSTERING

Clustering makes two or more servers appear to users as if they are one computer. The servers are connected not only physically by cables; they also are connected through the use of clustering software. This enables them to take advantage of features (such as fault tolerance and load balancing) that are unavailable to standalone server nodes. Clustered servers also can share disk drives that contain important information such as a database.

If you have installed Windows 2000 Advanced Server, clustering is a built-in component that you can take advantage of right away. When linked together, cluster service and network load balancing offer comprehensive availability and scalability. One good reason for using a cluster service is that it gives you reliable application, file, and printing services on a two-node cluster. When combined with Microsoft SQL Server Enterprise or Microsoft Exchange Enterprise (Microsoft's e-mail server application), cluster service adds trustworthy database and messaging services. (Server clustering is described in detail in Chapter 15.)

Network load balancing extends the IIS 5.0 clustering technology in several ways. For example, in a multi-tier application, Network Load Balancing supplies load balancing and high availability for the first tier, usually defined as the user interface. Because this kind of load balancing works through TCP/IP, a variety of workloads can benefit, including the load balancing of IIS 5.0 sessions and Point-to-Point Tunneling Protocol (PPTP) and Virtual Private Network (VPN) sessions.

As many as 32 servers can be formed into a Web cluster. Network load balancing is an extraordinary solution for the most demanding Web sites such as those that support tens of thousands of simultaneous connections. Microsoft Web sites, including the third-busiest Web site in the world, MSN, prove the value of network load balancing every day. (Network and server load balancing are described in detail in Chapter 15.)

Whereas cluster service reinforces the availability of database and messaging applications (back end), network load balancing delivers reliability to IIS 5.0 Web servers (front end). For example, on an e-commerce Web site you can cluster your front-end Web servers that are running IIS 5.0 with network load balancing, and have them access a back-end cluster that is running SQL Server Enterprise.

It should be noted that additional features in Windows 2000 Advanced Server make it easy to set up and manage clustering on your installation. These features include

▼ Improved usability, such as wizards for creating applications, establishing virtual servers, and configuring and managing clusters on your installation.

■ Fail over of system services, including all existing services— Web, file, print, and Message Queuing—plus support for Dynamic Host Configuration Protocol (DHCP), Windows Internet Name Service (WINS), and distributed file system (DFS).

**NOTE:** Fail over is an automated procedure in which, when the running application fails on one server, another server is immediately available to service user requests without the loss of data. The fail over process is seamless and protects against application downtime. In fact, the user will never know that the application or server failed. They will continue to work as normal, never experiencing any ill effects.

■ Orderly rolling upgrade to individual cluster nodes without taking the entire cluster offline.

■ Support for Windows Management Instrumentation (WMI) and the IIS snap-in, and integration with Active Directory.

■ Network adapter failure detection and forced fail over.

▲ Plug-and-play support for network adapters and disk drives (allowing hot-swappable components to be replaced without shutting down the system).

With Windows 2000 Server clustering you can set up applications on two servers in a cluster and provide a single, virtual image of the cluster to clients. If one node fails, the applications on the failed node become available on the other node. The actual content and applications are shared so that both machines have full access to them. Fail over times range from 20 seconds to 2 minutes.

Using the built-in clustering services for IIS 5.0 can greatly increase the availability of your Web site—and if your Web site is even minimally critical, you'll want to read Chapter 15 thoroughly.

## SUMMARY

One of the major but underlying changes to IIS 5.0 is its level of integration with Windows 2000 and Active Directory. Making IIS work within the parameters of the operating system makes it the best solution for providing a Web server that is always available, is easy to administer, and allows customized administrative solutions. The direct interface provided by ADSI gives you the ability to port Active Directory solutions to a Web application. If you are providing a Web presence within an enterprise structure, becoming familiar with how IIS 5.0 can benefit your directory service will allow you to implement more value for the organization.

# CHAPTER 14

# IIS 5.0 and Microsoft Exchange 2000

Because IIS 5.0 provides such a robust feature set and targets high availability, vendors are quick to develop applications around the strong Web server. During the past year Microsoft has publicized a new company direction for its software offerings. The focus for all future development at Microsoft is called *.Net* (pronounced *dot net*). In essence, .Net means everything you see from this point on will include Internet-based services. Already, Microsoft has positioned many of its servers as .Net capable. For more information on the new server types see http://www.microsoft.com/servers.

Microsoft's aim is to follow three simple rules:

▼ Everything must be capable of being administered as a Web service.

■ The Web services must integrate and aggregate in simple ways.

▲ The Web services must provide a compelling and simple user experience.

For more complete information on the .Net direction see the .Net home page at http://www.microsoft.com/net/default.asp.

# .NET AND EXCHANGE 2000

One of the first applications to exhibit the .Net experience is Microsoft Exchange 2000. Exchange is Microsoft's e-mail and collaboration tool, which has become a staple for the majority of Enterprise environments. Whereas IIS 5.0 includes simple e-mail and newsgroup features, and can be developed using its many compatible programming languages to provide collaboration, Exchange 2000 extends those capabilities with services that are built in. Exchange 2000 takes advantage of the IIS 5.0 architecture and its proven stability. Additionally, like IIS 5.0, Exchange 2000 has been developed to take full advantage of Windows 2000 and Active Directory.

Built around the IIS 5.0 structure, Exchange 2000 offers the following benefits:

▼ Exchange 2000 is fully integrated with the Windows 2000 Active Directory Service, enabling system administrators to create a single Enterprise directory for managing both messaging and network resources.

■ The Exchange 2000 database is optimized for high-performance streaming of multimedia data types such as voice and video. Exchange 2000 significantly increases the operation of Internet e-mail by allowing e-mail clients to store and retrieve Internet content directly from Exchange 2000 without format conversion. It also provides full compatibility with Simple Mail Transfer Protocol (SMTP), which provides superior routing capability.

■ Exchange 2000 supports a range of collaborative components, including group scheduling capabilities, discussion groups, and team folders, all of which are Web compatible.

■ With built-in content indexing and search functions, users can find and share information quickly, much like they have experienced while using a standard Web search engine.

■ Exchange 2000 combines powerful workflow tools with Web standards such as the Extensible Markup Language (XML) and Hypertext Transfer Protocol (HTTP). This results in a platform for superior Web applications such as knowledge management and e-commerce.

■ Information stored in Exchange 2000 can be accessed using a variety of client software including Microsoft Outlook, any Internet-standard e-mail client, and any Web browser. Exchange 2000 includes built-in content indexing, enabling high-speed, accurate full-text searches across a diverse set of information types such as e-mail messages, Web content, and Microsoft Office documents. All data stored in Exchange 2000 can be accessed through a Web browser with a user-friendly URL.

■ Exchange 2000 includes built-in services for building high-performance Web applications, including support for XML, Web Distributed Authoring and Versioning (WebDAV), and Active Server Pages (ASP). Data access technologies, such as OLE DB and Microsoft ActiveX Data Objects (ADO), enable developers to leverage their existing skills and applications when building Web Store applications. Web Store applications can be constructed with development tools such as Microsoft Visual Studio, Microsoft FrontPage 2000, and Microsoft Office Developer Edition.

■ Information in Exchange 2000 can be accessed using a wide range of client software options including Office 2000, a standard Web browser, Windows Explorer, cellular phones, and handheld computers. Performance, scalability, and ease of use in the Outlook Web Access client (discussed in this chapter) have been significantly improved over the last version. Exchange 2000 includes new capabilities that give knowledge workers access to their e-mail and Web Store content anytime, anywhere, and from any device.

**NOTE:**    The technology that pushes Exchange 2000 information to cellular phones and handheld computers is Microsoft's Mobile Information Server.

■ With instant messaging, users of Exchange 2000 can send spontaneous, urgent communications that appear instantly on another user's screen. Exchange 2000 also enables users to see presence information (similar to the "buddy list" concept on the Internet) for other users, indicating whether the user is online, out of the office, or busy.

▲ Exchange 2000 Conferencing Server (a separate add-on to Exchange 2000) includes a unified Web client experience for data and videoconferencing. It also includes a bridge to enable clients to fully participate with IP-multicast clients in videoconferences. End users have single-click access to conferences from their calendar. Scheduling can take place through the use of a Web browser using Outlook Web Access.

IIS 5.0 provides the base structure for the Internet (or .Net) functionality for Exchange 2000 and many other application servers down the road. Hopefully, you can comprehend the growing importance of IIS 5.0. It is critical to understand that, although there are other Internet server offerings available, Microsoft has spent a great deal of time developing Web services that can immediately provide benefit within the corporate structure.

This chapter outlines the IIS 5.0–specific components, tasks, and functions that are vital to Exchange 2000. Although this chapter focuses mainly on the interoperability between IIS 5.0 and Exchange 2000, there are a number of key tasks that will become useful knowledge when managing the IIS 5.0 Web server itself. As you read through this chapter, take special care to notice how much Exchange 2000 and OWA rely on the IIS 5.0 services. Many of the tasks and settings for OWA actually are administered using the Internet Services Manager MMC. This clarifies the extent of Microsoft's reliance on a secure and robust Internet server and explains why IIS 5.0 was developed.

Including a powerful Internet server in Windows 2000 enables Microsoft and other application vendors to develop their applications without having to worry about incorporating their own Web services. This accelerates and simplifies development so that newer technology can be made publicly available at a much faster rate. Working with the Web features for Exchange 2000 will be as comfortable as working with IIS 5.0 itself. The two applications provide tight integration. In fact, much of the Exchange 2000 Server's information is contained in the IIS 5.0 metabase. To provide a full disaster recovery plan for Exchange 2000 you also must include the metabase with your backups.

**NOTE:**  Most of the tasks outlined in this chapter use the same procedures outlined in Chapter 2. You might want to review Chapter 2 before continuing or keep an index finger inserted as a bookmark as you read through.

# OUTLOOK WEB ACCESS

Outlook Web Access (OWA), along with a default HTTP virtual server, is incorporated automatically when Exchange 2000 Server is installed. OWA gives users Web browser–based access to their e-mail boxes, personal calendars, group scheduling, contacts, and any *public folder* data stored on the Exchange 2000 Server. Public folders basically are containers that store information that can be read by anyone who has been granted access. These folders are a great way to establish a central location for common message threads that are important for a group of people to read; all the messages contained within should be available to all pertinent parties.

Any Internet browser that is fully HTML 3.2 compliant and supports DHTML can be used as the tool for direct access to the information stored on the Exchange 2000 Server. Two browsers that support these requirements are Microsoft Internet Explorer 4.0 or later and Netscape Navigator 4.0 or later.

Although OWA provides connection to many of the Exchange 2000 components, it is not currently meant to be a full replacement for Microsoft Outlook 2000. OWA makes accessing the Exchange 2000 mailboxes and folders convenient from a remote location and allows access from any workstation if someone is away from his or her own computer. However, there are a few items that OWA does not provide for which Outlook 2000 should still be held as a critical piece for business functions:

▼ **Offline use**   When OWA is used, all data is stored and kept on the Exchange 2000 Server. It cannot be downloaded to a local application for reading without a connection to the Exchange 2000 Server (for example, it cannot be read on an airplane).

■ **Tasks**   OWA does not provide access to the Tasks component of Outlook 2000 and Exchange 2000.

■ **Journal**   Journal capabilities are not included in OWA. The Journal feature enables you to keep track of business operations. Some organizations use this feature to gather information to bill clientele because it automatically keeps track of time spent on e-mail messages, documents, and sales calls.

■ **Printing templates**   Because an Internet browser is used as the connection to OWA, you are limited to the printing options of that particular brand of browser. Outlook 2000 provides many different preferences for printing e-mails, calendars, tasks, notes, and so forth.

■ **Outlook rules**   Using Outlook 2000, client-side and server-side rules are available to help organize how e-mail messages are received. For example, if it is time for annual salary increases and a message comes in from John Smith from human resources, you can configure an Outlook 2000 rule to notify you immediately. Or, if you subscribe to a sales e-mail newsletter that you like to read at your leisure, you might want those e-mails automatically moved from your Inbox to a custom e-mail folder. You can do this using Outlook 2000, but cannot when relying solely on OWA.

■ **Copying between public and mailbox folders**   Although OWA provides access to public folders and personal mailboxes, you cannot copy messages between the two like you can when using Outlook 2000.

■ **Robust mail features**   Outlook 2000 provides e-mail capabilities that cannot be utilized with OWA. For example, Outlook 2000 includes spell checking, e-mail expiration, and e-mail delivery schedules that are not available with OWA.

▲ **Appointment reminders**   Using Outlook 2000 you can set calendar and task items to alert you as the set dates and times approach. OWA provides only view capability for the personal and public calendars.

## Connecting to Outlook Web Access

Retrieving the Exchange 2000 Server data is as simple as typing the server's name in the browser's address line using standard Internet format. However, there are some small differences for using OWA when accessing over the corporate intranet versus connecting over a worldwide Internet link. To connect to a specific Exchange 2000 mailbox on a corporate intranet type the following address:

```
http://servername/exchange
```

This method displays a login screen, allowing users to enter their user ID and password. IIS 5.0 enables Integrated Windows authentication by default. This allows Microsoft Internet Explorer to attach automatically using the user's Windows 2000/Active Directory security ID.

Sometimes users will give others access to their folders. You can connect to a specific mailbox on the corporate intranet rather than your own by typing the browser address in the following format:

```
http://servername/exchange/userid/
```

Similarly, if you want to connect to a specific folder for a different user on the corporate intranet, such as the individual's calendar, add that information to the end of the OWA address like this:

```
http://servername/exchange/userid/calendar
```

To access a specific public folder through the Web browser over a corporate intranet, type the address in the following format:

```
http://servername/public/foldername/
```

To reach the Exchange 2000 folders over the Internet you would use the address formats as follows:

```
http://hostname/exchange/
```

and

```
http://hostname//exchange/userid/
```

The *hostname* moniker is the Internet format host name you are accustomed to seeing when doing general Internet surfing. For example, www.microsoft.com/exchange/ would be the URL to use if you were a Microsoft employee trying to access your Exchange 2000 e-mail box.

Similarly, accessing different public folders over the Internet follows the same format as accessing through the corporate intranet, except you utilize the hostname format like the following:

```
http://hostname/public/foldername
```

If you have changed the name of the virtual server's virtual mail or public folder directory to something other than the default

# IIS 5.0: A Beginner's Guide Blueprints

## Table of Contents

## Parallel Migration—Clean Installation

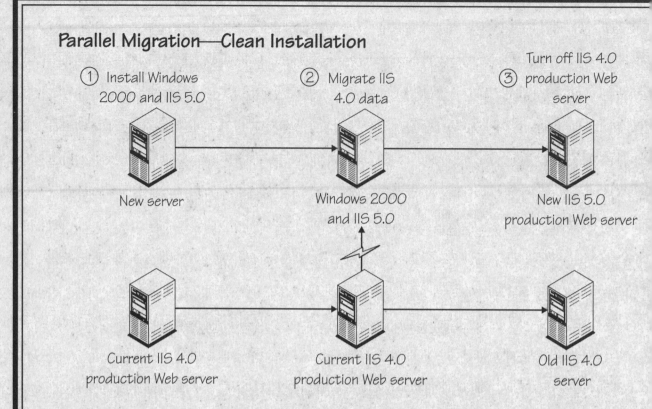

① Install Windows 2000 and IIS 5.0

New server

② Migrate IIS 4.0 data

Windows 2000 and IIS 5.0

Turn off IIS 4.0 ③ production Web server

New IIS 5.0 production Web server

Current IIS 4.0 production Web server

Current IIS 4.0 production Web server

Old IIS 4.0 server

## Parallel Migration—Install, Migrate, Upgrade

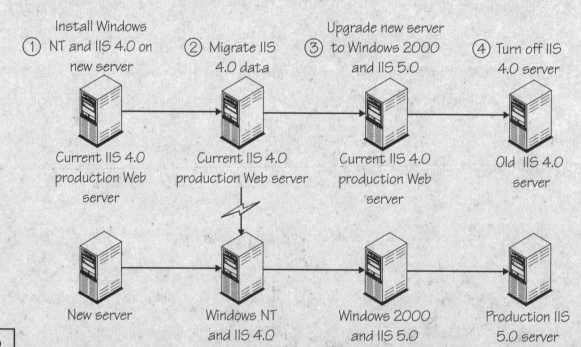

① Install Windows NT and IIS 4.0 on new server

Current IIS 4.0 production Web server

② Migrate IIS 4.0 data

Current IIS 4.0 production Web server

③ Upgrade new server to Windows 2000 and IIS 5.0

Current IIS 4.0 production Web server

④ Turn off IIS 4.0 server

Old IIS 4.0 server

New server

Windows NT and IIS 4.0

Windows 2000 and IIS 5.0

Production IIS 5.0 server

## Client-Side Script Processing

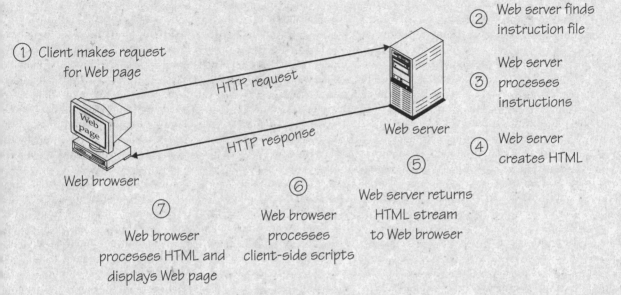

① Client makes request for Web page

② Web server finds instruction file

③ Web server processes instructions

④ Web server creates HTML

HTTP request

HTTP response

Web server

Web browser

⑤ Web server returns HTML stream to Web browser

⑥ Web browser processes client-side scripts

⑦ Web browser processes HTML and displays Web page

## Server-Side Script Processing

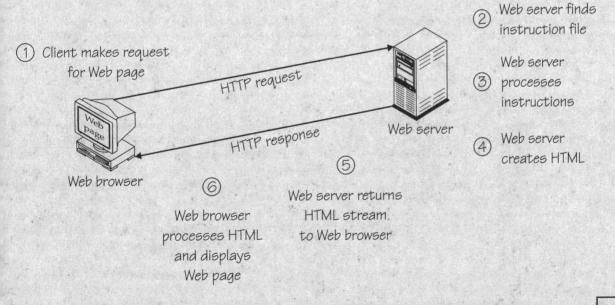

① Client makes request for Web page

② Web server finds instruction file

③ Web server processes instructions

④ Web server creates HTML

HTTP request

HTTP response

Web server

Web browser

⑤ Web server returns HTML stream to Web browser

⑥ Web browser processes HTML and displays Web page

# Network Load Balancing

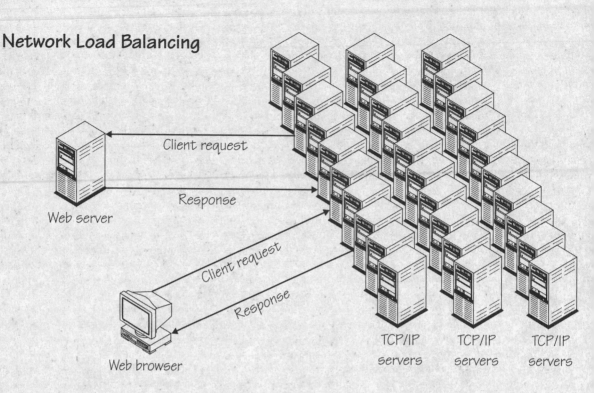

Web server

Client request

Response

Web browser

Client request

Response

TCP/IP servers    TCP/IP servers    TCP/IP servers

# Server Clustering

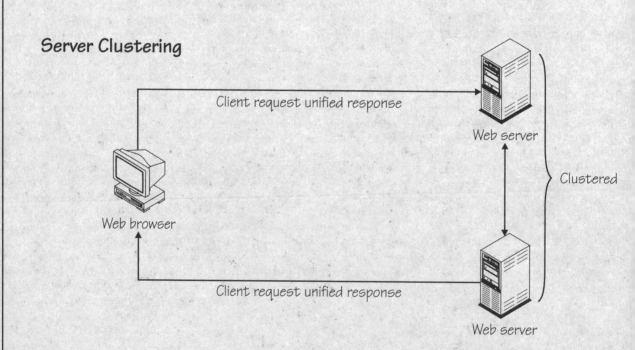

Client request unified response

Web server

Web browser

Clustered

Client request unified response

Web server

## HTTP Request and Delivery

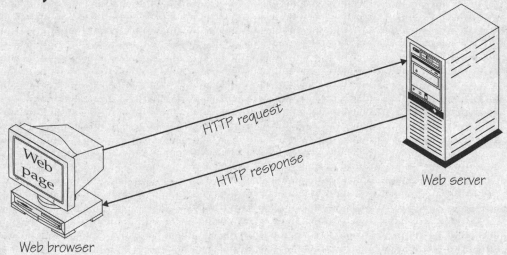

HTTP request

HTTP response

Web Page

Web browser

Web server

## ASP Request and Delivery

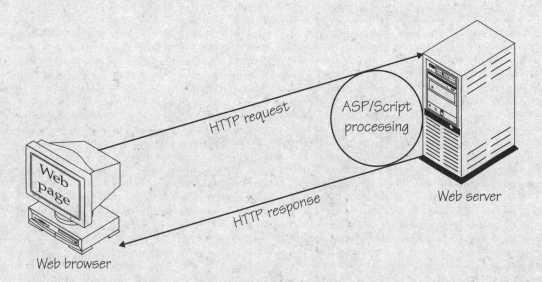

HTTP request

ASP/Script processing

HTTP response

Web Page

Web browser

Web server

## Firewall in Front of HTTP Server

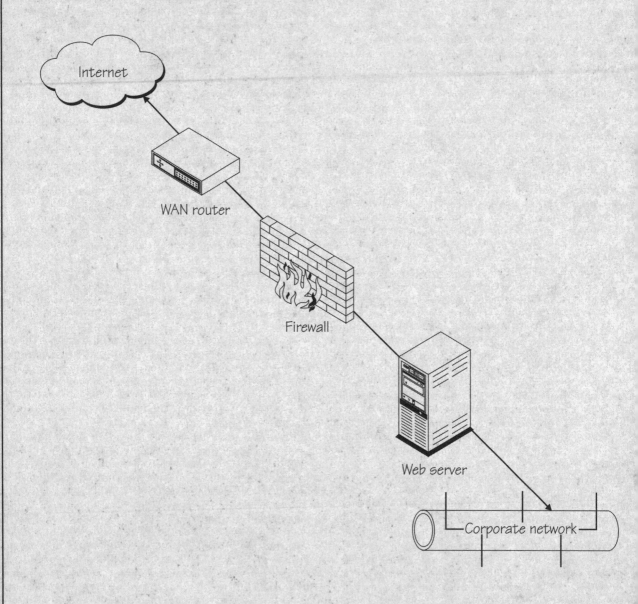

# Demilitarized Zone (DMZ)

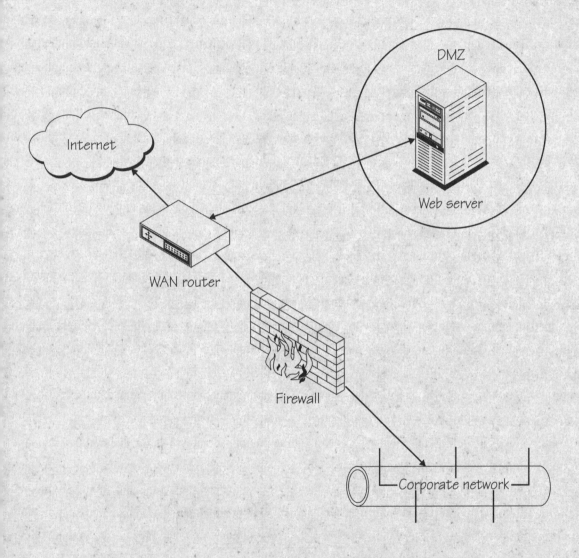

# IIS Metabase Structure

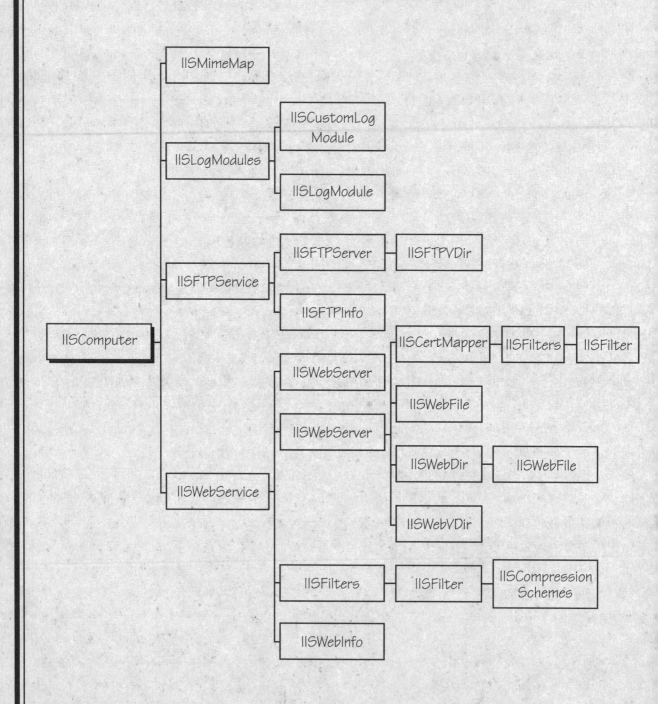

(exchange), you would need to alter the address line to match the custom location, as shown in the following:

```
http://hostname/custommaildirectory/userid/
```

Organizations generally change the default mail directory for added security because it is commonly known that the exchange directory is the default Exchange 2000 installation. Modifying or changing the virtual server's virtual mail directory is a common Exchange 2000 task and is outlined later in this chapter.

# Managing Outlook Web Access Security

Because OWA utilizes IIS 5.0 and IIS 5.0 runs on top of Windows 2000, the exchange information can be accessed through the Internet or a corporate intranet securely. You must gather some management information and be aware of some tasks to implement the best OWA security model for the organization. Unless you have lived under a rock for the past year, you know that security is the hottest technology news topic. It's understandable, as companies recognize the critical importance to have a direct link between the business and the Internet, that security becomes a concern requiring careful consideration. OWA is no different.

## Internet to Corporate Network Security

Using the detailed reference information in Chapter 2 to configure IIS 5.0, you can provide optimum security for OWA client connections through the corporate intranet. Windows 2000's NTFS file and folder permissions and Active Directory security model make Exchange 2000 the most secure e-mail and collaboration tool. Alternatively, for access to the Exchange 2000 Server through OWA over an Internet connection, there are a couple of other considerations. These are outlined in the next two sections describing the types of firewall configurations you should consider implementing.

**Firewall in Front of HTTP Server**    Because of the way the Internet allows connections across the large network, companies install firewalls. A firewall can be either a piece of hardware or an application running on a server. These firewalls provide an extra level of security against hackers who could gain access to the corporate network over the Internet's direct link.

When data is passed between the corporate network and the Internet and then back, it travels over ports. Each port has a specific port number that has been identified as a networking industry standard. A firewall enables configuring and filtering of these specific ports. When a firewall is in place and access to the Exchange 2000 Server over the Internet is a requirement, port 80 (the standard HTTP port) and port 443 must be open. Port 443 (the standard Secure Sockets Layer [SSL] port) is the tunnel for which access to the Exchange 2000 Server's IP address is enabled. If you have already configured access to the company intranet Web site for IIS 5.0, this port probably will already be open. This type of firewall is considered an *organizational* firewall.

**DMZ Firewall**    In addition to installing an organizational firewall for filtering corporate network-to-Internet access, you also can set up HTTP services on an isolated network called a Demilitarized Zone (DMZ). This not only provides additional protection for an IIS 5.0 Web site by putting the Web services on a separate network, it affords extra protection for the OWA connection. When a DMZ is installed, you actually must put in two firewalls: a DMZ firewall and the organization firewall.

In essence, this configuration provides multiple levels of protection against outside forces. You have OWA sitting on a front-end server on the network isolated from the corporate network, a firewall prohibiting unwanted access to the DMZ, and another firewall protecting the corporate network against potential attacks on the DMZ. In this two-firewall configuration, you must configure the OWA using the following steps:

1.  Set up and configure the DMZ.

2.  Open firewall ports 80 (HTTP) and 443 (SSL) to the front-end server's IP address.

3.  Install Exchange 2000 Server and OWA (with IIS 5.0) in the DMZ. This Exchange 2000 Server acts as the front-end server that will connect with the company's actual production (or back-end) Exchange 2000 Server. It basically serves as a connection point for users needing to access their mailbox and the public folders. The front-end server acts as a pass-through agent with the multiple firewalls providing the multiple levels of security.

4.  On the organizational firewall, open port 80 for access to the IP addresses of the back-end servers so the front-end server can connect through.

5.  Access to the Global Catalog server (server used for authentication; in this case the Windows 2000 Active Directory) also must be given. To grant this access you will need to open firewall ports 389 and 3268 on the organizational firewall.

**NOTE:** When SSL is enabled and it is required that all browsers must use SSL for connection, the DMZ firewall port 80 can remain closed; however, port 80 on the organizational firewall must still be opened.

If you are tasked with setting up and configuring the DMZ and organizational firewalls, it will help to know all of the Exchange 2000 ports that are used by the different services. Table 14-1 lists the different protocols, their port numbers, and the instance for which the protocol is used. Although a good number of these ports are specified for use with Exchange 2000, it also is a helpful reference for the specific ports you must consider when implementing IIS 5.0 services for access from an Internet connection.

| Protocol | Port Number | Used For |
|----------|-------------|----------|
| LDAP | 389 (TCP) | Lightweight Directory Access Protocol (LDAP), used by Active Directory and the Active Directory Connector. |
| LDAP/SSL | 636 (TCP) | LDAP over Secure Sockets Layer (SSL). When SSL is enabled, LDAP data that is transmitted and received is encrypted. To enable SSL, you must install a Computer certificate on the domain controller. |
| LDAP | 379 (TCP) | The Site Replication Service (SRS) uses TCP port 379. |
| LDAP | 390 (TCP) | Although not a standard LDAP port, TCP port 390 is the recommended alternate port to configure the Exchange Server 5.5 LDAP protocol when Exchange Server 5.5 is running on a Microsoft Windows 2000 Active Directory domain controller. |
| LDAP | 3268 (TCP) | Global Catalog. The Windows 2000 Active Directory Global Catalog listens on TCP port 3268. When you are troubleshooting issues that might be related to a Global Catalog, connect to port 3268 in LDAP. |
| LDAP/SSL | 3269 (TCP) | Global Catalog over SSL. Applications that connect to TCP port 3269 of a Global Catalog server can transmit and receive SSL encrypted data. To configure a Global Catalog to support SSL, you must install a Computer certificate on the Global Catalog. |

**Table 14-1.**   IIS 5.0/Exchange 2000 Protocol Ports

| Protocol | Port Number | Used For |
|---|---|---|
| IMAP4 | 143 (TCP) | Internet Message Access Protocol version 4 can be used by "standards-based" clients such as Microsoft Outlook Express or Netscape Communicator to access the e-mail server. IMAP4 runs on top of the Microsoft Internet Information Service (IIS) Admin Service (Inetinfo.exe), and allows client access to the Exchange 2000 information store. |
| IMAP4/SSL | 993 (TCP) | IMAP4 over SSL uses TCP port 993. Before an Exchange 2000 Server will support IMAP4 (or any other protocol) over SSL, you must install a Computer certificate on the Exchange 2000 Server. |
| POP3 | 110 (TCP) | Post Office Protocol version 3 allows "standards-based" clients such as Outlook Express or Netscape Communicator to access the e-mail server. As with IMAP4, POP3 runs on top of the IIS Admin Service and enables client access to the Exchange 2000 information store. |
| POP3/SSL | 995 (TCP) | POP3 over SSL. To enable POP3 over SSL, you must install a Computer certificate on the Exchange 2000 Server. |
| NNTP | 119 (TCP) | Network News Transport Protocol—sometimes called Usenet protocol—enables "standards-based" client access to public folders in the information store. As with IMAP4 and POP3, NNTP is dependent on the IIS Admin Service. |

**Table 14-1.**   IIS 5.0/Exchange 2000 Protocol Ports *(continued)*

| Protocol | Port Number | Used For |
|----------|-------------|----------|
| NNTP/SSL | 563 (TCP) | NNTP over SSL. To enable NNTP over SSL, you must install a Computer certificate on the Exchange 2000 Server. |
| HTTP | 80 (TCP) | Hypertext Transfer Protocol (HTTP) is used primarily by Microsoft Outlook Web Access (OWA), but also enables some administrative actions in Exchange System Manager. HTTP is implemented through the World Wide Web Publishing Service (W3Svc) and runs on top of the IIS Admin Service. |
| HTTP/SSL | 443 (TCP) | HTTP over SSL. To enable HTTP over SSL, you must install a Computer certificate on the Exchange 2000 Server. |
| SMTP | 25 (TCP) | Simple Mail Transfer Protocol is the foundation for all e-mail transport in Exchange 2000. The SMTP Service (SMTPSvc) runs on top of the IIS Admin Service. Unlike IMAP4, POP3, NNTP, and HTTP, SMTP in Exchange 2000 does not use a separate port for secure communication (SSL), but rather employs an *in-band security sub-system* called Transport Layer Security (TLS). |

**Table 14-1.** IIS 5.0/Exchange 2000 Protocol Ports *(continued)*

| Protocol | Port Number | Used For |
|----------|-------------|----------|
| SMTP/SSL | 465 (TCP) | SMTP over SSL. TCP port 465 is reserved by common industry practice for secure SMTP communication using the SSL protocol. However, unlike IMAP4, POP3, NNTP, and HTTP, SMTP in Exchange 2000 does not use a separate port for secure communication (SSL); it employs an *in-band security sub-system* called Transport Layer Security (TLS). To enable TLS to work on Exchange 2000, you must install a Computer certificate on the Exchange 2000 Server. |
| SMTP/LSA | 691 (TCP) | The Microsoft Exchange Routing Engine (RESvc) listens for routing link state information on TCP port 691. Exchange 2000 uses routing link state information to route messages and the routing table is constantly updated. The Link State Algorithm (LSA) propagates outing status information between Exchange 2000 Servers. This algorithm is based on the Open Shortest Path First (OSPF) protocol from networking technology, and transfers link state information between routing groups by using the X-LSA-2 command verb over SMTP and by using a Transmission Control Protocol (TCP) connection to port 691 in a routing group. |

**Table 14-1.**   IIS 5.0/Exchange 2000 Protocol Ports *(continued)*

| Protocol | Port Number | Used For |
|---|---|---|
| RVP | 80 (TCP) | RVP is the foundation for Instant Messaging in Exchange 2000. While RVP communication begins with TCP port 80, the server quickly sets up a new connection to the client on an ephemeral TCP port above 1024. Because this port is not known in advance, there are issues when you enable Instant Messaging through a firewall. |
| IRC/IRCX | 6667 (TCP) | Internet Relay Chat (IRC) is the chat protocol. IRCX is the extended version offered by Microsoft. Although TCP port 6667 is the most common port for IRC, TCP port 7000 also is very frequently used. |
| IRC/SSL | 994 (TCP) | IRC (or Chat) over SSL. IRC or IRCX over SSL is not supported in Exchange 2000. |
| X.400 | 102 (TCP) | ITU-T Recommendation X.400 really is a series of recommendations for what an electronic message handling system (MHS) should look like. TCP port 102 is defined in IETF RFC-1006, which describes OSI communications over a TCP/IP network. Briefly, TCP port 102 is the port that the Exchange message transfer agent (MTA) uses to communicate with other X.400-capable MTAs. |

**Table 14-1.** IIS 5.0/Exchange 2000 Protocol Ports *(continued)*

| Protocol | Port Number | Used For |
|---|---|---|
| MS-RPC | 135 (TCP) | Microsoft Remote Procedure Call is a Microsoft implementation of remote procedure calls (RPCs). TCP port 135 actually is only the RPC Locator Service, which is like the registrar for all RPC-enabled services that run on a particular server. In Exchange 2000 the Routing Group Connector uses RPC. Also, some administrative operations require RPC. To configure a firewall to allow RPC traffic, many more ports than just 135 must be enabled. |
| T.120 | 1503 (TCP) | ITU-T Recommendation T.120 is a series of recommendations that define data conferencing. Data conferencing is implemented on the server side as a Conferencing Technology Provider (CTP) in the Multipoint Control Unit (MCU), which is one component of the Exchange Conferencing Services (ECS). Data conferencing is implemented on the client side as Chat, Application Sharing, Whiteboard, and File Transferring in Microsoft NetMeeting. |
| ULS | 522 (TCP) | User Locator Service is a type of Internet directory service for conferencing clients, such as NetMeeting. Exchange 2000 Server and Exchange 2000 Conference Server do not implement a ULS; rather they take advantage of Active Directory for directory services (by TCP port 389). |

**Table 14-1.**    IIS 5.0/Exchange 2000 Protocol Ports *(continued)*

| Protocol | Port Number | Used For |
|---|---|---|
| H.323 (Video) | 1720 (TCP) | ITU-T Recommendation H.323 defines multimedia conferencing. TCP port 1720 is the H.323 (video) call setup port. After a client connects, the H.323 server negotiates a new, dynamic UDP port to be used for streaming data. |
| Audio | 1731 (TCP) | Audio conferencing is enabled in much the same way H.323 video conferencing is enabled in Exchange 2000. After clients connect to TCP port 1731, a new dynamic port is negotiated for further streaming data. |
| DNS | 53 (TCP) | Domain Name System (DNS) is at the heart of all of the services and functions of Windows 2000 Active Directory and Exchange 2000 Server. You cannot underestimate the impact that a DNS issue can have on the system. Therefore, when service issues arise, it is always wise to verify proper name resolution. |

**Table 14-1.** IIS 5.0/Exchange 2000 Protocol Ports *(continued)*

## Administration of User Access

When Exchange 2000 Server is installed, OWA is enabled by default for every user. You might have instances in which you need to disable access to a specific user. For example, if someone's employment has been terminated, you might be required to disable the person's access to their mailbox or to the public folders for which they have authorization. To disable OWA access for a single user, follow these steps:

1. Open the Active Directory Users and Computers Windows 2000 administration MMC component (select Start | Programs | Administrative Tools).

2. Click the View option on the top menu and select Advanced Features.

3. Find the user's name in the Active Directory Users and Computers list and double-click it.

4. Click the Exchange Advanced tab in the user properties. (The Exchange tab is added to all users' properties when Exchange 2000 is installed in the organization.)

5. Click the Protocol Settings dialog button.

6. Double-click HTTP.

7. Clear the Enable for Mailbox option, and continue to click OK until you have exited the user's properties. (Alternatively, you can enable OWA access for a single user by selecting the Enable for Mailbox option).

*CAUTION:*   If several different people share a computer to access the Exchange 2000 Server using OWA, it is recommended that local browser caching be disabled. If this is not turned off, messages retrieved during a session can remain on the computer's hard disk. This potentially allows the next user to read the messages from the previous session. It also is recommended that the browser be completely closed after every OWA session so the cache is completely emptied. Although disabling the local browser cache provides additional security, it also slows OWA performance. Watch out for this Catch-22.

**Allowing Users to Change OWA Passwords**   By default, the user cannot change their Exchange 2000 password using OWA because IIS 5.0's default configuration disallows this feature. However, you can modify the IIS 5.0 configuration. To enable users to change OWA passwords through IIS, you must employ the following steps on each IIS server to which Exchange users connect:

1.  Install and configure Secure Sockets Layer (SSL) on the server.

2.  Open Internet Services Manager (Start | Programs | Administrative Tools).

3.  Right-click the default Web site, select New, and then click on the Virtual Directory option.

4.  In the Virtual Directory Creation Wizard, type **IISADMPWD** in the Alias box, and then click Next.

5.  In the Directory box, type **&lt;*driveletter*&gt;:\winnt\system32\ inetsrv\iisadmpwd**.

6.  Click the Next button.

7.  Verify that only the read and run script check boxes are selected, click Next and then click the Finish button. If any other boxes are selected, uncheck them.

8.  Verify that the Iisadmpwd folder has the Anonymous Access authentication method enabled. It's okay if other authentication types also are selected, but Anonymous Access must be enabled.

9.  Change the Metabase PasswordChangeFlags setting to zero (0). To do this, perform the following steps at a command prompt:

    ■  cd &lt;*driveletter*&gt;:\inetpub\adminscripts adsutil

    ■  set w3svc/passwordchangeflags 1

*TIP:*   The available options for the PasswordChangeFlags setting are

▼  **0**   Requires password change by SSL.

■  **1**   Allows password change by non-secure ports.

■  **2**   Disables password changes.

▲  **4**   Disables advance notification of expiration.

You now can access the mailbox and change the account password by using the following address (notice the secure HTTP method—https):

```
https://servername/exchange/mailbox
```

# Managing Virtual Servers

As outlined previously in this book, a HTTP Virtual Server provides the transport services for users to access Web content and general documents in special Web-enabled directories on a Windows 2000 Server. When working with Exchange 2000 and OWA, you also will need to know how to manage these virtual servers for public access to additional folders and mailboxes. Creating additional HTTP virtual servers also helps distribute the load of increased traffic as the Web site becomes more popular or the company increases in head count.

## Creating Additional Virtual Servers

As the company continues to grow and the employee base increases, you will want to consider installing additional Exchange 2000 Servers. When doing this, you also will need to install additional HTTP Virtual Servers to accommodate increased access to mailboxes and public folders using OWA. After the additional Exchange 2000 Server is installed, you can create new HTTP Virtual Servers by walking through the following steps:

1. Run the Exchange 2000 System Manager.

2. Find the Protocols section in the Console Tree and expand the Servers group.

3. Locate the specific server for which you will be adding the HTTP Virtual Server and expand its properties.

4. Expand the Protocols item in the displayed list.

5. Right-click the HTTP option, navigate to New, and then select HTTP Virtual Server.

6. Identify a unique name and enter it in the Name field.

7. Click Finish to create the new virtual server.

There are other available configuration options such as limiting the number of connections, setting the connection timeout, and restricting access. Because Exchange 2000 uses the IIS 5.0 architecture, these options are described in detail in the reference in Chapter 2. However, it should also be noted that the IP address and TCP port combination must be unique for every virtual server. That is discussed in the next section.

### Davex.dll and Exchange 2000

When creating a virtual server that provides both Exchange content and file system content (files are run from a server directory through the Web browser) you can experience problems running the file system content. The message "HTTP/1.1 503 Service Unavailable" will display in the Web browser. This is because the davex.dll file is in the file system content virtual directory. When virtual servers are created on the Exchange 2000 Server using IIS 5.0, davex.dll is automatically copied to the new virtual server because it is assumed that you are creating the new virtual server to provide access to Exchange 2000 services. To fix this issue you must remove the davex.dll file from the virtual directory for which you want to provide file system content. To remove davex.dll, follow these directions:

1. Open Internet Services Manager and navigate to the specific Web site.

2. Click to expand the Web site folder.

3. Right-click the virtual directory of the Web site.

4. Select Properties.

5. Click the Virtual Directory tab.

6. Click Configuration.

7. Click the Apps Mappings tab.

8. Click the application mappings that looks like the following:

   ```
   C:\Program Files\Exchsrvr\bin\davex.dll (All)
   ```

9. Click Remove.

10. When you are prompted to Remove selected script mapping, click Yes.

11. Click OK twice.

This will remove the script value for the davex.dll file. Browse through the Web contents by right-clicking the virtual directory; then clicking Browse. You now should be able to browse through the Web contents.

Alternatively, if access to the davex.dll file is not set correctly for the Exchange specific virtual directory, the files and folders for the directory will be displayed in the Web browser instead of on the OWA logon page. If this happens, follow these directions to remedy the problem:

1. Open Internet Services Manager, right-click the Exchange virtual directory (the default name) under the default Web site, and then click Delete.

2. Choose Start | Programs | Administrative Tools | Services.

3. Right-click Microsoft Exchange System Attendant, and then click Restart to re-create the Exchange virtual directory.

4. Go back to Internet Information Manager, right-click the Exchange Virtual Directory, and then click Properties.

5. Click the Virtual Directory tab.

6. In the Application Setting section, click Create, and then click Configuration.

7. Click Add, and then in the Executable box type the path to the davex.dll file on your file system using the 8.3 naming convention; for example,

   ```
   C:\Progra~1\Exchsrvr\bin\davex.dll
   ```

8. Type an asterisk (*) in the Extension box.

9. Click OK and accept inheritance on any other objects if prompted.

## Configuring Virtual Servers

Every HTTP Virtual Server is identified on the network by using a combination of configuration settings. TCP port, SSL port, IP address, and host name all are pooled to give the virtual server its own identify. By default the TCP port is 80, the SSL port is 443, the IP address is configured to use any available, and the host name uses the exact server name on which Exchange 2000 is installed.

When OWA serves users in multiple Windows 2000 domains, the default configuration is not the optimal setting. For example, when all available IP addresses are used, all IP addresses on the specific server will be exploited for messaging services. Putting the messaging services on it's own IP address can significantly improve server performance and provide the best possible tracking for security purposes.

You can change any of the server's identity roles to give the messaging services their own unique presence on the company's network. To adjust these settings, follow these instructions:

1. Run the IIS 5.0 Internet Services Manager MMC snap-in (select Start | Programs | Administrative Tools).

2. Right-click the Internet Information Services and select Connect.

3. Type the name of the computer running the IIS 5.0 services for which you want to modify (if the Internet Services Manager is already connected to the server you will be modifying, you can skip steps 2 and 3).

4. Find the specific HTTP Virtual Server you want to amend and double-click it.

5. Right-click the specific Web site you want to manage and then select Properties.

6. On the Web Site tab click the Advanced button.

At this point you can use the reference section in Chapter 4 to provide necessary information to add, edit, and remove IP addresses, TCP ports, and SSL ports in the Advanced Web site configuration.

## Enabling SSL

Without the use of SSL, servers pass all data in clear text to the client computers. As described earlier in the book, SSL is composed of either 40-bit or 128-bit data encryption. This allows confidential information such as user passwords to be hidden from potential hackers. Exchange 2000 and OWA rely on the IIS 5.0 and Windows 2000 certificate services to provide SSL features to e-mail and public folder users. To enable SSL for Exchange 2000 and OWA you must configure the SSL component using the IIS 5.0 Internet Services Manager MMC. To enable SSL, follow these steps:

1. Run the IIS 5.0 Internet Services Manager MMC snap-in (choose Start | Programs | Administrative Tools).

2. Right-click the Internet Information Services; then select Connect.

3. Type in the name of the computer running the IIS 5.0 services you want to modify (if the Internet Services Manager is already connected to the server you will be modifying, you can skip steps 2 and 3).

4. Find the specific HTTP Virtual Server you want to amend and double-click it.

5. Right-click the specific Web site you want to manage and then select Properties.

6. On the Directory Security tab, click the Server Certificate button.

When the Server Certificate button is clicked, the Web Server Certificate Wizard starts. You will need to create a new certificate and submit it to a Certificate Authority before applying it to the HTTP Virtual Server. Use the methods described in Chapter 4 to complete the process.

## Managing Connections

A couple additional features you will want to consider for OWA are the ability to restrict incoming connections and setting the time-out values for the IIS 5.0 Web services. Limiting the incoming connections for OWA can help keep the Web services from becoming overloaded when a considerable amount of traffic passes through. Setting the connection time-out value helps ensure that the set number of OWA connections are available by disconnecting sessions when the server determines that a user link is idle.

Adjusting these values to the optimum settings for your environment will guarantee that Web access to the mailboxes and public folders is always available. To adjust the connection's limit and time-out values, follow these steps:

1. Run the IIS 5.0 Internet Services Manager MMC snap-in (choose Start | Programs | Administrative Tools).

2. Right-click the Internet Information Services and then select Connect.

3. Type the name of the computer running the IIS 5.0 services you want to modify (if the Internet Services Manager is already connected to the server you will be modifying, you can skip steps 2 and 3).

4. Find the specific HTTP Virtual Server you want to administer and double-click it.

5. Right-click the specific Web site you want to manage; then select Properties.

Chapter 4 outlines the additional steps for limiting connections and setting the time-out values for IIS 5.0, which directly relates to providing these functions for OWA.

## Controlling Access

In general, HTTP Virtual Servers provide three levels of authentication: anonymous, basic, and integrated (for more information on these three types of authentication, refer to Chapter 4). The optimum validation method for OWA is the Integrated Windows authentication. This method of authentication integrates the individual's user name and password from the Windows 2000/Active Directory login information with the Exchange 2000 services. Not only is this convenient for the user (not having to remember separate login information for e-mail and the network), but it also provides optimum barrier defense because it is based on the Windows 2000/ Active Directory security model.

By default, both basic and Integrated Windows authentication are enabled for the HTTP Virtual Servers. Additionally, although this default is perfectly fine for most organizations, it can be adapted to meet custom needs. When the authentication methods are modified, they are configured at the virtual directory level. Web enabling a directory on a server makes the directory available for access through a Web browser. For example, if you Web enabled the D:\Data directory on a specific server, it could easily be accessed from any Web browser by typing the following in the address field:

`http://servername/Data`

When Exchange 2000 is installed, there are two default directories that are Web enabled for user access through OWA:

- ▼ **Public**   The Public virtual directory contains all the default public folders for the organization.

- ▲ **Exchange**   The Exchange virtual directory contains the personal e-mail boxes for the organization.

In addition to the user access virtual directories, the following two additional directories are Web enabled for access:

- ▼ **Exadmin**   The Exadmin virtual directory contains the Web interface for access by those tasked with administering the Exchange 2000 Server. Not only are mailboxes and public folders available for the general user, Exchange 2000 provides the feature for using a Web browser to manage the server itself.

- ▲ **ExchWeb**   The ExchWeb virtual directory contains the graphics files that OWA uses for display on the initial OWA home page.

The Exchange 2000 HTTP Virtual Server allows anonymous connections, whereas the Exchange 2000 virtual directories (Public and Exchange) use integrated security. This allows anyone to access the OWA front end but you must have a valid user name and password to get any further into the virtual directory structure.

If you feel you need to alter the authentication settings on a virtual directory, follow these steps:

1. Run the IIS 5.0 Internet Services Manager MMC snap-in (select Start | Programs | Administrative Tools).

2. Right-click the Internet Information Services; then select Connect.

3. Type the name of the computer running the IIS 5.0 services you want to modify (if the Internet Services Manager is already connected to the server you will be modifying, you can skip steps 2 and 3).

4. Find the specific HTTP Virtual Server you want to adjust and double-click it.

5. Right-click the specific virtual directory that has the authentication settings you want to change, and then select Properties.

6. Click the Directory Security tab.

Next you'll want to amend the specific authentication settings per your organization's requirements. Chapter 4 outlines the detailed procedures and information on the different settings and their meanings.

## Configuring Mailbox and Public Folder Access

As described earlier in this chapter, you can create additional virtual servers to offload connections to keep Web server performance at its peak. When traffic increases because of increased number of employees, you will want to utilize virtual servers to make sure access to OWA continues to be efficient. After you have created a new virtual server for OWA access, you must configure it to access the public folders on the Exchange 2000 Server. To provide access to a public folder or public folder tree structure, use these steps:

1. Open the Exchange 2000 System Manager.

2. Find the Protocols container in the console tree and expand the Servers item.

3. Locate the specific server that houses the HTTP Virtual Server you want to modify and expand its properties.

4. Expand the Protocols item.

5. Highlight HTTP in the Protocols list, right-click the specific HTTP Virtual Server, and then select Properties.

6. On the General tab, highlight Public Folder and then click the Modify button.

7. In the Public Folder Selection window, highlight the specific public folder or public folder tree (denoted by a plus [+] sign); then click OK.

Once this process is complete, users will be able to access the public folder by typing the following in the address line of the Web browser:

```
http://servername/foldername
```

## Load Balancing

Another wise practice for improving the performance and availability of OWA and IIS 5.0 is to install and configure load balancing. Load balancing is the technique by which multiple servers handle Web requests to one IP address or host name. Basically, one IP address or host name is assigned to two or more Windows 2000 Servers, all running the IIS 5.0 and OWA services. When the user accesses OWA using the Web browser, Windows 2000 automatically determines which server will handle the request. When installed in a *round robin* DNS configuration, if one server goes down, another server automatically steps up to make sure that access to OWA is always available. This provides the utmost in reliability. Load balancing is covered in detail in Chapter 15.

## Troubleshooting IIS 5.0 After the Exchange 2000 Installation

There is one item of concern that you will want to focus on after the Exchange 2000 installation. Although Exchange 2000 relies completely on IIS 5.0's services, it does remove references to the NNTP and SMTP virtual server objects from the Internet Services Manager MMC. Because Exchange 2000 extends these objects using its services, they become available in the Exchange System Manager only after the installation is complete.

Although this method is convenient for Exchange 2000 Server administrators, it is inconvenient for individuals with Web server responsibilities. Most organizations combine services to provide an overall cost-effective model for owning equipment, but might distribute task administration between individuals. It's not unheard of to have a dedicated administrator for corporate e-mail and another whose expertise is Web services.

There is a fix for this issue that can help with the Exchange 2000 Server post installation; plus it also is helpful to know should future applications cause the same problem. Or, if the Internet Services Manager console becomes corrupt, you can use the following method to repair it and restore access back to the Web services:

1. Choose Start | Run.
2. In the space provided, type **regsvr32 c:\winnt\system32\inetsrv\smtpsnap.dll**
3. Click OK.
4. Select Start | Run.
5. In the space provided, type **regsvr32 c:\winnt\system32\inetsrv\nntpsnap.dll**
6. Click OK.

**NOTE:**   The preceding regsvr32 commands assume that IIS 5.0 has been installed in the default location. If you have used the custom installation method to install IIS 5.0 in an alternate location, change the command to point to the custom location.

7.  Choose Start | Programs | Accessories | Command Prompt.

8.  In the command prompt window, type the following: **cscript c:\inetpub\adminscripts\adsutil.vbs set smtpsvc/SmtpServiceVersion 5**

**NOTE:**   Again, if you have modified the IIS 5.0 default location, make sure the cscript command matches the correct inetpub location.

# SUMMARY

Hopefully, after reading this chapter you understand how important IIS 5.0 is to the prospective future applications from Microsoft (and other vendors). IIS 5.0 provides a very strong base of components for applications to be easily integrated with Web services. It provides scalability, reliability, tight integration, and a development architecture that makes it extremely secure.

Over the next few months you will notice other applications as part of the .Net experience that rely heavily on IIS 5.0 being installed and configured. In years to come the capability to integrate seamlessly with IIS 5.0 will be a requirement for any vendor functioning within the Windows 2000/Active Directory and .Net technology model. Knowledge of IIS 5.0 is already a critical aspect for many areas of information technology administration.

# CHAPTER 15

# IIS 5.0 Performance and Troubleshooting

Out of the box, IIS 5.0 probably will not be configured to provide optimum performance for your implementation. Any software application you set up generally is installed with only the vendor's defaults. Installing the default options and features is a method most software vendors use to make sure the application installs correctly. Many organizations immediately become disoriented and eventually frustrated when they install a new system and performance lags or problems occur.

Of course, neglecting to read the requirements and instructions tends to increase frustrations, but some technicians also fail to realize that a very important part of any installation is to perform the post-configuration procedures. The post-configuration procedures should include explicit steps based on the specific reasons the application was installed in the first place. For example, if IIS 5.0 will be providing access to data that resides on a SQL Server, there are configuration issues that must be addressed for both IIS and SQL.

Microsoft has done an excellent job providing a top-performing Web server and for most organizations the default installation will function without problem; however, paying special attention to some small configuration settings can increase the overall success of the installation. Each IIS 5.0 component, such as the HTTP, ASP, FTP, and SMTP, can be broken down into separate services and modified per instance.

Microsoft relates performance issues directly with troubleshooting—and vice versa. One key example of this is the Windows 2000 native tool, Windows Performance Monitor, which is used for troubleshooting system and performance issues.

# WINDOWS PERFORMANCE MONITOR

Before delving into the specific performance and troubleshooting techniques for each IIS service, it is useful to understand what is available to monitor performance and aid in troubleshooting. The Windows Performance Monitor, which is built into Windows 2000, is used for recording server and service data. The data that is collected can be used to set baselines for how the components should perform, and then compared to future data to determine whether the components are working as they should.

The items you scrutinize using the Performance Monitor tool are broken down into objects and counters. The object is the main component; each object has many counters associated with it. For example, if you want to see how much network traffic is flowing to the server, you would choose the Network Interface Performance Object; then select the Bytes Received/sec Performance Counter. To examine the traffic flowing out of the server, you would again select the Network Interface Performance Object; then choose the Bytes Sent/sec Performance Counter.

There are three distinct categories for Performance Monitor counters: performance, planning, and troubleshooting. Whereas many counters fall under one of the categories, several others actually qualify for two or more of the categories.

▼ **Performance**   Counters that fall under the performance category generally are used as a long-term monitoring system. The log file is created and left running so performance data can be collected and reviewed against history information. Performance problems can be caused by configuration settings, outdated hardware specifications, hardware driver problems, increase in IIS server demands, outside influences (other components that the IIS server relies on), and another program running on the server that is acting inefficiently by taking up more server resources than it should.

■ **Planning**   A counter used for planning enables you to determine when the server hardware should be upgraded because of increased use. For example, if SMTP began by servicing one hundred users and has steadily grown to several hundred, you can use the planning counters to identify which hardware components should be upgraded and when it should be done to meet the growing demands on the server.

▲ **Troubleshooting**   Troubleshooting counters enable you to verify that there are problems or errors with some of the IIS services. When using a troubleshooting counter generally you'll want to construct an alert to notify you when problems arise.

Windows Performance Monitor is accessed by navigating to Start | Programs | Administrative Tools | Performance. When the program is executed, the window shown in Figure 15-1 is displayed. As you can see, the Windows Performance Monitor tool is a snap-in to the MMC like the Internet Services Manager, so you actually could add this tool to your custom MMC and have the performance information available along with the tool to manage your IIS server. Another great feature of the Performance Monitor is that you can review performance and troubleshooting data for the IIS 5.0 server from your workstation or any remote computer running Windows 2000. You don't have to be sitting at the IIS 5.0 server to gather and review the information.

In addition to providing the standard log files for output of gathered data, the Windows Performance Monitor tool permits output to .HTM files. This gives you a convenient way of pushing the logs to your IIS server directory, or creating another Virtual Server to allow

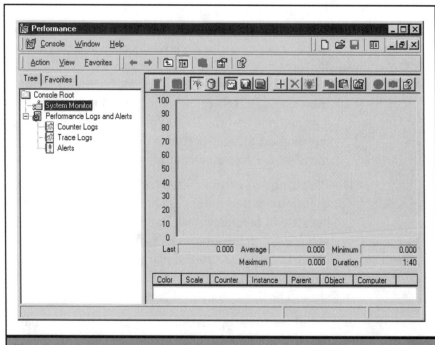

**Figure 15-1.** Windows Performance Monitor MMC

access to the log files remotely through your Web browser. Additionally, the .HTM file is updated automatically while open in the Web browser, as shown in Figure 15-2.

As Figure 15-1 depicts, there are three types of Performance Monitor tools under the Performance Logs and Alerts heading: Counter Logs, Trace Logs, and Alerts.

▼ **Counter logs** Counter logs are not meant to run continuously. They operate for a short or moderate period of time—preferably a short one (such as several hours instead of several days). While the Counter log is activated it uses the most resources of all the Performance Monitor logs, because it is gathering real-time data and constantly writing the results to a file. It is a wise practice to create a Counter log when you first install or

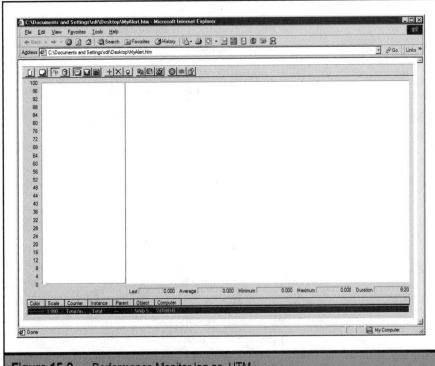

**Figure 15-2.**  Performance Monitor log as .HTM

enable a service, such as each of the various IIS components. Let it run for a time and save the log file for future use to compare to more current data. This first log file is your baseline of how the specific service should run under the initial load. You also can create periodic Counter logs to monitor how the increased use is affecting the server. This method can help justify the purchase and implementation of additional equipment for long-term investment. It's also a good way to identify how much use the component receives or how popular the particular service has become.

■ **Trace logs** A Trace log watches the system and when a specific event occurs it is recorded in the log file. This type of log runs continuously, but does not tax the server severely because it records data to a file only when the defined incident occurs.

▲ **Alerts** A Windows Performance Monitor Alert is created to perform an action when a specific event occurs. Shown in Figure 15-3, you can customize how the Alert reacts to the events a number of different ways:

■ **Write an entry in the Windows 2000 Application Event log** Windows 2000 enables its own Application Event log by default. It records all application-specific occurrences generated on the server including errors, warnings, and informational messages. The Application Event log is a great troubleshooting tool and because IIS 5.0 is considered an application, all of its events also will be recorded in this log.

■ **Send a message across the network to a logged-in user** For this to function, the Messaging Service must be running on both the originating computer (server) and the recipient computer. This alert displays on the recipient computer immediately in a pop-up alert box. This is an efficient way to perform proactive administration. You can effectively resolve an issue before the user base is even aware that a problem exists.

■ **Start a performance data log** When you choose this action, a log that you have created previously starts

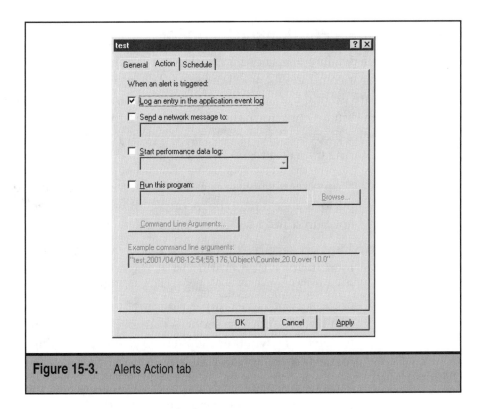

**Figure 15-3.**   Alerts Action tab

collecting data immediately. The available log files will be listed in the drop-down list of this action.

■ **Run an external program**   Using any external application, the alert can run the program; for example, you might want to use this particular action when sending an e-mail to a specific person who generally would be interested in the event. Several freeware programs on the market allow the sending of an e-mail through SMTP via a command-line. One example, mail.exe, is bundled in the Windows NT Resource Kit Clone Utilities, located at http://maxx.mc.net/ ~jlh/nttools/html/nttools.htm. Because the alert allows the configuration of an external program, including any command-line switches or arguments, there really are unlimited possibilities to what action you can cause the alert to take.

## Using Windows Performance Monitor

Before detailing the steps for creating the various Windows Performance Monitor components, you'll need a bit of information to make sure you are getting the most out of the Performance Monitor tool. When using Windows Performance Monitor keep these points in mind; ignoring them can have an adverse effect on your overall performance-monitoring plan and result in bad data:

▼ **Stop screen-saver programs**    Screen savers can cause performance data to be inconsistent when they "kick-in" and run during a monitoring session.

■ **Turn off services that are not essential or relevant to monitoring**    Certain Windows 2000 or third-party services directly affect performance because of their constant polling of the server. For example, you might not necessarily need real-time file backup services running when you are trying to determine whether the Web service is processing user requests in an appropriate amount of time.

▲ **Increase the paging file to physical memory size plus 100 MB** Performance Monitoring itself can tax the server. Windows 2000 uses a special file on the server's hard disk that serves as a temporary repository for data that is passed in and out of RAM. This paging file is utilized by all services that interact with the server, including Performance Monitor. Increasing the size of the paging file gives the server more room to process Performance Monitor's requests.

> **NOTE:**   To create or modify a log, you must have Full Control permission for the following registry key, which controls the Performance Logs and Alerts service: HKEY_LOCAL_MACHINE\SYSTEM\CurrentControlSet\Services\ SysmonLog\Log Queries. Administrators usually have this permission by default. Administrators can grant permission to users by using the Security menu in the Registry Editor (Regedt32.exe). To run the service (which runs in the background when you configure a log), you must have permission to start or otherwise configure services on the system. Administrators have this right by default and can grant it to users by using Group Policy. To log data on a remote computer, the Performance Logs and Alerts service must run under an account that has access to the remote system.

The steps for creating each of the Performance Monitor components, Counter log, Trace log, and Alert, are outlined in the next few sections. Memorizing these steps will save you time later, because these log files are used to provide critical troubleshooting data for IIS and all aspects of the Windows 2000 operating system.

## Creating a Counter Log

As described previously, the counter log file allows you to compare statistics from an initial period of time to a future time. By comparing the changes, you can effectively determine how popular a service has become, or even if the server hardware needs to be upgraded.

To create a Counter log, follow these steps:

1. Run the Performance tool.

2. Double-click Performance Logs and Alerts; then click Counter Logs.

3.  Any existing logs will be listed in the Details pane. A green icon indicates a log is running; a red icon indicates a log has been stopped.

4.  Right-click a blank area of the Details pane and click New Log Settings.

5.  In Name, type the name of the log; then click OK.

6.  On the General tab click Add. Select the counters you want to log.

7.  If you want to change the default file and schedule information, make the changes on the Log Files tab and the Schedule tab.

## Creating a Trace Log

To constantly monitor the server and have it report on specific, defined parameters, you'll want to create a Trace log. The Trace log will help you understand when changes in the services are affecting overall performance, or when a problem arises that needs immediate attention. The Trace log, however, is not a proactive tool like the Alert. You must remember to review the log file.

To create a Trace log, complete the following steps:

1.  Run the Performance tool.

2.  Double-click Performance Logs and Alerts, and then click Trace Logs.

3.  Any existing logs will be listed in the Details pane. A green icon indicates the logs are running; a red icon indicates logs have been stopped.

4.  Right-click a blank area of the Details pane and click New Log Settings.

5. In Name, type the name of the Trace log you want to create; then click OK.

By default, the log file is created in the PerfLogs folder in the root directory of the server. A sequence number is appended to the file name you enter. The file is assigned a sequential trace file type with an .etl extension. Trace logging of file details and page faults can generate an extremely large amount of data. It is recommended that you limit trace logging using the file details and page fault options to a maximum of two hours. Only one instance of each trace provider can be enabled at any given time.

## Creating an Alert

Alerts are the proactive components of the Windows Performance Monitor. Based on how you configure them, alerts can notify you when problems arise using any number of methods.

To create an Alert, do the following:

1. Run the Performance tool.

2. Double-click Performance Logs and Alerts; then click Alerts.

3. Any existing alerts will be listed in the Details pane. A green icon indicates the alerts are running; a red icon indicates alerts have been stopped.

4. Right-click a blank area of the Details pane and click New Alert Settings.

5. In Name, type the name of the alert; then click OK.

6. To define a comment for your alert, along with counters, alert thresholds, and the sample interval, use the General tab. To define actions that should occur when counter data triggers an alert, use the Action tab; to define when the service should begin scanning for alerts, use the Schedule tab.

# WEB SERVICE PERFORMANCE AND TROUBLESHOOTING

IIS 5.0 provides the best Web performance possible but there are instances in which even the best can be improved. The Web services of IIS tend to be the most anticipated portion of its many services. Depending on the amount of traffic your Web site will experience, you should work through the following sections to ensure your Web services are configured to meet the requirements of your situation.

## Making Sure You Have the Latest Updates

Microsoft makes the HotFix Check tool available to ensure your IIS 5.0 servers are up to date on all patches. The tool can be run continuously or periodically, against the local machine or a remote one, using either a database on the Microsoft Web site or a locally hosted copy. When the tool finds a patch that hasn't been installed it can display a dialogue window or write a warning to the Event log.

The HotFix Check tool consists of two Windows Script Host files: HFCHECK.WSF and NOTIFY.JS. HFCHECK.WSF is the actual tool; NOTIFY.JS can be used to customize and extend the functionality. HFCHECK.WSF refers to an XML file list for the catalog of hotfixes available for IIS; then compares this list to the hotfixes installed on the local system. The XML file list, hosted on the Microsoft site, can either be queried on the Microsoft site or downloaded to the local machine and queried locally. If a hotfix is missing, the tool calls the Notify function in NOTIFY.JS (JavaScript file). The downloaded HotFix tool reports an error on the command line and writes a warning message to the Application Event log. However, you can customize Notify to perform other actions such as stopping or recycling the IIS services or sending an e-mail to the administrator. The Notify function is in the separate NOTIFY.JS file, so you can rework the Notify function to meet your requirements.

If you call HFCHECK.WSF without any command-line parameters, it checks the local machine for missing hotfixes. The following command-line switches are available to extend HFCHECK's functionality:

▼ **/B <path bulletins file>**   If you want to query the bulletins file in your intranet (or if your servers don't have access to the Microsoft Web site), you can host the bulletins file on your own server. The file is available at http://www.microsoft.com/ technet/security/search/bulletins.xml; just save it to your local storage. You'll want to set up a routine that will grab the latest version of the file periodically; for example, HFCHECK.WSF /B c:\tools\bulletins.xml.

■ **/M <machine1,machine2>**   HFCHECK.WSF also can check the hotfix status on remote machines through WMI. You can specify multiple machine names by separating each with a comma and making sure to exclude spaces between them; for example, HFCHECK.WSF /M iislive,iistest,iisdev.

■ **/U <Domain\Username or Computername\Username> /P <Password>**   If a user name and password are not specified, WMI connects using the current logon credentials to the remote machine. WMI must be able to connect to the remote computer using an administrator-equivalent account and password. You can specify a different user name and password using this example: HFCHECK.WSF /M iislive,iistest,iistest /U iisdomain\Administrator /P adminpassword.

▲ **Using the /?, d**   Displays all the command-line options available for the HFCHECK program.

The HotFix Check tool for IIS is available for download, from http://download.microsoft.com/download/win2000platform/Patch/ IIS5_HFC_1.0/NT5/EN-US/HFCINST.EXE.

## Enabling HTTP Compression

HTTP compression increases the transmission rate when Web pages are processed by the Web server and sent along to a compression-enabled Web browser. Note that the client browser must also have compression capability. Generally, the newer browsers can operate this way, but you should check with the specific vendor to ensure it allows this capability.

To enable HTTP compression, do the following:

1. In the Internet Services Manager, right-click the Web server and choose Properties from the context pop-up menu.

2. On the Internet Information Services tab, make sure that WWW Service is selected in the Master Properties drop-down box; if not, select it.

3. Click the Edit button.

4. Select the Service tab from the Master Properties window.

5. On the Service tab you'll see the HTTP Compression section. You should select the options to configure based on your requirements:

   ■ Selecting Compress Static Files only compresses static files for transmission to compression-enabled clients.

   ■ Selecting Compress Static Files and Compress Application Files compresses application files (you have to have both selected for application compression to work).

6. In the Temporary Folder box enter a valid path (directory) that resides on the IIS 5.0 server. You also can browse for this directory and select it in a folder selection window.

**NOTE:** The directory you select must be on the server's local drive, must be formatted using NTFS (not FAT or FAT32), cannot be a shared directory, and cannot be configured as a Windows 2000 compressed directory.

7. Set the maximum size of the data that will be contained in the directory. This can be Unlimited or Limited To a specific size in megabytes (MB).

**NOTE:** Although HTTP compression could help speed access to the content, if you have a lot of dynamic material on the Web site it actually could slow the Web server because of the additional processing power required to compress the data stream. If the percentage of Processor Time is already more than 80 percent, it's best to leave HTTP compression alone. Using Windows Performance Monitor, log the %Processor Time counter of the Processor object over a three-day period to establish a baseline. Then, enable HTTP compression using the previous steps and compare the data.

## Enabling HTTP Keep-Alives

When a Web browser contacts the server periodically to keep the connection open, this is referred to as "HTTP Keep-Alives." For example, if HTTP Keep-Alives were not present, a new connection for each graphic element on a page would need to be made by the client browser. HTTP Keep-Alive allows the browser to connect and keep a pipe open until the entire page has been downloaded. Although this provides a big benefit for the Internet browser, it does require additional server activity and resources. If your server could use the extra performance power, you can turn HTTP Keep-Alives off by stepping through this short instruction:

1. In the Internet Services Manager right-click the specific Web site in which you need to modify the HTTP Keep-Alives setting and choose Properties from the context menu.

2. On the Web Site tab of the Web site's property window, in the Connections section clear the check box for the HTTP Keep-Alives Enabled.

## Socket Pooling

You might want to disable socket pooling if you are not hosting a large number of sites or you have special security concerns. Socket pooling causes IIS 5.0 to listen to all IP addresses. For some organizations this might present a possible security risk for secure domains with multiple networks. Both bandwidth throttling and performance adjustments will apply to all Web sites configured for the same port. If you intend to use bandwidth throttling or do performance tuning on a per-site basis, you must disable socket pooling for it to work properly.

To disable socket pooling, type the following (as one complete line) in a command prompt window on the IIS 5.0 server:

```
c:\inetpub\adminscripts\cscript adsutil.vbs set w3svc/
disablesocketpooling true
```

## Bandwidth Throttling

One of the key new features of IIS 5.0 is Bandwidth Throttling. Bandwidth Throttling allows you to limit the amount of bandwidth that is available to the IIS 5.0 services. For example, if the server also participates in the company as an e-mail or news server, you might want to limit the Web portion so that there is plenty of bandwidth available for the other services. However, Bandwidth Throttling affects only the request for static HTML files. Before choosing to specify the amount of bandwidth available to the Web services, you should determine exactly how much bandwidth the server is using in the first place. It's possible that the connections to and from the server are fine.

To determine the amount of bandwidth the server is currently using, complete these steps:

1. Employ Windows Performance Monitor, use the Bytes Total/sec counter for the Network Interface object. (If instead you want to compare the difference between incoming and outgoing traffic, examine the variation between the Bytes Sent/sec and the Bytes Received/sec counters.)

2. Compare the Bytes Total/sec with the Current Bandwidth counter. If the percentage of bandwidth is more than 50 percent, consider enabling Bandwidth Throttling.

To throttle IIS 5.0's bandwidth, follow these steps:

1. In the Internet Service Manager, right-click either the IIS 5.0 server or one of the Web sites contained within the IIS 5.0 server (you can throttle bandwidth across the entire server or per each Web site), and choose Properties on the context menu.

2. On the Internet Information Services tab (for the server) or the Performance tab (for a single Web site), select the Enable Bandwidth Throttling option.

3. In the Maximum Network Use box, enter the maximum number of kilobytes per second (KBps) you want IIS to use.

## Process Throttling

If you are hosting multiple Web sites on one computer you should consider enabling Process Throttling. Applying Process Throttling, you can limit the percentage of time that the Web services can use when processing out-of-process applications (applications that run outside the confines of the Web services). Not only does this distribute processor time across the different Web sites; it restricts the processor's usage for non-Web applications if the server is housing other applications.

Before enabling Process Throttling, you should determine whether your Web server or the Web sites could benefit from it. To do this follow these instructions:

1. Using Windows Performance Monitor, inspect the %Processor Time counter of the Processor object and the Maximum CGI Requests and Total CGI Requests of the Web Service object.

2. In Internet Services Manager, enable Process Accounting. Process Accounting ensures that the Job Object counter is included in the IIS log files. To enable Process Accounting:

   ■ In Internet Services Manager, right-click the server or the Web site where Process Accounting should be enabled; then choose Properties from the context menu.

   ■ Verify that the Enable Logging check box is enabled and that the log format type is W3C Extended Log File Format.

   ■ Click the Properties button next to the Active Log Format drop-down list.

   ■ Select the Extended Properties tab, and then cursor down the extended properties list until you see Process Accounting.

   ■ Click the check box to enable Process Accounting.

3. After a time, review the IIS log file to determine the number of out-of-process applications that are being accessed. If the number of out-of-process applications is high, consider enabling Process Throttling. To do this:

   ■ Using Internet Services Manager, select the specific Web site for which you want to enable Process Throttling; then right-click the site and choose Properties from the context menu.

   ■ Choose the Performance tab.

- Check the box next to Enable Process Throttling.
- Enter the CPU time (in percentage) to which you want this specific Web site limited.
- Check the Enforce Limits if you want the IIS server to adhere to the different levels of consequence if the process utilization limit is overrun.

When Enforce Limits is enabled, the IIS service follows more stringent guidelines for imposing the configured limit (CPU percentage). There are three levels of consequence that the IIS server follows if the limit is exceeded.

▼ **Level 1**   When total processor has exceeded the specified time limit, an event is written to the Windows 2000 Event Log.

■ **Level 2**   When the processor use exceeds 150 percent of the limit, an event is written to the Windows 2000 Event Log and the CPU priority for all of the out-of-process applications is set to Idle.

▲ **Level 3**   When the processor use exceeds 200 percent of the limit, an event is written to the Windows 2000 Event Log and the out-of-process applications are forced to shut down.

If you find that Process Throttling does not help your situation, there are other considerations you can pursue; generally in the following order:

1. Upgrade the CPU to a faster speed.
2. Add additional CPUs.
3. Replicate the Web site to another server and distribute traffic across both servers.
4. Move co-existing applications to another server so that IIS has dedicated resources (CPU, Disk, RAM, and so forth).

**NOTE:** Keep in mind that network utilization also plays a part in processor usage. To verify that the network is not involved, you will want to check the Windows Performance Monitor counters for the Network Adapter in conjunction with the Processor counters. When the Network Adapter utilization stays low and the Processor utilization is high, the Processor is providing the bottleneck for your Web site's performance problems.

## Web Service Performance Monitor Counters

In addition to those specific performance and troubleshooting items detailed in the previous sections, the Web service also can be monitored conveniently using the installed counters. When IIS 5.0 is installed on the Windows 2000 Server, there are several counters that are installed for use with the Windows Performance Monitor tool. Those specific counters are listed in Table 15-1. Each is listed by name and category with a brief description.

| Web Service Counter | Category | Description |
| --- | --- | --- |
| Anonymous Users/sec | Performance | The rate at which users are making anonymous connections using the Web service. |
| Bytes Received/sec | Performance | The rate at which data bytes are received by the Web service. |
| Bytes Sent/sec | Performance | The rate at which data bytes are sent by the Web service. |

**Table 15-1.** Web Service Performance Monitor Counters

| Web Service Counter | Category | Description |
|---|---|---|
| Bytes Total/sec | Performance | The sum of Bytes Sent/sec and Bytes Received/sec. This is the total rate of bytes transferred by the Web service. |
| CGI Requests/sec | Performance | The rate of CGI requests that are being simultaneously processed by the Web service. |
| Connection Attempts/sec | Performance | The rate at which connections using the Web service are being attempted. |
| Copy Requests/sec | Performance | The rate at which HTTP requests using the COPY method are made. Copy requests are used for copying files and directories. |
| Current Anonymous Users | Performance | Current Anonymous Users is the number of users who currently have an anonymous connection using the Web service. |
| Current Blocked Async I/O Requests | Performance/ Troubleshooting | Current requests temporarily blocked because of bandwidth throttling settings. |
| Current CAL Count for Authenticated Users | Performance | The current count of licenses used simultaneously by the Web service for authenticated connections. |

**Table 15-1.**    Web Service Performance Monitor Counters *(continued)*

| Web Service Counter | Category | Description |
|---|---|---|
| Current CAL Count for SSL Connections | Performance | Current CAL count for SSL connections is the current count of licenses used simultaneously by the Web service for SSL connections. |
| Current CGI Requests | Performance | The current number of CGI requests that are simultaneously being processed by the Web service. |
| Current Connections | Performance | The current number of connections established with the Web service. |
| Current ISAPI Extension Requests | Performance | The current number of Extension requests that are simultaneously being processed by the Web service. |
| Current NonAnonymous Users | Performance | The number of users who currently have a nonanonymous connection using the Web service. |
| Delete Requests/sec | Performance | The rate at which HTTP requests using the DELETE method are made. Delete requests generally are used for file removals. |
| Files Received/sec | Performance | The rate at which files are received by the Web service. |

**Table 15-1.**    Web Service Performance Monitor Counters *(continued)*

| Web Service Counter | Category | Description |
|---|---|---|
| Files Sent/sec | Performance | The rate at which files are sent by the Web service. |
| Files/sec | Performance | The rate at which files are transferred; that is, sent and received by the Web service. |
| Get Requests/sec | Performance | The rate at which HTTP requests using the GET method are made. Get requests generally are used for basic file retrievals or image maps, although they can be used with forms. |
| Head Requests/sec | Performance | The rate HTTP requests using the HEAD method are made. Head requests generally indicate a client is querying the state of a document they already have to see if it needs to be refreshed. |
| ISAPI Requests/sec | Performance | The rate at which ISAPI Extension requests are being simultaneously processed by the Web service. |
| Lock Requests/sec | Performance | The rate at which HTTP requests using the LOCK method are made. Lock requests are used to lock a file for one user so that only that user can modify the file. |

**Table 15-1.** Web Service Performance Monitor Counters *(continued)*

| Web Service Counter | Category | Description |
|---|---|---|
| Locked Errors/sec | Performance | The rate of errors due to requests that couldn't be satisfied by the server because the requested document was locked. These generally are reported as an HTTP 423 error code to the client. |
| Logon Attempts/sec | Performance | The rate at which logons using the Web service are being attempted. |
| Maximum Anonymous Users | Performance | The maximum number of users who established concurrent anonymous connections using the Web service (counted since service startup). |
| Maximum CAL Count for Authenticated Users | Performance | The maximum count of licenses used simultaneously by the Web service for authenticated connections. |
| Maximum CAL Count for SSL Connections | Performance | The maximum count of licenses used simultaneously by the Web service for SSL connections. |
| Maximum CGI Requests | Performance | The maximum number of CGI requests simultaneously processed by the Web service. |

**Table 15-1.** Web Service Performance Monitor Counters *(continued)*

| Web Service Counter | Category | Description |
|---|---|---|
| Maximum Connections | Performance | The maximum number of simultaneous connections established with the Web service. |
| Maximum ISAPI Extension Requests | Performance | The maximum number of Extension requests simultaneously processed by the Web service. |
| Maximum NonAnonymous Users | Performance | The maximum number of users who established concurrent nonanonymous connections using the Web service (counted since service startup). |
| Measured Async I/O Bandwidth Usage | Performance/ Troubleshooting | Measured bandwidth of asynchronous I/O averaged over a minute. |
| Mkcol Requests/sec | Performance | The rate at which HTTP requests using the MKCOL method are made. Mkcol requests are used to create directories on the server. |
| Move Requests/sec | Performance | The rate at which HTTP requests using the MOVE method are made. Move requests are used for moving files and directories. |

**Table 15-1.**    Web Service Performance Monitor Counters *(continued)*

| Web Service Counter | Category | Description |
|---|---|---|
| NonAnonymous Users/sec | Performance | The rate at which users are making nonanonymous connections using the Web service. |
| Not Found Errors/sec | Performance/ Troubleshooting | The rate at which errors occur because of requests that couldn't be satisfied by the server because the requested document could not be found. These are generally reported as an HTTP 404 error code to the client. |
| Options Requests/sec | Performance | The rate at which HTTP requests using the OPTIONS method are made. |
| Other Request Methods/sec | Performance | The rate at which HTTP requests are made that do not use the OPTIONS, GET, HEAD, POST, PUT, DELETE, TRACE, MOVE, COPY, MKCOL, PROPFIND, PROPPATCH, MS-SEARCH, LOCK or UNLOCK methods. These can include LINK or other methods supported by gateway applications. |

**Table 15-1.** Web Service Performance Monitor Counters *(continued)*

| Web Service Counter | Category | Description |
|---|---|---|
| Post Requests/sec | Performance | The rate at which HTTP requests using the POST method are made. Post requests generally are used for forms or gateway requests. |
| Propfind Requests/sec | Performance | The rate at which HTTP requests using the PROPFIND method are made. Propfind requests retrieve property values on files and directories. |
| Proppatch Requests/sec | Performance | The rate at which HTTP requests using the PROPPATCH method are made. Proppatch requests set property values on files and directories. |
| Put Requests/sec | Performance | The rate at which HTTP requests are made using the PUT method. |
| Search Requests/sec | Performance | The rate at which HTTP requests are made using the MS-SEARCH method. Search requests are used to query the server to find resources that match a set of conditions provided by the client. |

**Table 15-1.**   Web Service Performance Monitor Counters *(continued)*

| Web Service Counter | Category | Description |
|---|---|---|
| Service Uptime | Troubleshooting | Uptime for W3SVC Service or W3 sites. |
| Total Allowed Async I/O Requests | Troubleshooting/ Planning | Total requests allowed by bandwidth throttling settings (counted since service startup). |
| Total Anonymous Users | Troubleshooting/ Planning | Total Anonymous Users is the total number of users who established an anonymous connection with the Web service (counted since service startup). |
| Total Blocked Async I/O Requests | Troubleshooting/ Planning | Total requests temporarily blocked because of bandwidth throttling settings (counted since service startup). |
| Total Common Gateway Interface (CGI) Requests | Troubleshooting/ Planning | Custom gateway executables (.exe) the administrator can install to add forms processing or other dynamic data sources. CGI requests spawn a process on the server, which can be a drain on server resources. The count is the total since service startup. |
| Total Connection Attempts (all instances) | Troubleshooting/ Planning | The number of connections that have been attempted using the Web service (counted since service startup). This counter is for all instances listed. |

**Table 15-1.**   Web Service Performance Monitor Counters *(continued)*

| Web Service Counter | Category | Description |
|---|---|---|
| Total Copy Requests | Troubleshooting/ Planning | The number of HTTP requests using the COPY method (counted since service startup). Copy requests are used for copying files and directories. |
| Total Count of Failed CAL Requests for Authenticated Users | Troubleshooting/ Planning | The number of HTTP requests that failed because of a license being unavailable for an authenticated user. The count is the total since service startup. |
| Total Count of Failed CAL Requests for SSL Connections | Troubleshooting/ Planning | The total count of HTTP requests that failed because of a license being unavailable for SSL connections. |
| Total Delete Requests | Troubleshooting/ Planning | The number of HTTP requests using the DELETE method (counted since service startup). Delete requests generally are used for file removals. |
| Total Files Received | Troubleshooting/ Planning | The total number of files received by the Web service (counted since service startup). |
| Total Files Sent | Troubleshooting/ Planning | The total number of files sent by the Web service (counted since service startup). |

**Table 15-1.** Web Service Performance Monitor Counters *(continued)*

| Web Service Counter | Category | Description |
|---|---|---|
| Total Files Transferred | Troubleshooting/ Planning | The sum of Files Sent and Files Received. This is the total number of files transferred by the Web service (counted since service startup). |
| Total Get Requests | Troubleshooting/ Planning | The number of HTTP requests using the GET method (counted since service startup). Get requests generally are used for basic file retrievals or image maps, although they can be used with forms. |
| Total Head Requests | Troubleshooting/ Planning | The number of HTTP requests using the HEAD method (counted since service startup). Head requests generally indicate a client is querying the state of a document they already have to see if it needs to be refreshed. |

**Table 15-1.** Web Service Performance Monitor Counters *(continued)*

| Web Service Counter | Category | Description |
| --- | --- | --- |
| Total ISAPI Extension Requests | Troubleshooting/ Planning | Custom gateway Dynamic Link Libraries (.dll) that the administrator can install to add forms processing or other dynamic data sources. Unlike CGI requests, ISAPI requests are simple calls to a DLL library routine; thus they are better suited to high-performance gateway applications. The count is the total since service startup. |
| Total Lock Requests | Troubleshooting/ Planning | The number of HTTP requests using the LOCK method (counted since service startup). Lock requests are used to lock a file for one user so that only that user can modify the file. |

**Table 15-1.** Web Service Performance Monitor Counters *(continued)*

| Web Service Counter | Category | Description |
|---|---|---|
| Total Locked Errors | Troubleshooting/ Planning | The number of requests that couldn't be satisfied by the server because the requested object was locked. These generally are reported as an HTTP 423 error code to the client. The count is the total since service startup. |
| Total Logon Attempts | Troubleshooting/ Planning | The number of logons that have been attempted using the Web service (counted since service startup). |
| Total Method Requests | Troubleshooting/ Planning | The number of all HTTP requests (counted since service startup). |
| Total Method Requests/sec | Troubleshooting/ Planning | The rate at which all HTTP requests are made. |
| Total Mkcol Requests | Troubleshooting/ Planning | The number of HTTP requests using the MKCOL method (counted since service startup). Mkcol requests are used to create directories on the server. |
| Total Move Requests | Troubleshooting/ Planning | The number of HTTP requests using the MOVE method (counted since service startup). Move requests are used for moving files and directories. |

**Table 15-1.**    Web Service Performance Monitor Counters *(continued)*

| Web Service Counter | Category | Description |
|---|---|---|
| Total NonAnonymous Users | Troubleshooting/ Planning | The total number of users who established a nonanonymous connection with the Web service (counted since service startup). |
| Total Not Found Errors | Troubleshooting/ Planning | The number of requests that couldn't be satisfied by the server because the requested document could not be found. These generally are reported as an HTTP 404 error code to the client. The count is the total since service startup. |
| Total Options Requests | Troubleshooting/ Planning | The number of HTTP requests using the OPTIONS method (counted since service startup). |
| Total Other Request Methods | Troubleshooting/ Planning | The number of HTTP requests that are not OPTIONS, GET, HEAD, POST, PUT, DELETE, TRACE, MOVE, COPY, MKCOL, PROPFIND, PROPPATCH, MS-SEARCH, LOCK, or UNLOCK methods (counted since service startup). These can include LINK or other methods supported by gateway applications. |

**Table 15-1.**    Web Service Performance Monitor Counters *(continued)*

| Web Service Counter | Category | Description |
|---|---|---|
| Total Post Requests | Troubleshooting/ Planning | The number of HTTP requests using the POST method (counted since service startup). Post requests generally are used for forms or gateway requests. |
| Total Propfind Requests | Troubleshooting/ Planning | The number of HTTP requests using the PROPFIND method (counted since service startup). Propfind requests retrieve property values on files and directories. |
| Total Proppatch Requests | Troubleshooting/ Planning | The number of HTTP requests using the PROPPATCH method (counted since service startup). Proppatch requests set property values on files and directories. |
| Total Put Requests | Troubleshooting/ Planning | The number of HTTP requests using the PUT method (counted since service startup). |
| Total Rejected Async I/O Requests | Troubleshooting/ Planning | Total requests rejected because of bandwidth throttling settings (counted since service startup). |

**Table 15-1.** Web Service Performance Monitor Counters *(continued)*

| Web Service Counter | Category | Description |
|---|---|---|
| Total Search Requests | Troubleshooting/ Planning | The number of HTTP requests using the MS-SEARCH method (counted since service startup). Search requests are used to query the server to find resources that match a set of conditions provided by the client. |
| Total Trace Requests | Troubleshooting/ Planning | The number of HTTP requests using the TRACE method (counted since service startup). Trace requests enable the client to see what is being received at the end of the request chain and use the information for diagnostic purposes. |
| Total Unlock Requests | Troubleshooting/ Planning | The number of HTTP requests using the UNLOCK method (counted since service startup). Unlock requests are used to remove locks from files. |

**Table 15-1.**    Web Service Performance Monitor Counters *(continued)*

| Web Service Counter | Category | Description |
|---|---|---|
| Trace Requests/sec | Performance | The rate at which HTTP requests using the TRACE method are made. Trace requests enable the client to see what is being received at the end of the request chain and use the information for diagnostic purposes. |
| Unlock Requests/sec | Performance | The rate at which HTTP requests using the UNLOCK method are made. Unlock requests are used to remove locks from files. |

**Table 15-1.** Web Service Performance Monitor Counters *(continued)*

# FTP SERVICE PERFORMANCE AND TROUBLESHOOTING

The FTP Service relies heavily on disk space (for storing files retrievable through the FTP connection) and the network connection. IIS does not provide much in the way of modifying performance parameters for the FTP service. However, if FTP is a critical component and it is taxing the server because of the coexistence with the Web and SMTP services, you should consider pushing the FTP service to a separate server. You can identify whether the FTP service would benefit from this migration by using Windows Performance Monitor with the Performance Objects and Counters listed in the next section.

# FTP Service Performance Monitor Counters

In addition to those specific performance and troubleshooting items detailed in the previous sections, the FTP service can be watched using the counters that are part of the IIS 5.0 installation. During the IIS 5.0 installation, several counters are installed for use with the Windows Performance Monitor tool. The FTP service-specific counters are detailed in Table 15-2. Each is listed by name and category with a brief description.

| FTP Service Counter | Category | Description |
| --- | --- | --- |
| Bytes Received/sec | Performance | The rate at which data bytes are received by the FTP service. |
| Bytes Sent/sec | Performance | The rate at which data bytes are sent by the FTP service. |
| Bytes Total/sec | Performance | The sum of Bytes Sent/sec and Bytes Received/sec. This is the total rate of bytes transferred by the FTP service. |
| Current Anonymous Users | Performance | The number of users who currently have an anonymous connection using the FTP service. |
| Current Connections | Performance | The current number of connections established with the FTP service. |

**Table 15-2.**   FTP Service Performance Monitor Counters

| FTP Service Counter | Category | Description |
|---|---|---|
| Current NonAnonymous Users | Performance | The number of users who currently have a nonanonymous connection using the FTP service. |
| FTP Service Uptime | Troubleshooting | FTP Service and FTP site uptime in seconds. |
| Maximum Anonymous Users | Performance | The maximum number of users who established concurrent anonymous connections using the FTP service (since service startup). |
| Maximum Connections | Performance | The maximum number of simultaneous connections established with the FTP service. |
| Maximum NonAnonymous Users | Performance | The maximum number of users who established concurrent nonanonymous connections using the FTP service (since service startup). |
| Total Anonymous Users | Troubleshooting/ Planning | The total number of users who established an anonymous connection with the FTP service (since service startup). |
| Total Connection Attempts (all instances) | Troubleshooting/ Planning | The number of connections that have been attempted using the FTP service (since service startup). This counter is for all instances listed. |
| Total Files Received | Troubleshooting/ Planning | The total number of files received by the FTP service since service startup. |

**Table 15-2.**   FTP Service Performance Monitor Counters *(continued)*

| FTP Service Counter | Category | Description |
|---|---|---|
| Total Files Sent | Troubleshooting/ Planning | The total number of files sent by the FTP service since service startup. |
| Total Files Transferred | Troubleshooting/ Planning | The sum of Files Sent and Files Received. This is the total number of files transferred by the FTP service since service startup. |
| Total Logon Attempts | Troubleshooting/ Planning | The number of logons that have been attempted using the FTP service (since service startup). |
| Total NonAnonymous Users | Troubleshooting/ Planning | The total number of users who established a nonanonymous connection with the FTP service (since service startup). |

**Table 15-2.**   FTP Service Performance Monitor Counters *(continued)*

# SMTP SERVICE PERFORMANCE AND TROUBLESHOOTING

The SMTP service's performance relies primarily on the routing capabilities of the servers and network equipment involved in getting e-mail messages from your server to the recipient. If you can ensure that the hops to the destination are minimal and that the network equipment from here to there works properly, the SMTP service should function well.

There are some specific items that can be configured to improve how well the IIS server interacts with the messages. Using the SMTP reference in Chapter 5, you can limit the size of messages, limit the overall user session size (in kilobytes), limit the messages per connection, and decrease the retry intervals. To understand when it's time to make these specific changes to improve SMTP performance, you should use the SMTP Windows Performance Monitor Objects and Counters listed in the following section.

## SMTP Service Performance Monitor Counters

Along with the specific performance and troubleshooting information detailed in the previous sections on SMTP, the service's availability and execution can be monitored using its installed performance counters. During the IIS 5.0 installation, there are several counters installed that are used with the Windows Performance Monitor tool. In fact, there are more SMTP-specific counters than any other IIS 5.0 service. The SMTP service counters are itemized in Table 15-3. Each is listed by name with the category it falls under and its description.

| SMTP Service Counter | Category | Description |
|---|---|---|
| % Recipients Local | Performance | The percentage of recipients that will be delivered locally. |
| % Recipients Remote | Performance | The percentage of recipients that will be delivered remotely. |
| Avg Recipients/ msg Received | Performance | The average number of recipients per inbound message received. |
| Avg Recipients/ msg Sent | Performance | The average number of recipients per outbound messages sent. |
| Avg Retries/ msg Delivered | Performance/ Troubleshooting | The average number of retries per local delivery. |
| Avg Retries/ msg Sent | Performance/ Troubleshooting | The average number of retries per outbound message sent. |

**Table 15-3.**    SMTP Service Performance Monitor Counters

| SMTP Service Counter | Category | Description |
|---|---|---|
| Badmailed Messages (Bad Pickup File) | Troubleshooting | The number of malformed pickup messages sent to badmail. |
| Badmailed Messages (General Failure) | Troubleshooting | The number of messages sent to badmail for reasons not associated with a specific counter. |
| Badmailed Messages (Hop Count Exceeded) | Troubleshooting | The number of messages sent to badmail because they exceeded the maximum hop count. |
| Badmailed Messages (NDR of DSN) | Troubleshooting | The number of Delivery Status Notifications sent to badmail because they could not be delivered. |
| Badmailed Messages (No Recipients) | Troubleshooting | The number of messages sent to badmail because they had no recipients. |
| Badmailed Messages (Triggered via Event) | Troubleshooting | The number of messages sent to badmail at the request of a server event sink. |
| Bytes Received Total | Performance/ Planning | The total number of bytes received. |
| Bytes Received/sec | Performance | The rate at which bytes are received. |
| Bytes Sent Total | Performance | The total number of bytes sent. |
| Bytes Sent/sec | Performance | The rate at which bytes are sent. |
| Bytes Total | Performance/ Planning | The total number of bytes sent and received. |

**Table 15-3.** SMTP Service Performance Monitor Counters *(continued)*

| SMTP Service Counter | Category | Description |
|---|---|---|
| Bytes Total/sec | Performance | The rate at which bytes are sent and received. |
| Cat: Address lookup completions | Performance/ Planning | The number of address lookup completions processed. |
| Cat: Address lookup completions/sec | Performance | The number of address lookup completions processed per second. |
| Cat: Address lookups | Performance/ Planning | The number of Directory Service (DS) lookups for individual addresses. |
| Cat: Address lookups not found | Troubleshooting | The number of address lookups that did not find any DS object. |
| Cat: Address lookups/sec | Performance | The number of address lookups dispatched to the DS per second. |
| Cat: Categorizations completed | Performance | The total number of messages submitted to the categorizer that have finished categorization. |
| Cat: Categorizations completed successfully | Troubleshooting | The number of categorizations that completed without any errors. |
| Cat: Categorizations completed/sec | Performance | The rate of categorizations completed. |
| Cat: Categorizations failed (DS connection failure) | Troubleshooting | The number of categorizations that failed due to a DS connection failure. |

**Table 15-3.** SMTP Service Performance Monitor Counters *(continued)*

| SMTP Service Counter | Category | Description |
|---|---|---|
| Cat: Categorizations failed (DS logon failure) | Troubleshooting | The number of categorizations that failed due to a DS logon failure. |
| Cat: Categorizations failed (non-retryable error) | Troubleshooting | The number of categorizations that failed with a hard error (not retry-able). |
| Cat: Categorizations failed (Out of Memory) | Troubleshooting | The number of categorizations that failed because of lack of available memory. |
| Cat: Categorizations failed (retryable error) | Troubleshooting | The number of categorizations that failed with a retry-able error. |
| Cat: Categorizations failed (sink retryable error) | Troubleshooting | The number of categorizations that failed with a generic retry-able error. |
| Cat: Categorizations in progress | Performance | The number of categorizations in progress. |
| Cat: LDAP bind failures | Troubleshooting | The total number of Lightweight Directory Access Protocol (LDAP) bind failures. |
| Cat: LDAP binds | Troubleshooting | The total number of successful LDAP binds performed. |
| Cat: LDAP connection failures | Troubleshooting | The total number of failures encountered connecting to LDAP servers. |

**Table 15-3.**    SMTP Service Performance Monitor Counters *(continued)*

| SMTP Service Counter | Category | Description |
|---|---|---|
| Cat: LDAP connections | Performance | The total number of LDAP connections opened. |
| Cat: LDAP connections currently open | Performance | The number of LDAP connections currently open. |
| Cat: LDAP general completion failures | Troubleshooting | Number of LDAP completions with a generic failure. |
| Cat: LDAP paged search completion failures | Troubleshooting | Number of LDAP paged searches that completed with a failure. |
| Cat: LDAP paged search failures | Troubleshooting | Number of failures to dispatch an async paged LDAP search. |
| Cat: LDAP paged searches | Troubleshooting | LDAP paged searches successfully dispatched. |
| Cat: LDAP paged searches completed | Performance | Number of paged LDAP completions processed. |
| Cat: LDAP search completion failures | Troubleshooting | Number of LDAP searches that completed with a failure. |
| Cat: LDAP search failures | Troubleshooting | Number of failures to dispatch an async LDAP search. |
| Cat: LDAP searches | Troubleshooting | LDAP searches successfully dispatched. |
| Cat: LDAP searches abandoned | Troubleshooting | Number of LDAP searches abandoned. |
| Cat: LDAP searches completed | Troubleshooting | Number of LDAP search completions processed. |
| Cat: LDAP searches completed/sec | Performance | LDAP search completions processed/sec. |

**Table 15-3.** SMTP Service Performance Monitor Counters *(continued)*

| SMTP Service Counter | Category | Description |
| --- | --- | --- |
| Cat: LDAP searches pending completion | Performance/ Troubleshooting | Number of LDAP searches pending async completion. |
| Cat: LDAP searches/sec | Performance | LDAP searches successfully dispatched/sec. |
| Cat: mailmsg duplicate collisions | Troubleshooting | The number of times a duplicate recipient address was detected by mailmsg/categorizer. |
| Cat: Messages aborted | Troubleshooting | The number of messages marked to be aborted by the categorizer. |
| Cat: Messages bifurcated | Troubleshooting | The number of new messages created by the categorizer (bifurcation). |
| Cat: Messages Categorized | Performance | The number of messages categorizer has submitted to the queue. |
| Cat: Messages submitted | Performance/ Planning | The total number of messages submitted to the categorizer. |
| Cat: Message submitted/sec | Performance | The rate at which messages are being submitted to the categorizer. |
| Cat: Recipients after categorization | Performance/ Planning | The number of mailmsg recipients submitted from the categorizer to the queue. |
| Cat: Recipients before categorization | Performance/ Planning | The number of mailmsg recipients submitted to categorizer. |
| Cat: Recipients in categorization | Performance | The number of recipients the categorizer is currently processing. |

**Table 15-3.** SMTP Service Performance Monitor Counters *(continued)*

| SMTP Service Counter | Category | Description |
|---|---|---|
| Cat: Recipients NDRd (ambiguous address) | Planning | The number of recipients with addresses that match multiple DS objects. |
| Cat: Recipients NDRd (forwarding loop) | Troubleshooting | The number of recipients NDRd by the categorizer because of a forwarding loop detection. |
| Cat: Recipients NDRd (illegal address) | Troubleshooting | The number of recipients with illegal addresses detected by the categorizer. |
| Cat: Recipients NDRd (sink recip errors) | Troubleshooting | The number of recipients NDRd by the categorizer due to a generic recipient failure. |
| Cat: Recipients NDRd (unresolved) | Troubleshooting | The number of unresolved recipients (local addresses not found). |
| Cat: Recipients NDRd by categorizer | Troubleshooting | The number of recipients set to be NDRd by the categorizer. |
| Cat: Senders unresolved | Troubleshooting | The number of senders not found in the DS. |
| Cat: Senders with ambiguous addresses | Troubleshooting | The number of senders with addresses that match multiple DS objects. |
| Categorizer queue length | Performance | The number of messages in the categorizer queue. |
| Connection Errors/sec | Troubleshooting | The number of connection errors per second. |

**Table 15-3.** SMTP Service Performance Monitor Counters *(continued)*

| SMTP Service Counter | Category | Description |
|---|---|---|
| Current Messages in Local Delivery | Performance/ Planning | The number of messages that are currently being processed by a server event sink for local delivery. |
| Directory Drops total | Performance/ Planning | The total number of messages placed in a drop directory. |
| Directory Drops/sec | Performance | The number of messages placed in a drop directory per second. |
| DNS Queries Total | Planning | The total number of Domain Naming System (DNS) lookups. |
| DNS Queries/sec | Performance | The rate of DNS lookups. |
| ETRN Messages Total | Planning | The total number of ETRN messages received by the server. |
| ETRN Messages/sec | Performance | The number of ETRN messages per second. |
| Inbound Connections Current | Performance | The total number of connections currently marked as inbound. |
| Inbound Connections Total | Performance/ Planning | The total number of inbound connections received. |
| Local Queue Length | Performance/ Planning | The number of messages in the local queue. |
| Local Retry Queue Length | Troubleshooting | The number of messages in the local retry queue. |

**Table 15-3.**    SMTP Service Performance Monitor Counters *(continued)*

| SMTP Service Counter | Category | Description |
|---|---|---|
| Message Bytes Received Total | Performance/ Planning | The total number of bytes received in messages. |
| Message Bytes Received/sec | Performance | The rate at which bytes are received in messages. |
| Message Bytes Sent Total | Performance/ Planning | The total number of bytes sent in messages. |
| Message Bytes Sent/sec | Performance | The rate at which bytes are sent in messages. |
| Message Bytes Total | Performance/ Planning | The total number of bytes sent and received in messages. |
| Message Bytes Total/sec | Performance | The rate at which bytes are sent and received in messages. |
| Message Delivery Retries | Performance/ Troubleshooting | The total number of local deliveries that were retried. |
| Message Send Retries | Performance/ Troubleshooting | The total number of outbound message sends that were retried. |
| Messages Currently Undeliverable | Troubleshooting | The number of messages that have been reported as currently undeliverable by routing. |
| Messages Delivered Total | Performance/ Planning | The total number of messages delivered to local mailboxes. |
| Messages Delivered/sec | Performance | The rate at which messages are delivered to local mailboxes. |
| Messages Pending Routing | Performance/ Troubleshooting | The number of messages that have been categorized but not routed. |

**Table 15-3.**    SMTP Service Performance Monitor Counters *(continued)*

| SMTP Service Counter | Category | Description |
|---|---|---|
| Messages Received Total | Performance/ Planning | The total number of inbound messages accepted. |
| Messages Received/sec | Performance | The rate at which inbound messages are being received. |
| Messages Refused for Address Objects | Troubleshooting | The total number of messages refused for lack of address objects. |
| Messages Refused for Mail Objects | Troubleshooting | The total number of messages refused for lack of mail objects. |
| Messages Refused for Size | Troubleshooting/ Planning | The total number of messages rejected because they were too big. |
| Messages Sent Total | Performance/ Planning | The total number of outbound messages sent. |
| Messages Sent/sec | Performance | The rate at which outbound messages are being sent. |
| NDRs Generated | Performance/ Troubleshooting | The number of non-delivery reports that have been generated. |
| Number of MailFiles Open | Performance | Number of handles to open mail files. |
| Number of QueueFiles Open | Performance | Number of handles to open queue files. |
| Outbound Connections Current | Performance/ Planning | The number of connections currently outbound. |
| Outbound Connections Refused | Troubleshooting | The number of outbound connection attempts refused by remote sites. |

**Table 15-3.**    SMTP Service Performance Monitor Counters *(continued)*

| SMTP Service Counter | Category | Description |
|---|---|---|
| Outbound Connections Total | Performance/ Planning | The total number of outbound connections attempted. |
| Pickup Directory Messages Retrieved Total | Performance/ Planning | The total number of messages retrieved from the mail pickup directory. |
| Pickup Directory Messages Retrieved/sec | Performance | The rate at which messages are being retrieved from the mail pickup directory. |
| Remote Queue Length | Performance/ Planning | The number of messages in the remote queue. |
| Remote Retry Queue Length | Performance/ Planning | The number of messages in the retry queue for remote delivery. |
| Routing Table Lookups Total | Performance/ Planning | The total number of routing table lookups. |
| Routing Table Lookups/sec | Performance | The number of routing table lookups per second. |
| Total Connection Errors | Troubleshooting | The total number of all connection errors. |
| Total DSN Errors | Troubleshooting | The total number of failed DSN generation attempts. |
| Total messages submitted | Performance/ Planning | The total messages submitted to queuing for delivery. |

**Table 15-3.** SMTP Service Performance Monitor Counters *(continued)*

# ASP PERFORMANCE AND TROUBLESHOOTING

If you will be employing ASP technology within your Web sites, you should understand that this technology creates additional work for the Web server. That's not to say that ASP should not be used. In fact, if you want to create robust Web-based applications, ASP is the recommended method. Following the recommendations and troubleshooting procedures in the next sections can help you focus on how ASP can improve your Web site's capabilities.

## Isolating a Poorly Performing Web Application

When troubleshooting an IIS application, it is standard practice to isolate the specific Web application by running it in a separate memory space. This is referred to as running an application *Out-of-Process* (OOP). However, when a component is used on multiple ASP pages and in multiple applications, it can be a bit more difficult to completely isolate the application module (DLL) file from the rest of the Web site. To properly troubleshoot application problems you must isolate a COM DLL into a separate process to determine whether it is adversely affecting the Web server's performance. The Windows 2000 Component Services (COM+) 1.0 enables you to isolate a COM DLL into a separate process.

Using the following steps, you can successfully isolate a specific DLL. Once the DLL is isolated, any process that uses the isolated DLL makes *Remote Procedure Calls* (RPC) to the Dllhost.exe program that contains the isolated DLL, rather than loading the DLL within its own process space. You can perform this procedure for each DLL file you think might be generating errors until you determine the exact application that is causing problems for the Web server.

To isolate a COM DLL, follow these steps:

1. Click Start, point to Programs, point to Administrative Tools, and then click Component Services.

2. Expand the Computers folder, expand My Computer, and then select the COM+ Applications folder.

3. Right-click the COM+ Applications folder, click New, and then click Application. This creates a new Application.

4. Click Next.

5. Click Create Empty Application.

6. Assign a Name to the application (that is, the same name as the COM DLL). Do not include any periods.

7. Select Server Application.

8. Click Next.

9. Set the Security Context required by the DLL by

   ■ Selecting either the Interactive (Logged on) user, or

   ■ Specifying credentials to impersonate "this" user.

10. Click Next.

11. Click Finish.

12. To add the DLL to the new COM+ Application, right-click the Components folder that is inside the new COM+ Application.

13. Choose New | Component.

14. Click Next.

15. Select Install new component(s).

16. Browse to the folder that contains the DLL to isolate.

17. Select the DLL to isolate.

18. Click Open.

**NOTE:** You must select a COM or COM+ DLL, otherwise the following error message will display: One or more files do not contain components or type libraries. These files cannot be installed.

19. Click Next.

20. Click Finish.

21. You must reset the IISADMIN service; Initiate this by choosing Start | Run.

22. In the Run dialog box type **iisreset**.

23. Click OK.

# Tuning ASP Performance

Using the Adsutil.vbs (VBScript) file included in the AdminScripts directory, you can quickly tune ASP to demonstrate immediate performance enhancements. The next few sections deal with the specific ASP parameters that can be tweaked for improved operation. For each of the ASP properties, you will need to use a specific command line for the Adsutil.vbs utility to change a property in the Metabase. To do this you will need to run the Adsutil.vbs utility from the <%SYSTEMDRIVE%>\inetpub\adminScripts directory, and append the precise ASP parameter and its new data value. For example, to reconfigure the AspRequestQueueMax metabase property, type the following command (all on one line):

```
adsutil.vbs set w3svc/AspRequestQueueMax <NewValue>
```

Where *<NewValue>* is the number of requests that ASP should use per processor.

**NOTE:**   For all entries, these settings change the value at the Master WWW Properties level. They are inherited by all new Web applications and all existing applications that have not been explicitly set to a different value.

## AspProcessorThreadMax

The AspProcessorThreadMax Metabase property specifies the maximum number of worker threads per processor that is automatically created by IIS 5.0. The setting can dramatically increase the scalability of your Web applications and improve the performance of your server in general. This setting defines the maximum number of ASP requests that can run simultaneously. Unless your ASP applications are spending extended time making calls to external programs or components, you should leave this setting at its default; the AspProcessorThreadMax default is 25.

AspProcessorThreadMax is one of the few ASP Metabase attributes for which you must obtain statistics before tuning. To determine the performance statistics for this attribute, observe the following System Monitor counters during the peak load time using a one-second chart interval in Windows Performance Monitor:

- ▼ Processor: %Processor Time (for each processor)
- ■ Active Server Pages: Requests/Sec
- ■ Active Server Pages: Requests Rejected
- ■ Active Server Pages: Requests Queued
- ▲ Web Service: Connections/Sec

Based on the output of these combined counters, if the Requests Queued counter never increases and the processor(s) utilization is low, the site has more capacity than it currently needs, and you should leave the AspProcessorThreadMax value alone. If the Requests Queued counter consistently moves up and down, and the listed processor(s) are running well below 50 percent, you should increase the ASPProcessorThreadMax Metabase entry. When the Requests Queued counter grows at an unmanageable rate with CPU utilization, look at custom or third-party components as the source of the problem. If the Requests Queued counter grows and CPU utilization increases to an intolerable level, this indicates there is a problem with connectivity to an external database. The connectivity issue generally can be attributed to a slow network connection, a large query, or a slow back-end computer.

## AspRequestQueueMax

The AspRequestQueueMax Metabase property specifies the maximum number of concurrent ASP requests that are permitted entry into the request queue. Web browsers attempting to request ASP files when the queue is filled to the configured capacity are shown the familiar HTTP 500 "Server too busy" error message. The default setting for AspRequestQueueMax is 3,000.

## AspQueueConnectionTestTime

IIS 5.0 inserts all received ASP requests into a queue. If the request has been in the queue for longer than the number of seconds specified in the AspQueueConnectionTestTime Metabase property, ASP double-checks that the client is still connected before executing the request. If the client is no longer connected, the request is promptly deleted from the queue without processing. You can use the AspQueueConnectionTestTime metabase property to make sure that IIS does not squander its processing time if a connection has been abandoned. The AspQueueConnectionTestTime default value is 3.

## AspScriptEngineCacheMax

The AspScriptEngineCacheMax property specifies the maximum number of scripting engines that the ASP pages will store in memory. The default AspScriptEngineCacheMax Metabase value is 125. This value should be adequate. If you have a large amount of RAM in the server, you can safely increase this value, but only in increments of 10.

## AspSessionTimeOut

The AspSessionTimeOut property specifies the default amount of time that a session object is preserved in memory after the last request for the object has been made. The AspSessionTimeOut Metabase attribute can be used to tune your ASP applications. Because session objects consume memory resources, limiting the lifetime of an individual session with this property makes your applications more scalable. The default value for AspSessionTimeOut is 20 (minutes).

# ASP Buffering

Setting the Buffer property to TRUE can significantly improve the performance of large ASP applications in which users primarily connect to the application through a modem. You can enable buffering for your applications from the Internet Services Manager MMC snap-in. Alternatively, if you want to add this property on a single page, you must add the <% Response.Buffer = True %> statement in the HTML of only the selected pages. Adding it per page enables you to target only those specific ASP applications that could cause a significant amount of overhead.

**NOTE:** If you have upgraded from IIS 4.0, the Buffer property is set to FALSE. This is the default setting for IIS 4.0; the installation of IIS 5.0 over IIS 4.0 migrates the previous version's settings.

## ASP Performance Monitor Counters

As with the performance and troubleshooting counters installed for the Web, FTP, and SMTP services, a specific counter is available for ASP. The ASP counters are itemized in Table 15-4; each is listed by name and category with a brief description. Utilizing these counters you can effectively determine if ASP is having problems or causing problems for the IIS services.

| ASP Counter | Category | Description |
|---|---|---|
| Debugging Requests | Troubleshooting | Number of debugging document requests. |
| Error During Script Runtime | Troubleshooting | Number of requests failed because of runtime errors. |
| Errors from ASP Preprocessor | Troubleshooting | Number of requests failed due to preprocessor errors. |
| Errors from Script Compilers | Troubleshooting | Number of requests failed because of script compilation errors. |
| Errors/Sec | Troubleshooting/ Performance | The number of errors per second. |

**Table 15-4.** ASP Performance Monitor Counters

| ASP Counter | Category | Description |
| --- | --- | --- |
| Request Bytes In Total | Performance | The total size, in bytes, of all requests. |
| Request Bytes Out Total | Performance | The total size, in bytes, of responses sent to clients. This does not include standard HTTP response headers. |
| Request Execution Time | Performance | The number of milliseconds it took to execute the most recent request. |
| Request Wait Time | Performance | The number of milliseconds the most recent request was waiting in the queue. |
| Requests Disconnected | Troubleshooting | The number of requests that were disconnected due to communication failure. |
| Requests Executing | Performance | The number of requests currently executing. |
| Requests Failed Total | Troubleshooting | The total number of requests failed because of errors, authorization failure, and rejections. |
| Requests Not Authorized | Troubleshooting | Number of requests failed because of insufficient access rights. |
| Requests Not Found | Troubleshooting | The number of requests for files that were not found. |
| Requests Queued | Performance | The number of requests waiting for service from the queue. |

**Table 15-4.** ASP Performance Monitor Counters *(continued)*

| ASP Counter | Category | Description |
|---|---|---|
| Requests Rejected | Troubleshooting | The total number of requests not executed because there were insufficient resources to process them. |
| Requests Succeeded | Troubleshooting | The number of requests that executed successfully. |
| Requests Timed Out | Troubleshooting/ Performance | The number of requests that timed out. |
| Requests Total | Troubleshooting/ Planning | The total number of requests since the service was started. |
| Requests/Sec | Performance | The number of requests executed per second. |
| Script Engines Cached | Performance | The number of script engines in cache. |
| Session Duration | Performance | The number of milliseconds that the most recent session persisted. |
| Sessions Current | Performance | The current number of sessions being serviced. |
| Sessions Timed Out | Performance/ Troubleshooting | The number of sessions timed out. |
| Sessions Total | Troubleshooting/ Planning | The total number of sessions since the service was started. |
| Template Cache Hit Rate | Performance | Percent of requests found in template cache. |
| Template Notifications | Troubleshooting | The number of templates invalidated in the cache because of change notification. |

**Table 15-4.**    ASP Performance Monitor Counters *(continued)*

| ASP Counter | Category | Description |
| --- | --- | --- |
| Templates Cached | Performance | The number of templates currently cached. |
| Transactions Aborted | Troubleshooting | The number of transactions aborted. |
| Transactions Committed | Troubleshooting/ Performance | The number of transactions committed. |
| Transactions Pending | Performance | Number of transactions in progress. |
| Transactions Total | Troubleshooting/ Planning | The total number of transactions since the service was started. |
| Transactions Total/sec | Performance | Transactions started per second. |

**Table 15-4.**    ASP Performance Monitor Counters *(continued)*

# FRONTPAGE EXTENSIONS TROUBLESHOOTING

If you have a perfectly tuned IIS 5.0 server, you will have little trouble utilizing the FrontPage extensions. Microsoft developed the FrontPage extensions to take advantage of the key technologies in IIS 5.0 to provide a bridge between its FrontPage editing and authoring utility and the Windows 2000–oriented Web server. Maximizing the Web services performance enables FrontPage extensions to perform as a tool to manage the Web site through Microsoft FrontPage. With the FrontPage extensions installed, Microsoft FrontPage is transformed beyond its HTML authoring and editing capabilities. It becomes an additional administration tool for creating Virtual Servers and modifying Web permissions.

Troubleshooting the FrontPage extensions is a relatively quick process. Right-click the Web site that has the extensions installed, navigate to All Tasks, and choose Check Server Extensions. This process literally takes a few seconds, but catches any errors that might have occurred during the extension's use and corrects them.

Beyond checking the server extensions, there are four little-known utilities that are installed with the FrontPage extensions that can help troubleshoot connections problems and minimize the work involved with administering the FrontPage extensions. These four utilities are described in the next sections.

Before installing the FrontPage extensions, there are a couple of "gotchas" that you need to be aware of:

▼ Some anti-virus utilities can prevent FrontPage extensions from installing correctly. Disable the anti-virus protection during the installation and re-enable it after the installation is complete.

▲ If you install Microsoft FrontPage onto the server where the FrontPage extensions are installed, all of the known database drivers are included with the installation. If you do not install Microsoft FrontPage, you will need to install the database components separately. These are included in the MDAC 2.1 (Microsoft Data Access Components) update from Microsoft's Web site: http://www.microsoft.com/data/21info.htm.

## FrontPage Extensions Snap-in

The FPMMC.msc file is an MMC snap-in that can run by itself or insert into your current Internet Services Manager console. This snap-in allows interaction and administration of just the server components that are utilizing the FrontPage extensions. Opening this console application displays the Virtual Directories on the IIS 5.0 server that are being utilized by the extensions and allows you to:

▼ Install the FrontPage server extensions on a Web server.

■ Extend a virtual server with the FrontPage server extensions.

■ Check and fix the FrontPage server extensions on a Web.

■ Upgrade the FrontPage server extensions on a Web.

■ Remove the FrontPage server extensions from a Web.

- Delete a subWeb that you have extended with the FrontPage server extensions.

- Convert a subWeb into a folder, and vice versa.

- Recalculate all hyperlinks in a Web.

- Add an administrator.

- Enable or disable authoring on a Web.

- Tune Web performance.

- Log authoring operations.

- Require Secure Sockets Layer (SSL) for authoring.

- Specify that a folder can contain executable scripts or programs.

- Enable source control.

▲ Set e-mail options.

There are only a couple of tasks that you cannot perform using the FrontPage MMC snap-in. You cannot administer the FrontPage server extensions from a remote computer (use the Fpremadm utility instead). Additionally, you cannot perform command-line scripting (use the Fpsrvadm utility instead). These tasks are provided by two command-line utilities discussed in the following sections.

## TCPTest.exe

TCPTest.exe does just what its name implies: It verifies the TCP/IP connection of the server where the FrontPage extensions are installed. Shown in Figure 15-4, you only need to click the Start Test button to retrieve the status of the following:

▼ **32-bit Winsock**   The FrontPage extensions use a specific TCP driver on Windows systems. This driver must be active and the right version.

■ **Server's Localhost IP Address**   To use Microsoft FrontPage on a specific computer, the computer must have a Localhost presence, meaning that the computer has to be set up as a Web host. You should be able to type **http://localhost** in the address line of the Internet browser and see a page display.

- **Server's Host Name** All Web servers must be able to allow connections using the server's actual computer name. This TCPTest option ensures the capability works and displays the name of the computer if it is successful.

- **IP Address Assigned to the Server** After ensuring the server's host name passes, TCPTest verifies that the host name matches the server's actual TCP/IP address and displays the IP address it finds.

- ▲ **Localhost Resolution** In addition to identifying that the localhost resolution works, TCPTest also verifies and retrieves the localhost IP address assigned to the server.

## Fpremadm.exe

The Fpremadm is a command-line utility that enables you to administer the FrontPage server extensions from a Microsoft Windows-based PC that is not the computer on which the Web server is running. It has an interface based on the Fpsrvadm utility and performs all the commands of Fpsrvadm. Use Fpremadm when you want to remotely administer the FrontPage server extensions from a Windows-based PC from the command line or a batch file.

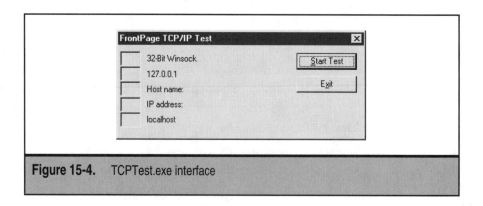

**Figure 15-4.** TCPTest.exe interface

Fpremadm has the following command-line syntax and options:

```
fpremadm.exe -targetserver <url>
 [-adminusername username
 -adminpassword password]
 [-command value]*
```

## Fpsrvadm.exe

The Fpsrvadm utility is an application for UNIX, Microsoft Windows NT, and Windows 2000 operating systems. It offers a complete set of FrontPage server extensions operations. Use Fpsrvadm from the command line or from batch files. Fpsrvadm must be run on the server computer.

Fpsrvadm has the following command-line syntax and options:

```
Usage: fpsrvadm.exe [-help]
 [-operation <install | upgrade | create | merge
 | uninstall | fulluninstall | check | security
 | delete | rename | setDirExec | setDirNoExec
 | enable | disable | recalc
 | putfile | recalcfile>]
 [-port <nnnn>]
 [-Web <Web name>]
 [-type <msiis | frontpage | Website
 | netscape-enterprise | netscape-fasttrack>]
 [-servconf <server config file>]
 [-multihost <hostname or IP address>]
 [-username <username>]
 [-password <password>]
 [-ipaddress <IP address>]
 [-access <remove|administrators|authors|users>]
 [-destination <destination Url>]
 [-filename <file name>]
```

If you type Fpsrvadm alone at the command prompt (without any of the command-line options), the menu shown in Figure 15-5 displays in the MS-DOS window; so you don't necessarily need to enter any of

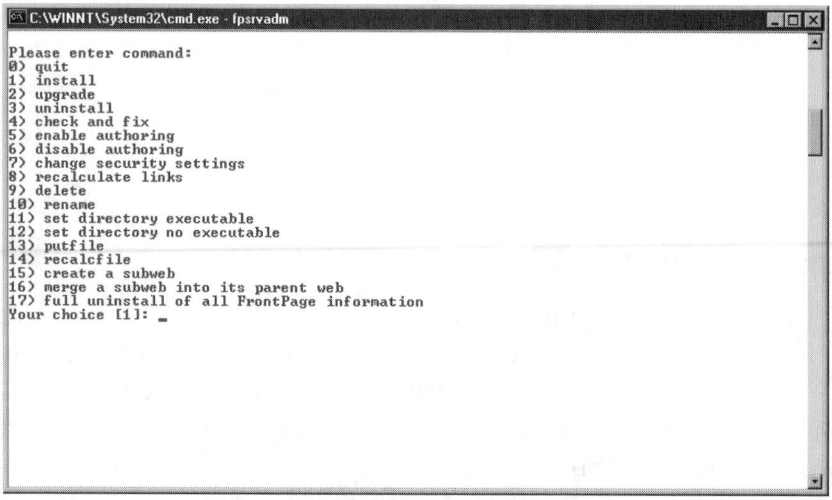

**Figure 15-5.** Fpsrvadm MS-DOS menu

the command-line options to use the tool's functionality. If there are specific commands you use consistently, you might want to place the precise commands in a batch file so you must run only the batch file to execute the process instead of typing out the full command each time.

# WINDOWS 2000 PERFORMANCE AND TROUBLESHOOTING

Because IIS 5.0 runs on top of Windows 2000, it makes sense to identify any Windows 2000 performance configurations that specifically affect the Web services. During the Windows 2000 installation process, comprehensive scans are performed to allow the operating system to be tuned for optimum operation as a file and print server. The installation does not take into account that the server has been designated as the primary Web server; thus, there are a few configuration changes that can help the overall performance for Web services.

# Windows 2000 Service Pack

When Microsoft releases a service pack for the operating system, it is a serious event. In general, the life cycle of each operating system is dotted with several service pack releases before a major new OS announcement. You should always keep track of the latest revision of the operating system and apply any new offerings when they are available. Operating system service packs include bug fixes, feature additions, and enhancements to system components and performance. Watching the Microsoft servers Web site, located at http://www.microsoft.com/ servers/, will enable you to keep on top of the constantly evolving operating system. The Web page specifically designated for Windows 2000 is at http://www.microsoft .com/windows2000/default.asp. Applying the latest service pack will ensure that the operating system is running properly. This is important because if there are IIS issues, you would rather spend your time identifying and resolving any Web server problems instead of fighting with the underlying operating system.

To better understand how critical it is to install the latest operating system service pack, look through the following IIS 5.0 specific fixes that are included in Windows 2000 Service Pack 1. The fixes outlined are just those that Microsoft intended for the IIS services. The Windows 2000 Service Pack also includes a horde of fixes for the operating system itself. By applying the latest fixes, you ensure a server environment that is as error-free as possible.

## SMTP Service Fixes in Windows 2000 SP1

The following fixes included in Windows 2000 SP1 are designated to repair key pieces of the SMTP service. These areas were identified as being problematic after the original release of Windows 2000.

▼ **Q262685 XADM**   SMTP causes messages to loop when you move a mailbox

■ **Q262327**   SMTP service stops unexpectedly

- **Q257217**  SMTP service stops unexpectedly or does not relay correctly

- **Q253606**  Memory and critical section leak in CExpire::GetExpireBlockProperties

- **Q253284**  Large number of alias domains causes 550 error for valid domains

▲ **Q257358**  Cdosys.dll may cause an access violation when the mail header contains DBCS characters

## NNTP Service Fixes in Windows 2000 SP1

The following pair of fixes are included in Windows 2000 SP1 and are specifically positioned to repair the NNTP service. Utilizing these fixes will ensure that the NNTP service operates correctly.

▼ **Q253611**  Rebuild of corrupted NNTP hash table does not work

▲ **Q253607**  Windows 2000 NNTP service works incorrectly with Exchange Server 2000 (RC1)

## Web Service Fixes in Windows 2000 SP1

The Web service is the main IIS component, so it's no wonder that Microsoft included the most fixes for this service. The following list depicts all of the fixes included in Windows 2000 SP1.

▼ **Q262666**  Indexing service cannot index or search based on document summary information

- **Q261116**  ASP incorrectly decodes the QUERY_STRING and may reveal the metabase path information

- **Q260933**  IIS Convlog stops processing IIS log file if the URL ends with a comma

- **Q260838**  IIS stops servicing HTR requests

- **Q260353** Use of Java/COM components in COM+ enabled systems can cause delays

- **Q260205** HTTP request with a large number of dots or dot-slashes causes high CPU utilization

- **Q258189** IIS log contains wrong data when ISAPI uses default for file size

- **Q258075** Indexes larger than four gigabytes may become corrupted

- **Q257880** COM+ does not run IComponentRegistrar:: UnregisterComponent()

- **Q257332** Access violation in W3svc.dll on secure connection to Nonexistant IP:PORT

- **Q256093** IIS may generate access violation for certain HTTP requests

- **Q255054** COM+ does not reach SetMaxThreads for the package

- **Q252934** Passing objects in reference leaks Visual Basic Object Reference in COM+

- **Q252463** Index server error message reveals physical location of Web folders

- **Q252313** Index server query timeout does not function

- **Q250397** Content is lost at SF_NOTIFY_AUTH_COMPLETE

- **Q249599** Virtual Directory mapped to UNC returns server-side script code when URL contains additional characters at the end of the request

- **Q246806** Access denied for the default document file mapped to Ssinc.dll

- **Q244998** Port number is not returned with content location when specified by URL

- ▲ **Q197401** Convlog tool stops processing NCSA files when reaching short host name

# Windows 2000 Disk Performance

A Windows 2000 Server hard disk can be a serious bottleneck for Web sites that house large files that are accessed frequently. If the amount of RAM installed in the server is small, IIS is unable to preserve copies of the files in RAM to simulate faster access. In this scenario, IIS must access the files directly from the hard disk. The access speed and size of the hard disk determine how quickly IIS can locate a requested file.

To monitor your disk drives, use the Windows 2000–specific counters in Performance Monitor to log the percentage of CPU utilized, network card saturation, and the % Disk Time counter of the Physical Disk object. If the % Disk Time counter is high, but the CPU and network card are not saturated, the disk drive is creating a bottleneck. If the Web server is used heavily for access to databases, you will want to increase the amount of RAM significantly or install a hard disk controller that has a large RAM cache built onto it.

# Windows 2000 Server Role

Microsoft Windows 2000 Server and IIS 5.0 have been developed so you can get the best performance from your server. The server can be configured to run as either an application server or a file server. These two types of servers have different memory needs and the chosen setting directly influences the performance of the server.

By default, Windows 2000 Server is installed as a file server. For best performance, IIS 5.0 requires that the Windows 2000 Server be configured as an application server. Changing this value adds immediate benefits when the server is primarily used as a Web server.

To configure your server as an application server, follow these steps:

1. Click Start, point to Settings, and click Network and Dial-up Connections.

2. Select Local Area Connection and open its properties.

3. Select File and Printer Sharing for Microsoft Networks and open its properties.

4. On the Server Optimization tab, select Maximize data throughput for network applications.

# Accessing Performance Information Natively

One of the most exciting aspects of Microsoft's operating systems is that there is so much to learn and eventually you will encounter some hidden gems. Windows 2000 includes a repository database that contains volumes of information about the computer on which it is installed. Products such as Microsoft Systems Management Server utilize this wealth of information. However, you can take advantage of this native data warehouse by just understanding how to access it and which tools are available to you.

## Windows Management Instrumentation

Web-Based Enterprise Management (WBEM) is a set of technologies created by the standards committee, Distributed Management Task Force (DMTF), http://www.dmtf.org/wbem/. These standards were created to provide for the unification of Enterprise Management technologies. Any vendor working within these standards will be able to create enterprise-level applications that work across different platforms.

WBEM enables the industry to deliver a well-integrated set of standard-based management tools leveraging emerging technologies such as Common Information Model (CIM, described in more detail in this chapter), XML (Extensible Markup Language), Desktop Management Interface (DMI), and Managed Object Format (MOF). The WBEM model is a framework that includes Application Programming Interfaces (API), syntax, and an object model; it is the mediator between the application layer and the provider. These applications can be developed around any language that allows interaction with the WBEM interface. Some of these languages are VBScript, JScript, COM, and Windows Scripting Host.

WBEM provides a point of integration through which data from management sources can be accessed, and it complements and extends existing management protocols and instrumentation such as Simple Network Management Protocol (SNMP), Desktop Management Interface (DMI), and Common Management Information Protocol (CMIP).

Windows Management Instrumentation (WMI) is Microsoft's version of WBEM. WMI provides a layer of services to make 32-bit operating systems easier to manage. WMI extends the CIM to represent management objects in Windows-based managed environments.

The WMI technology provides the following:

▼ Access to monitor, command, and control any managed object through a common, unifying set of interfaces, regardless of the underlying instrumentation mechanism. WMI is an access mechanism.

■ A consistent model of Windows 2000 operating system operation, configuration, and status.

■ A COM Application Programming Interface (API) that supplies a single point of access for all management information.

■ Interoperability with other Windows 2000 management services. This approach can simplify the process of creating integrated, well-designed management solutions.

■ A flexible, extensible architecture. Developers can extend the information model to cover new devices, applications, and so on, by writing code modules called WMI providers.

■ Extensions to the Windows Driver Model (WDM) to capture instrumentation data and events from device drivers and kernel-side components.

■ A powerful event architecture. This allows management information changes to be identified, aggregated, compared, and associated with other management information. These changes also can be forwarded to local or remote management applications.

■ A rich query language that enables detailed queries of the information model.

▲ A scriptable API that developers can use to create management applications. The scripting API supports several languages including Microsoft Visual Basic, Visual Basic for Applications, Visual Basic Scripting Edition (VBScript), Microsoft JScript, and Perl. Additionally, you can use the Windows Scripting Host or Internet Explorer to write scripts that use this interface. Windows Scripting Host, like Internet Explorer, serves as a controller engine of ActiveX scripting engines. Windows Scripting Host supports scripts written in VBScript, JScript, and Perl.

Version 1.5 is the current revision of WMI. This version comes installed as part of the Windows 2000 operating system. A key feature of version 1.5 is the ability to gather information from the computer's BIOS (basic input/output system). The BIOS stores information about the manufacturer, the product, the version, the serial number, and the default hardware settings. Hardware vendors whose product supports SMBIOS version 2.1 (Systems Management BIOS, formerly known as DMI BIOS) will be able to take full advantage of the WMI version 1.5.

## Using VBScript to Retrieve WMI Information

For those who take the time to become VBScript and WMI literate, accessing the WMI repository is straightforward. Abundant information is available with just a few lines of code, as you'll see in the VBScript examples in this section. If past chapters have not convinced you that VBScript is a critical component that will keep you happily employed in the future, hopefully this section will entice you to become a VBScript enthusiast. And, just as important as managing your career, VBScript provides the best tools to manage your IIS 5.0 server.

**NOTE:** The following example scripts require that the latest Microsoft Scripting Engines (http://msdn.microsoft.com/scripting/) are installed on the computer that is running the scripts, and that WMI version 1.5 or greater (http://msdn.microsoft.com/code/sample.asp?url=/msdn-files/027/001/576/msdncompositedoc.xml) is installed on the remote computer against which the script is being run.

**Example: Getting Service Information**    The following VBScript prompts for a computer name, connects to the specified computer, and then retrieves information about all of the services that are running on the chosen computer. It is run using the command-line cscript filename.vbs.

```
ComputerName = InputBox("Enter the name of the computer for which
you want service information")
winmgmt1 = "winmgmts:{impersonationLevel=impersonate}!//"&
ComputerName &""
Set ServSet = GetObject( winmgmt1 ).InstancesOf ("Win32_service")
for each Serv in ServSet
 GetObject("winmgmts:").InstancesOf ("win32_service")
      WScript.Echo ""
      WScript.Echo Serv.Description
      WScript.Echo " Executable: ", Serv.PathName
      WScript.Echo " Status: ", Serv.Status
      WScript.Echo " State: ", Serv.State
      WScript.Echo " Start Mode: ", Serv.StartMode
      WScript.Echo " Start Name: ", Serv.StartName
Next
```

Here is an example of the output of the previous script:

```
Indexing Service
 Executable: C:\WINNT\System32\cisvc.exe
 Status: OK
 State: Stopped
 Start Mode: Manual
 Start Name: LocalSystem
```

```
IIS Admin Service
 Executable: C:\WINNT\System32\inetsrv\inetinfo.exe
 Status: OK
 State: Running

 Start Mode: Auto
 Start Name: LocalSystem
FTP Publishing Service
 Executable: C:\WINNT\System32\inetsrv\inetinfo.exe
 Status: OK
 State: Running
 Start Mode: Auto
 Start Name: LocalSystem
Simple Mail Transport Protocol (SMTP)
 Executable: C:\WINNT\System32\inetsrv\inetinfo.exe
 Status: OK
 State: Running
 Start Mode: Auto
 Start Name: LocalSystem
World Wide Web Publishing Service
 Executable: C:\WINNT\System32\inetsrv\inetinfo.exe
 Status: OK
 State: Running
 Start Mode: Auto
 Start Name: LocalSystem
Windows Management Instrumentation
 Executable: C:\WINNT\System32\WBEM\WinMgmt.exe
 Status: OK
 State: Running
 Start Mode: Auto
 Start Name: LocalSystem
```

**Example: Displaying Process and Memory Counters**    The following VBScript example connects to the WMI repository of the local or remote computer and retrieves the Performance Monitor data in a MS-DOS Prompt window; it is run using cscript filename.vbs. This script is extremely useful when you need the performance data quickly and the graphical interface of Performance Monitor is not required.

**NOTE:** In addition to the WMI 1.5 and current Scripting Engines requirements, a specific Managed Object Format (MOF) file must be compiled on the computer for which the data will be retrieved. This MOF file, perfmon.mof, is available for download in the WMI Software Developer Kit (SDK): http://msdn.microsoft.com/code/sample.asp?url=/msdn-files/027/001/566/ msdncompositedoc.xml. When the MOF file is compiled, the information contained within is inserted into the computer's WMI repository so that the Performance Monitor counter provider is initialized for use. MOF files generally are compiled using the Mofcomp.exe utility in Windows 2000. Compiling a MOF file is as simple as running the command-line *mofcomp filename.mof.*

```
set processes = GetObject("winmgmts:root/perfmonScriptExample")
.InstancesOf ("NTProcesses")
WScript.Echo "Displaying Process Counters"
WScript.Echo "==========================="
WScript.Echo
for each process in processes
    WScript.Echo " " & process.Process & ": #Threads=" &
process.Threads & " Working Set=" & process.WorkingSet
    WScript.Echo
next
WScript.Echo "Displaying Memory Counters"
WScript.Echo "=========================="
WScript.Echo
set memorySet = GetObject("winmgmts:root/perfmonScriptExample")
.InstancesOf ("NTMemory")
for each memoryItem in memorySet
    WScript.Echo " " & memoryItem.Memory & ": Committed Bytes=" &
memoryItem.CommittedBytes
next
```

Here is the output of the example script:

```
Displaying Process Counters
============================
 Idle: #Threads=1 Working Set=1638
 System: #Threads=47 Working Set=217088
 services: #Threads=30 Working Set=6938624
 WinMgmt: #Threads=12 Working Set=2908160
 inetinfo: #Threads=25 Working Set=8880128
 explorer: #Threads=22 Working Set=9846784
 sqlmangr: #Threads=4 Working Set=4182016
 iexplore: #Threads=14 Working Set=7897088
 _Total: #Threads=380 Working Set=179949568
Displaying Memory Counters
============================
 @: Committed Bytes=193974272
```

# Windows 2000 Performance Monitor Counters for IIS 5.0

Windows 2000 itself provides the most available objects and counters for the Windows Performance Monitor tool. Each component that can have a significant effect on the operation of the server has an object and counter associated with it. However, there are a specific few that can impact the performance of the IIS 5.0 services. Those Objects and Counters are listed and described in Table 15-5.

| Object\Counter | Recommendation |
| --- | --- |
| Memory\Pages/sec | 0–20 (more than 80 indicates trouble). |
| Memory\Available Bytes | At least 4 MB. |
| Memory\Committed Bytes | Not more than about 75 percent of physical memory size. |

**Table 15-5.**   Windows 2000 Performance Monitor Counters that Affect IIS 5.0

| Object\Counter | Recommendation |
|---|---|
| Memory\Pool Nonpaged Bytes | Steady—a slow rise might indicate a memory leak. |
| Processor\%Processor Time | Less than 75 percent. |
| Processor\Interrupts/sec | Depends on processor; up to 1,000 for 486/66 processors; 3,500 for P90; more than 7,000 for P200. Lower is better. |
| Processor\System Processor Queue Length | Less than 2. |
| Disk (Logical or Physical)\ % Disk Time | As low as possible. |
| Disk (Logical or Physical)\ Queue Length | Less than 2. |
| Disk (Logical or Physical)\ Avg Disk Bytes/Transfer | As high as possible. |

**Table 15-5.**    Windows 2000 Performance Monitor Counters that Affect IIS 5.0 (continued)

# OPTIMIZING FOR SQL SERVER

For any application you work with, it is critical that the latest service pack is applied to bring the application up to the most current revision. Not only does a service pack fix bugs and incorporate new features; it also provides performance enhancements. If you will be connecting your IIS 5.0 Web pages to SQL Server data, definitely visit Microsoft's SQL Server Web site to retrieve the latest service pack: http://www.microsoft.com/sql/downloads/default.htm.

# IIS 5.0 and SQL Server on the Same Server

When IIS 5.0 and SQL Server exist on the same computer, there are several hardware areas you can look at to tune the connection between the Web site and the database you want to access. Keeping note of these areas can help you create an operating environment where IIS can thrive, and the database is highly accessible. SQL Server, by itself, can take a lot of processing power. When you combine IIS and SQL you'll want to take extra steps to ensure the hardware is "up-to-snuff."

## Hardware

The larger the SQL Server database, the greater the hardware requirements will be. There are other factors such as the number of concurrent users/sessions, transaction throughput, and database operations that also determine hardware requirements. For example, a database housing data that is updated infrequently generally has lower hardware requirements than a 1-terabyte (TB) data warehouse that records critical sales figures, product, and customer information for a large corporation.

Aside from the assumed disk storage requirements, adding memory and faster processors will increase the space available for data to be cached in memory and queries referencing large amounts of data to be processed quickly. If you are using IIS 5.0 on the same server as SQL you should count on beefing up the hardware to match the additional requirements. Taking care of the SQL requirements first can save you a lot of time later.

# IIS 5.0 and SQL Server on Separate Servers

In addition to identifying the specific components outlined in the previous section, if SQL Server resides on a computer other than the IIS 5.0 server, you must take additional measures to ensure top performance. One measure is to verify that you have a connection between the two servers that is free of extraneous network congestion. Basically, you'll want to make sure that the network route between the Web site and the database is free of unnecessary traffic. For example, connecting the two servers to the same network switch will minimize the distance the data has to travel as the ASP page requests information from the SQL database and the data is returned and formatted for output.

When speed is a critical issue, you also should purchase high-performance network interface cards (NICs) for each server so that data travels faster (to and from) across the connection. For data that is critical to the organization, it is not unheard of to purchase 100Mbit (or faster) network cards to ensure that the network will not be a factor if performance degrades. When you have the fastest connection available you can generally overlook, or casually glance at, this component when troubleshooting performance issues.

## SQL Server Performance Monitor Counters

When working with SQL Server and IIS there are specific SQL performance issues that can complicate the overall Web site workings. If you are using the Web site to connect to data, you'll want to identify any SQL concerns by ensuring that SQL is running at its optimum level. When SQL Server is installed, it automatically makes its own Performance Monitor Objects and Counters available to the Windows Performance Monitor tool.

There are many objects and counters installed that allow monitoring of the databases, the database connections, and other SQL processes. The list of SQL Server Objects in Table 15-6 outlines those objects that can affect the overall Web site performance when you use ASP to connect to external data. Each of these objects contains numerous counters with which to monitor and then tune SQL Server for use with your Web site.

| SQL Server Object | Description |
|---|---|
| SQL Server: Access Methods | Searches through and measures allocation of SQL Server database objects (for example, the number of index searches or number of pages that are allocated to indexes and data). |
| SQL Server: Buffer Manager | Provides information about the memory buffers used by SQL Server, such as free memory and buffer cache hit ratio. |
| SQL Server: Databases | Provides information about a SQL Server database, such as the amount of free log space available or the number of active transactions in the database. There can be multiple instances of this object. |
| SQL Server: General Statistics | Provides information about general server-wide activity, such as the number of users who are connected to an instance of SQL Server. |
| SQL Server: Latches | Provides information about the latches on internal resources (such as database pages) that are used by SQL Server. |
| SQL Server: Memory Manager | Provides information about the SQL Server memory usage, such as the total number of lock structures currently allocated. |

**Table 15-6.**   SQL Server Performance Monitor Counters that Affect IIS 5.0

**NOTE:** SQL Server has a performance-monitoring tool of its own called SQL Server Profiler. This tool is SQL-centric so it provides much more in the way of rich performance data. SQL Server is a robust application and database product that deserves much more coverage than can be included in this book. If you are interested in learning more about SQL Server and the SQL Server Profiler tool, investing in a good SQL Server book is recommended. The *Microsoft SQL Server Administrator's Companion*, from Microsoft Press (ISBN: 0735610517), is an excellent resource for understanding the many features of SQL Server.

# CLUSTERING

As applications and processes steadily migrate away from being standalone solutions, high availability for the Web site will increasingly be a significant concern for every organization. There are a couple of additional technologies that Microsoft has incorporated into the Windows 2000 series of servers from which you can reap huge benefits for your Web site. Utilizing these technologies will improve performance and minimize the potential for outages. The technologies, Server Clustering and Network Load Balancing, allow redundancy and fail-over services that are critical for a Web site in which high availability is necessary.

## Server Clustering

Two special versions of Windows 2000, Windows 2000 Advanced Server and Windows 2000 Datacenter, offer the Server Clustering service. This service ensures that the applications required to run the business are always available. The Cluster service enables you to link two servers together so that if one fails because of software or hardware failure the other server takes over, providing uninterrupted service.

For your IIS 5.0 Web site, this feature can be a lifesaver. The Clustering technology can ensure your Web site will always be available. Even though Windows 2000 Server by itself provides key technologies to help eliminate downtime, combining two servers further decreases the probability that the Web site would become unavailable. Of course, to take advantage of this technology you must install either Windows 2000 Advanced Server or Windows 2000 Datacenter. This technology is not available to Windows 2000 Server.

Using Server Clustering, you can build a reliable Web site using lower-cost hardware and the clustering technologies in Windows 2000 Advanced Server and Windows 2000 Datacenter. By letting two or more servers work together as if they were a single system, you can ensure your Web site is available despite unplanned outages. Another great feature of Server Clustering is the ability to minimize interruption in service during a planned maintenance cycle. As one server is brought down for maintenance, the Web site automatically fails over to the available server.

Cluster Service can be installed on either domain controllers or two-member servers. Windows 2000 Advanced Server supports two servers in a cluster and Windows 2000 Datacenter supports up to four. There are two modes supported by Windows 2000 Server Clusters; use the following guidelines to choose the mode that will provide the best value for your IIS server.

▼   **Active/Active Clustering**   Active/Active Clustering is the mode you want to use when processing time is critical. When this mode is employed, all of the servers that are part of the cluster share processing time for the installed applications. Basically, there are several servers providing application use. The combined servers act as one computing unit and share the responsibilities for providing application usage and data. Active/Active Clustering turns many servers into one computing powerhouse. New servers can be added at any time using the Comclust.exe command-line utility (see the upcoming section on Configuring IIS Clustered Virtual Servers for more information on Comclust.exe). If one or more servers fail, the remaining nodes immediately provide the fail-over and still share processing power. This is the best method of clustering—but it also is the most costly in terms of hardware purchasing.

▲   **Active/Passive Clustering**   In Active/Passive Clustering one server provides the entire processing power for the applications and data; when the server goes down or becomes unavailable, the mirror node takes over. This is a valuable tool to provide redundancy and fail-over, but it does not provide the processing power of Active/Active Clustering. However, when you need clustering services and want to keep the hardware budget low, this clustering mode is the way to go.

**NOTE:** Server Clustering provides complete fail-over services when either a server or an application fails. This is different from Network Load-Balancing (described at the end of the "Clustering" section). Network Load-Balancing provides redundancy only for the server itself; not the specific applications that are housed on the server.

There are two utilities for managing and administering the cluster services: Cluster Administrator and the Cluster.exe command-line utility. Cluster Administrator is an MMC snap-in that provides the same functionality as any snap-in. Cluster.exe is a command-line tool with many options for managing the clustered environment in an MS-DOS window. Cluster.exe includes the options shown in Figure 15-6.

For complete information on how to install and configure Windows Server Clustering, see the Windows 2000 Advanced Server or Windows 2000 Datacenter documentation. It is highly recommended that you purchase a good book on Windows 2000 so that you can understand the concepts behind the installation and configuration. One extremely useful book is *Windows 2000: The Complete Reference,* by Kathy Ivens and Kenton Gardinier, ISBN: 0072119209, from Osborne/McGraw-Hill.

```
Command Prompt                                                          _ □ ✕
The syntax of this command is:

CLUSTER /LIST[:domain-name]
CLUSTER [[/CLUSTER:]cluster-name] <options>

<options> =
  /PROP[ERTIES] [<prop-list>]
  /PRIV[PROPERTIES] [<prop-list>]
  /PROP[ERTIES][:propname[,propname ...] /USEDEFAULT]
  /PRIV[PROPERTIES][:propname[,propname ...] /USEDEFAULT]
  /REN[AME]:cluster-name
  /VER[SION]
  /QUORUM[RESOURCE][:resource-name] [/PATH:path] [/MAXLOGSIZE:max-size-kbytes]
  /SETFAIL[UREACTIONS][:node-name[,node-name ...]]
  /REG[ADMIN]EXT:admin-extension-dll[,admin-extension-dll ...]
  /UNREG[ADMIN]EXT:admin-extension-dll[,admin-extension-dll ...]
  NODE [node-name] node-command
  GROUP [group-name] group-command
  RES[OURCE] [resource-name] resource-command
  <RESOURCETYPE:RESTYPE> [resourcetype-name] resourcetype-command
  NET[WORK] [network-name] network-command
  NETINT[ERFACE] [interface-name] interface-command

<prop-list> =
  name=value[,value ...][:<format>] [name=value[,value ...][:<format>] ...]

<format> =
  BINARY:DWORD:STR[ING]:EXPANDSTR[ING]:MULTISTR[ING]:SECURITY:ULARGE

CLUSTER /?
CLUSTER /HELP
```

**Figure 15-6.**   Cluster.exe command-line options and syntax

**NOTE:**   Microsoft supports Cluster Server only when it is used on a validated, listed cluster configuration. Validation is available only for complete configurations that are tested together; not on individual components. For a listing of approved complete systems, see the following Microsoft Web site: http://www.microsoft.com/hcl. Query on the "Cluster" category. This category lists complete systems that have attained certification. The entire configuration with all components installed must be certified as a complete solution.

## Configuring IIS Clustered Virtual Servers

Before installing IIS server instances on a cluster server, make sure the Cluster Service is installed correctly and fail-over works. To verify that fail-over is working, you must shut down (power off) only one of the clustered nodes and look to see that the other server continues to provide the Windows 2000 services.

To configure the IIS Clustered Virtual Server, follow these steps:

1. Open a command prompt on the first node server and run Comclust.exe. Follow the screen instructions; then repeat the procedure on the second node server. Ignore the message indicating that component load balancing (CLB) will not be installed.

   Comclust.exe has the following command-line options:

   Usage: ComClust [flags]

   Flags:

   - -a: Add current machine to a new cluster

   - -r: Remove current machine from the cluster

   - -j: Join this machine to a cluster

   This initial step prepares the server by setting up Microsoft Distributed Transaction Coordinator (MSDTC) on both nodes and automatically installing the MSDTC resource group on the cluster server. MSDTC resource setup for IIS virtual servers is needed only when Web applications are using transaction mode or calling MSDTC related applications. It is not necessary to be dependent on the MSDTC resource for an IIS virtual server instance if the Web sites will not be using transactions.

2. Move the IIS virtual server shared-disk group to the first node. Create a Web site content directory on the shared disk (for example: R:\Inetpub\Wwwroot). Place your default pages (default.asp, default.htm, index.htm, etc.) in this new directory.

3. Create an IP address resource for an IIS virtual server in the disk group in the Cluster Administrator. Use a different IP address for each virtual server. Be certain to make the IP address depend on both the MSDTC and shared disk resources.

4.  Create a network name resource in the same group for the IIS virtual server network name; it depends on the IP address resource previously created.

5.  In Internet Service Manager on the first node, create a brand new Web site (do not make it a default Web site). This will serve as the clustering Web site.

6.  Give the IP address as the IP address resource IP parameter provided in the cluster administrator. Map the Web content to the directory on the shared disk (in this case, R:\Inetpub\Wwwroot).

7.  Back in Cluster Administrator create an IIS server instance. Step through the Clustering Wizard and map the IIS server instance to the new Web site that is now available in the drop-down list.

The IIS virtual server is now ready to be accessed on the first node. You can manually move the group to the second node and create a new Web site using the Internet Services Manager on the second node. Give the new Web site the exact same directory path (R:\Inetpub\Wwwroot) and IP address. To automatically synchronize the Web site across the two nodes you also can use the IISSync utility, as described in the next section.

The only thing left at this point is to test the new IIS virtual Web site. Do this by simply opening a Web browser and typing in the address of the server. The virtual Web site should open as you would expect any other Web site to do.

**Using IISSync**    IISSync is available on Windows 2000 Advanced Server and Windows 2000 Datacenter. IISSync is used to synchronize the Metabase of clustered Web servers. Because IISSync was originally included in IIS 4.0, specific steps are needed to ensure that IISSync will run within the Windows 2000 clustered environment. The default anonymous user accounts (IUSR_servername and IWAM_servername) used for authentication to the Web site are accounts that are local to Windows 2000 Server where IIS is installed. To use IISSync to automatically synchronize the Metabase to both nodes of a clustered node environment, domain accounts need to be created to replace those two accounts.

The following steps are required to run IISSync when the clustered nodes are both member servers:

**NOTE:** If the clustered nodes are domain controllers, you can skip steps 1–4.

1. On a Windows 2000 domain controller, choose Start | Programs, and then choose Administrative Tools.

2. Run the Active Directory and choose Users and Computers.

3. Expand the tree under the domain name, and then click to highlight the Users folder. Right-click and select New User.

4. Create two new domain accounts in the Domain Users group. You should consider keeping the IUSR and IWAM conventions but inventing a unique name to finish out the user account. For example, make the account names: IUSR_<*uniquename*> and IWAM_<*uniquename*>.

5. On each of the two cluster nodes, right-click My Computer, and then select Manage.

6. With the Computer Management snap-in, expand Local Users and Groups, expand Groups, and then click Users. Add the two new user accounts as domainname\IUSR_uniquename and domainname\IWAM_uniquename.

7. The new domain accounts need to have the "Log on Locally" user right to function correctly. To manually assign the two new domain accounts the "Log on Locally" right, open Administrative Tools and select Local Security Policy. In Security settings, expand Local Policies and User Right Assignment. Click Log on Locally; then click Add. Add the two new domain accounts from the available domain list.

8. Open the Internet Services Manager on the first node. From the clustered Web site's Properties page, select Directory Security, select Anonymous Access, and then choose Edit. Replace the default anonymous user account with the domain user account (IUSR_*uniquename*) and password you specified.

9.  From the command prompt on the first node, go to the directory systemdrive:\inetpub\adminscripts and run the following two commands:

```
Cscript adsutil.vbs SET W3SVC/WAMUserName IWAM_uniquename

Cscript adsutil.vbs SET W3SVC/WAMUserPass "userpassword"
```
(without the quotes)

10.  Still on the first node, from the command prompt go to the directory systemdrive:\winnt\system32\inetsrv and run the following command:

```
iissync secondnodecomputername
```

IISSync will return a status of 0 that indicates that IISSync finished successfully. The second node now is synchronized with the same Metabase settings from the first node.

If IISSync returns a status other than 0, refer to Table 15-7 to isolate the reason for the failure.

| Status Code | Meaning and Probable Cause |
| --- | --- |
| 0 | Successful Synchronization. |
| 3 | The Metabase is inaccessible on Target Server. (The Metabase might be corrupt or in use.) |
| 1060 | Communications problem between Nodes. (This occurs when the Dcom default protocols do not match on both Nodes.) |
| 1722 | The Remote Procedure Call (RPC) server is unavailable. Invalid Target Server Name or Communications Problem between Nodes. |
| 1726 | The remote procedure call failed. |
| 2147500037 | Microsoft Transaction Server (MTS) Replication is not configured. (See the Knowledge Base article Q191138.) |

**Table 15-7.**    IISSyncStatus Codes

| Status Code | Meaning and Probable Cause |
| --- | --- |
| 2148007941 | Administrator account not logged in on Target Server. (If MTS is configured for Local Administration instead of Remote Administration, it is necessary to have a Local Administrator Equivalent account logged on the Target Server when IISSync is run.) |
| 2148598792 | Communications problem between Nodes. (Possible IP Conflict. Make sure all IP addresses on both Nodes and in the IIS Resource group are in the same subnet and valid.) |
| 2148598794 | Invalid share in MTS replication settings. (Set the MTS replication share to the administration share on which MTS is installed on the Target Server.) |
| 2148599041 | User logged on to Target Server has insufficient rights for MTS replication. (Log on to Target Server as Local Administrator.) |
| 2148598801 | The component's CLSID is missing or corrupt. |
| 2148598808 | Application file CLSIDs or IIDs do not match corresponding DLLs |
| 2148598800 | One or more users in the application file are not valid. |
| 2148598785 | Errors occurred accessing one or more objects. |
| 2148598797 | An error occurred copying the file. |
| 2148598828 | The server catalog version is not supported. |

**Table 15-7.** IISSync Status Codes *(continued)*

## Configuring SMTP in a Clustered Environment

Installing the IIS Web services in a clustered environment is a relatively quick and easy process. However, the SMTP service requires special steps to ensure that it will work correctly in a clustered environment. If the Web and SMTP services are on the same IIS server, and you require clustering functionality, walk through the following steps to correctly set up SMTP service.

*TIP:*   Before attempting the steps in this section you need to ensure that IIS 5.0 is set up as a cluster resource using the instructions in the previous section on Configuring IIS Clustered Virtual Servers.

To configure SMTP in the Clustered environment, walk through the following steps:

1.  Ensure that SMTP Service is installed on both cluster nodes by following these steps:

    ■   Select Start | Control Panel | Add/Remove Programs.

    ■   Click the Add/Remove Windows Components, and then verify that SMTP Service is listed under Internet Information Services. If it is indeed installed, close the Add/Remove Programs applet.

2.  Make sure to configure the SMTP service to start manually and that it is using the local system account. You can confirm this using the following steps:

    ■   Choose Start | Programs | Administrative Tools, and then run the Services application.

    ■   Double-click Simple Mail Transport Protocol (SMTP).

    ■   On the General tab, set Startup Type to Manual.

    ■   On the Log On tab, select the Local System account setting.

    ■   Repeat this process for both nodes in the cluster.

**NOTE:** The remainder of the steps in this process will be completed on a single node. Once the process is complete, you will run the IIS Synchronization command to synchronize all IIS information on your node with the other nodes in the server cluster.

3. Right-click the My Computer icon on the Windows desktop, click Manage, expand Services and Applications in the left pane, and then expand Internet Information Services.

4. Right-click the default SMTP Virtual Server, click Properties, and then click Advanced on the General tab.

5. Under IP address, double-click All Unassigned.

6. In the Identification dialog box, change TCP Port from the default number, "25" to any unassigned port number. It is important to change this port number to avoid conflict with the new SMTP Virtual Server that you will be creating for clustering. Type in the new port number—make sure it is indeed a unique port number—and then click OK.

7. Create a new SMTP Virtual Server.

8. Right-click Internet Information Services in the left pane, click New, and then click SMTP Virtual Server.

9. When you get to the Select Home Directory, and Default Domain screen of the New SMTP Virtual Server Wizard, be sure to type the paths to the shared resource to be used in clustering; not to a local hard drive.

10. In Select IP address, use the default All Unassigned.

11. In Select Default Domain, type the name of your domain.

12. Once you create the new SMTP Virtual Server, you might have to manually start this new SMTP Virtual Server from within the Services item. Make sure to use the default TCP port on the new virtual server, port 25.

13. Start Cluster Administrator. Follow the wizard and associate a resource type to the new SMTP Virtual Server.

14. In Cluster Administrator, select the group that contains Internet Information Server, right-click Internet Information Server in the left pane, click New, and then click Resource.

15. Click SMTP Server Instance from the Resource type list, type a descriptive name in the Name box (this is used for cluster administration purposes only), and then click Next.

16. Make sure all nodes are listed under Possible Owners; then click Next.

17. In the Dependencies dialog box, add IIS server, physical disk, network name, and the IP address resources from the IIS group.

18. In the Parameters dialog box, be sure to select your new SMTP virtual server from the list; not the default SMTP Virtual Server.

19. Click the Finish button.

20. Run the IIS Synchronization command to synchronize all IIS information on your node with the other nodes in the server cluster.

21. At a command prompt, go to the \WINNT\System32\Inetsrv folder on your node; then type **iissync** *servername*, where *servername* is another node in the server cluster. See your IIS documentation for more information on the IIS Synchronization command.

## Network Load-Balancing

Another component of the Windows Clustering Services is Network Load-Balancing (NLB). For your business-critical applications, Microsoft Windows 2000 Advanced Server and Windows 2000 Datacenter Server extend the reliability provided by Windows 2000 Server by using the Network Load-Balancing technology, which includes features to increase system availability. This technology enables you to spread incoming requests across as many as 32 servers; thus you can expand enterprise-wide services such as Web services and still ensure that they'll respond quickly, even under heavy loads.

Server Clustering, described in the previous section, provides full server and application fail-over. Network Load-Balancing, on the other hand, works with the network requests that are made of the servers. The requests that come in are distributed across the many servers to simulate high network availability and provide faster and continuous connections.

Network Load-Balancing automatically detects the failure of a server and quickly reassigns client traffic among the remaining servers. This safeguard will help you provide uninterrupted, continuous service for your critical business applications. However, keep in mind that Network Load-Balancing is only affected by a server failure; it has nothing to do with application failures. Server Clustering solves these issues.

Network Load-Balancing distributes IP traffic to multiple copies of a TCP/IP service, such as a Web server. NLB transparently partitions the client requests among the hosts and lets the clients access the cluster using one or more virtual IP addresses. From the client's point of view, the cluster appears to be a single server that answers the client requests. As enterprise traffic increases, network administrators can add servers to the cluster to increase the capacity of the network. NLB can be used in conjunction with Server Clustering to provide the most redundant, high-capacity system for your Web sites. The main feature of NLB is network performance but it offers much in the way of availability and scalability for the Web site.

Because NLB provides enhanced network services, it's not unusual that it is installed and assigned to the network interface installed in the server. In fact, the installation is performed the same way you would install an additional network component using the Windows 2000 Network and Dial-Up Connections applet (choose Start | Settings | Control Panel | Network and Dial-Up Connections). You only need to add the NLB network service to the current local area network connection; then configure NLB to work across the different nodes. For full information on the installation and configuration of NLB, refer to either the Windows 2000 Advanced Server or Windows 2000 Datacenter documentation, or invest in the book mentioned earlier in the Server Clustering section (*Windows 2000: The Complete Reference*).

## Quick Configuration of NLB in Windows 2000

Because of its functionality, Network Load-Balancing sounds like a complicated component to set up. It's really not. Using the following steps, you can quickly configure your Web environment to use NLB.

1. If Network Load Balancing is already enabled, skip to step 2. If not:

   - Choose Start | Settings | Network and Dial-up Connections.

   - Right-click the interface that should act as the virtual adapter (for example, the network card to which you will be assigning NLB); then click Properties.

2. Click to select the Network Load Balancing check box.

3. Click the Network Load Balancing component, and then click Properties.

4. Type your cluster-specific data on the Cluster Parameters, Host Parameters, and Port Rules tabs.

5. Click Internet Protocol (TCP/IP), and then click Properties. Click Use the Following IP Address and type the virtual IP address in the IP Address box.

# SUMMARY

As you have read in this chapter, IIS performance and troubleshooting go hand in hand. If you periodically take the time to determine whether the Web site is performing optimally, you will minimize the chances of troubleshooting a serious problem down the road. Microsoft has provided the tools you need to retrieve and store the performance statistics, to immediately know of potential problems, and to keep the Web site running by enabling you to upgrade consistently with the increase of traffic.

There is no such thing as a perfect piece of technology. To get the best out of your hardware and software investments you will need to carefully identify areas where specific actions could increase the value. By understanding where potential problems exist for IIS 5.0, you can enable a Web environment that is easy to manage, a breeze to maintain, and performs as well as technology allows.

# CHAPTER 16

## Client Connectivity

Getting IIS 5.0 installed and configured, and understanding how it works as a robust Web server, certainly is key to ensuring a successful Web site rollout. However, making the server available means nothing if people don't visit or if they have trouble accessing your Web site. If they are faced with consistent error messages, they might not return.

There will always be those select few people who have installed applications on their computers that keep them from using their Web browsers successfully. Unfortunately, there also are those folks that have a tough time with the operations of a computer no matter how many training classes they attend. However, another part of rolling out a Web server such as IIS 5.0 is ensuring that the visiting client can connect effectively. Again, there will be those circumstances that you cannot control but if you pay special attention to some of the more common client connectivity issues, you can rest assured that the majority of visitors to the Web site will be successful in connecting and navigating through the structure of your Web.

This chapter serves to identify common client connectivity issues and provide a reference for those famous error messages that are displayed in the Web browser from time to time. By keeping the HTTP error reference at your side, you can quickly determine whether the Web error received by the client's Web browser is a problem with the client or the Web server. Sometimes the best troubleshooting and alerting system is the end user. You can always rely on users to voice an opinion when something is wrong; particularly when they feel it is not their own fault. Having a good handle on the client issues can help you keep the site running and determine when to suggest that the end user seek training or contact a desktop support person.

## CLIENT "GOTCHAS"

Before delving into the specific error messages that can arise when certain functions of the Web site are not working properly, it is important to identify those issues that really have nothing to do with the IIS server at all. These issues generally are Web browser specific and can seem to the end user as if the Web site is not functioning properly. Understandably, there are Web browser offerings on the market other than those developed by Microsoft.

The purpose of a Web site is to give something to the visitor, whether it is information, programs for download, or products and services. To make this happen efficiently, the Web site must be available to all visitors, no matter what Web browser they decide to use—a non-partisan Web site. Thus, to fully support the vehicles the user rides in on, you have to understand complications ahead of time. This section will outline some of the more common issues for which you need to be prepared.

## AOL Netscape and Files Without Extensions

Netscape has been a long-standing Web browser, popular with a lot of people. In the early days Netscape was, in essence, the only Web browser. Since then a number of Web browsers have been offered that are very palatable for surfing the Web. Microsoft of course is one; another very interesting Web browser is Opera (http://www.opera.com).

America Online (AOL) purchased the Netscape browser a few years ago and promised to keep the Internet tool current with the newer Internet technologies. Unfortunately, this has not happened. One issue that seems to cause quite a bit of trouble for Netscape users is the use of files that don't have a file extension on an Internet server. When IIS locates a requested file that does not have a file extension, the Content-Type that is sent back to the Web browser is set to *application/octet stream*. Because of the file's header information the AOL browser will not display the file but will attempt to download it.

You can fix this issue by making a modification to the IIS 5.0 metabase. After installing the MetaEdit program from the IIS Resource Kit, follow these directions:

1. Execute MetaEdit.

2. Expand the LM tree in the left-hand pane.

3. Open the MimeMap folder.

4. In the right-hand pane, double-click ID 6015 MimeMap.

5. In the Data list box find the listing for .*,application/octet-stream.

6. Change the value to **.*,test/html**.

7. Click OK to close MetaEdit.

8. Now stop and restart IIS:

   ■ Open a command prompt window.

   ■ Type **net stop iisadmin /y**.

   ■ Press ENTER.

   ■ Type **net start w3svc**.

   ■ Press ENTER.

   ■ Close the command prompt window.

## AOL Netscape Can't Browse an Intranet Site

Another Netscape "gotcha" can be found when a user tries to navigate around a Web site that is internal to the company. For Intranets, most companies prefer to configure the IIS site to authenticate users based on their network login account information. AOL Netscape will not work with this feature; it will work with only Basic authentication. This feature (NTLM, NT challenge/response authentication) works as expected with a Microsoft Web browser. There are a couple of ways to fix the problem: One is to standardize on the Microsoft Web browser, Internet Explorer, and enforce its use; the other is to change the authentication method for the Web site by doing the following:

1. Start Internet Service Manager.

2. Right-click the specific Intranet Web site.

3. On the context menu, click Properties.

4. When the property screen displays, click the Directory tab.

5. Click the Edit button in the Anonymous Access and Authentication Control section.

6. Select the Basic Authentication method on the Authenticated Access window.

7. Click OK until the property screen is closed.

**NOTE:** Although this fix will enable AOL Netscape to connect, setting Basic Authentication for any Web browser is a severe security risk. Basic Authentication allows passwords to be sent across the connection as plain text. This gives hackers just the vehicle they need to steal passwords and gain access to the system. If security is a major concern in your company, check with the browser manufacturer for a fix or choose a different browser that offers better security.

# HTTP ERROR REFERENCE

It's safe to say that the majority of everyday Web surfers have encountered browser error messages. It wasn't too long ago that these error messages, displayed in the Web browser window, truly were cryptic, puzzling pieces of information. The general Web populace had no idea what the error numbers meant or what to do to fix the problem. In many cases the user had typed in the wrong Web address or tried to access an HMTL page that existed yesterday but was removed for one reason or another.

Microsoft has done a remarkable job of trying to offset the obscure information with usable, understandable data. As mentioned earlier in this book, you actually can customize the displayed messages to help the visitor understand more about what is happening when an error occurs. Although this definitely will help the Web surfer to understand more about an issue when it arises, there generally are several different methods for fixing each problem. The resolution could be as simple as the user verifying the Web address he or she typed into the Web browser; however, it also could be something with the IIS server or configuration itself. When the latter becomes the solution, you need to know how to minimize the user's downtime. The following sections reference the common error messages that can be displayed to the user and the possible fixes.

## 400

The 400 error message is the most commonly seen and normally happens because the user has typed the wrong address into the Web browser. This generally is not a big concern for the administrator of the Web site. However, it is possible that a file has inadvertently been moved or deleted from the Web so you might want to verify that the file is still available.

The specific 400 error is displayed to the user as HTTP 400 – Bad Request, with the following instructions:

▼ If you typed the page address in the Address bar, make sure it is spelled correctly.

■ Open the http:// home page; then look for links to the information you want.

▲ Click the Back button to try another link.

If the user has typed in the correct address and the file still exists on the IIS server, it is possible that either the file is corrupt and should be restored from backup, or that there is a Get package corruption. When a request is made of a particular page on the Web server, IIS uses an internal Get command to fulfill the request. If the client trying to access the page has a faulty network connection, the request packet cannot be read by the IIS Web services.

If the Web site actually is an Intranet page, you can determine whether the connection between the client and the IIS server is suspect by utilizing Network Monitor, a Microsoft utility that captures and analyzes the packets in network traffic. For more information on Network Monitor, see the Microsoft Knowledge Base article Q148942. Microsoft's Knowledge Base is located at http:// search.support.microsoft.com/.

## 401-1

The 401-1 error message is displayed when the user does not have the proper rights to view the page they are trying to access. For example, when the Web browser attempts access to a page that does not allow anonymous access the user will not be authenticated. This error message can arise from several different problems; the most common are

▼  The user's credentials (the username and password) are not correct.

▲  The user account might not have permission to log on to the computer interactively (the Log On Locally right).

If you have turned off the right for anonymous access to the specific Web page or Web site, you must verify that the person should be able to access the page. If he or she should not have access, case closed. However, if he or she should be granted access to the Web site, check the username and the password of the user to make sure they are correct. If they are correct, be sure the user has the Log On Locally right granted to it.

To verify user rights, do the following:

1.  Open the Local Security Policy tool from the Administrative Tools folder.

2.  Select Local Policies, choose User Rights Assignment, and then click the Log On Locally user right.

If the user account or group that the user belongs to is not listed, add it.

# 401-2

The 401-2 error message is displayed when the visiting user does not have the appropriate authority to access the specific page. The user is presented with the following information in the Web browser:

▼  Click the Refresh button to try again with different credentials.

■  If you believe you should be able to view this directory or page, please contact the Web site administrator by using the e-mail address or phone number listed on the file:// home page.

▲ HTTP 401.2 – Unauthorized: Logon failed due to server configuration.

Although this error message indicates that the proper rights have not been applied to the Web page, it also is possible that a specific server-side script is not providing the appropriate rights to the user when it runs. This means the authentication method that the user's computer is trying to use might not be enabled on the IIS server, or the user is trying to access the page through a proxy server and the Integrated Windows Authentication is the only option selected.

If the user should have access to the Web page, modify the authentication methods so that the user and the IIS server can handshake:

1. From the Start menu, point to Programs, point to Administrative Tools, and then click Internet Services Manager.

2. Under the Tree pane, browse to the desired Web site.

3. Right-click the Web site, and then click Properties.

4. On the Directory Security tab, under Anonymous access and authentication control, click Edit.

5. Select (and implement) at least one type of authentication method.

## 401-3

The 401-3 error message is displayed when the user tries accessing the Web site using a username and password that have not been configured for access on the IIS server itself. The 401-3 error message is different from 401-2 in that it specifies access problems with the entire Web site instead of just a Web page. The following information is displayed to the user:

▼ Click the Refresh button to try again with different credentials.

■ If you believe you should be able to view this directory or page, please contact the Web site administrator by using the e-mail address or phone number listed on the file:// home page.

▲ HTTP 401.3 – Access denied by ACL on resource.

Access to the Web site with the user's credentials depends on whether the Windows 2000 NTFS permissions have been applied to a specific file or directory. This error message indicates that the user has successfully logged on to the server but the Windows 2000 file and directory security mechanism has denied access to the file he or she was requesting. If the user should have the right to use the chosen file, you will need to modify the specific file rights to allow him or her to gain access.

Modifying file and directory permissions is completed through the Internet Services Manager interface. To modify the permissions for a specific file:

1. Open Internet Services Manager.

2. Navigate to the specific Web site that requires the permissions change and then find the file that needs to be modified.

3. Right-click the file and choose Properties from the context menu.

4. Click the File Security tab.

5. Click the Edit button in the first section entitled Anonymous Access and Authentication Control.

6. Make sure the proper authentication methods are selected; then exit the file properties, clicking OK to save any changes.

7. Click the My Computer icon on the IIS server's desktop; then select Manage on the context menu. The Computer Management tool will display as shown in Figure 16-1.

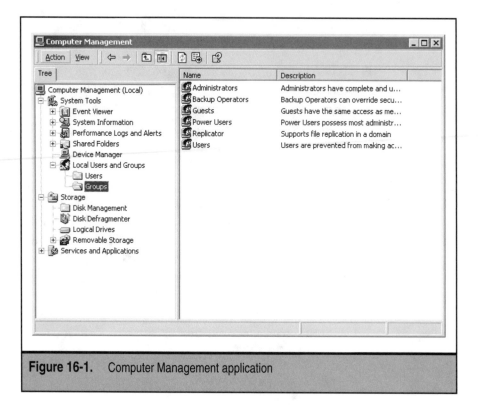

**Figure 16-1.** Computer Management application

8. Expand Local Users and Groups.

9. In the Groups folder, find the group of which the user should be a member to access the specific file that was modified in the previous steps.

10. Add the user to the appropriate group to grant him or her access to the file.

## 401-4

HTTP error 401-4 describes yet another authentication issue for the user. However, this error message is more related to the use of a program external to IIS that supplies authentication services before the user is passed on for a second verification by the IIS server security. An additional Filter program can be used to authenticate incoming users. Error 401-4 indicates that the authentication failed. If you are using an additional program to grant users access to the Web site, look for support with that program for how to identify and fix the issue.

The user is presented with the following information:

▼ Click the Refresh button to try again with different credentials.

■ If you believe you should be able to view this directory or page, please contact the Web site administrator by using the e-mail address or phone number listed on the file:// home page.

▲ HTTP 401.4 – Unauthorized: Authorization denied by filter.

This error message also can be displayed if you are using Digest Authentication. This error typically occurs because the user's password either is not stored in reversible encryption, or the password has not been reset (for the hashing to take place).

Digest Authentication is new to Windows 2000 and IIS 5.0. This form of authentication encrypts the user's password information and helps prevent some common server attacks. To use Digest Authentication in Windows 2000, the server must have access to an Active Directory Server that is set up for Digest Authentication. If the server running IIS is not an Active Directory Server or does not have access to the Active Directory, this authentication scheme will not work.

If the server is already a Directory Server, perform the following steps:

1. Open the Active Directory Users and Computers.

2. Open the domain that you want to administer.

3. Double-click the username that you want to use with Digest Authentication.

4. In Account Options, select Store password using reversible encryption.

5. Click OK.

6. Reset the user's password now in order for the encryption to take place. To reset the user's password, right-click the user name in the directory and click Reset Password.

7. Click OK.

In order for Internet Information Services 5.0 to use Digest Authentication, you must select it in Internet Service Manager. To do this, perform the following steps:

1.  Open Internet Services Manager.

2.  Expand the Web server in which you want to make the change, and then open the Web site's properties.

3.  Click the Directory Security tab.

4.  Under Anonymous Access and Authentication Control, click Edit.

5.  Select Digest Authentication from the list, and then click OK.

## 401-5

The 401-5 error message tells the user that a script that runs on the Web server has denied access to the login information. When a CGI or ISAPI script is running to surpass the IIS authentication method and the user's credentials fail, this error message will display. The user should verify that the information he or she has given is correct, and if not contact the system administrator to have the issue resolved. You should make sure the script you have put in place is working correctly. Verify the script's code to ensure it has not been tampered with or formatted incorrectly, or that you have not inadvertently made changes that stop the script from performing its functions correctly.

When this error occurs, the user is confronted with the following information in the Web browser window:

▼   Click the Refresh button to try again with different credentials.

■   If you believe you should be able to view this directory or page, please contact the Web site administrator by using the e-mail address or phone number listed on the file:// home page.

▲   HTTP 401.5 – Unauthorized: Authorization by ISAPI or CGI application failed.

# 403

The 403 error indicates there is a synchronization discrepancy between the metabase and the Windows 2000 file system, with the object the user is trying to access. The user will be presented with the following information:

▼ Click the Refresh button to try again with different credentials.

■ If you believe you should be able to view this directory or page, please contact the Web site administrator by using the e-mail address or phone number listed on the file:// home page.

▲ HTTP Error 403 – Forbidden.

The AccessPerm key for the object being requested exists in the metabase but not in the file system. Presently, there is no synchronization between the file system and properties in the metabase. You must manually synchronize the various properties in the metabase and File System. There are two ways to accomplish this task, as discussed in the following sections.

## Synchronize the Metabase and File System—Option 1

Option 1 involves manually deleting and re-creating the object, using the following steps:

1. Re-create the object in the file system.

2. Open the MMC and delete the old object.

3. Open Windows Explorer and delete the object from the file system.

## Synchronize the Metabase and File System—Option 2

Option 2 uses one of the VB Admin scripts installed with IIS. Use the Adsutil.vbs script to delete the metabase entry for the object in question.

## 403-1 and 403-10

403-1 and 403-10 are error messages that the user will see when they try to access an executable file on the IIS server that has not been configured to allow execution. The user will see the following information:

▼ Open the file:// home page, and then look for links to the information you want.

■ Click the Refresh button, or try again later.

■ HTTP 403.1 Forbidden: Execute Access Forbidden.

▲ HTTP 403.10 – Access Forbidden: Invalid configuration.

Verify that the appropriate execute right has been granted to the Web site. You do this by opening the property sheet on either the Default Web Site, or the Virtual Directory that is affected. If you have set script permissions for the entire IIS server, the Default Web Site properties will be used to modify the value. Alternatively, if you have configured script security on a site-by-site basis, you will want to drill down to the specific Virtual site in Internet Services Manager and make the changes there. For the Default Web Site, the Home Directory tab contains the script permissions information; for a Virtual Directory, the Virtual Directory tab will be used. On the specific property sheet for either one, the Application Settings section houses the Execute Permissions options. As outlined earlier in the book, there are three explicit options for script permissions: None, Scripts Only, Script and Executables. If the 403-1 error message is being displayed, there's a good chance this value is set to None.

In addition to the script permissions not being configured correctly, the 403-1 error can be the result of an erroneous naming scheme on the virtual directory. This error can occur when there is a period (.) in the name of the virtual directory; for example

```
http://www.mycompany.com/test.test
```

If this is the case, you will need to delete the virtual directory with the period (.) in its name; then re-create the virtual directory in question and make sure the new virtual directory name does not contain a period.

# 403-2

403-2 is the error message displayed when no default page has been configured for the Web site, or if the directory containing the file being accessed is set to allow only script execution.

The user is faced with the following information:

▼  Open the file:// home page, and then look for links to the information you want.

■  Click the Refresh button, or try again later.

▲  HTTP 403.2 – Forbidden: Read Access Forbidden.

To further expand on this issue, the following are the most common problems when the 403-2 error message is displayed:

▼  The resource being accessed does not have Read access set. For example, the SCRIPTS directory does not have Read access by default. Run Internet Services Manager, navigate to the virtual directory in question, open its properties, and verify that Read access has been granted to the directory; then do the following:

1.  Run Internet Services Manager.

2.  Navigate to the virtual directory that is causing the error message.

3.  Right-click and choose Properties from the context menu.

4.  Verify that the Read permission has been selected for this directory, as shown in Figure 16-2.

■  The default document specified is either not correct, or the default document does not exist. For example, the default

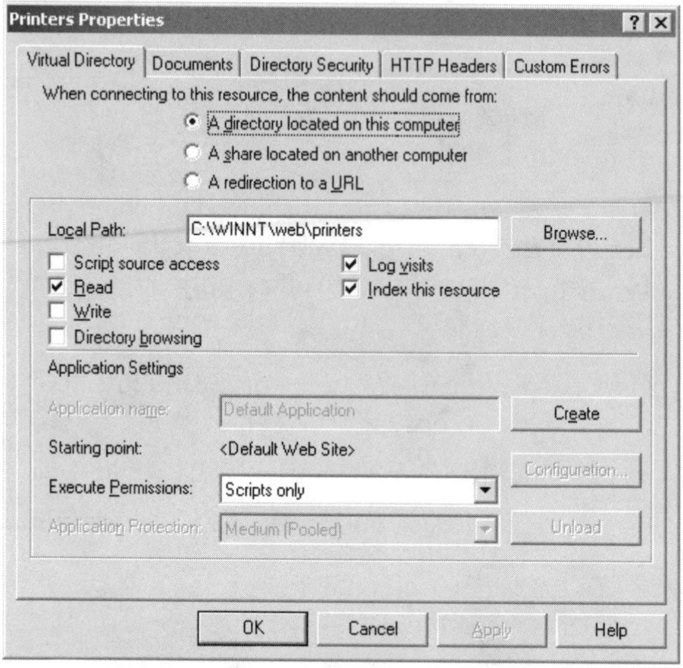

**Figure 16-2.** Virtual Directory with Read Permission selected

document might be set to Default.htm but the one uploaded by the Web publisher is Index.htm. If a file named Default.htm is not on that Web site, this error message occurs. Either create the default document and place it in the affected directory, or modify the default document information by doing the following:

1. Run Internet Services Manager.

2. Navigate to the virtual directory that is causing the error message.

3. Right-click and choose Properties from the context menu.

4. Click the Documents tab and verify that the correct startup documents have been configured. Add the appropriate startup document if it doesn't exist in the list, as shown in Figure 16-3.

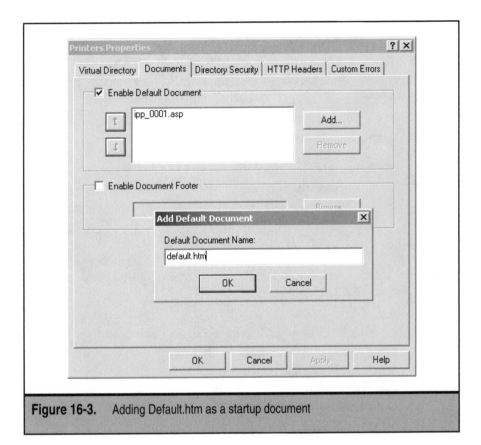

**Figure 16-3.**    Adding Default.htm as a startup document

▲  Directory browsing is not enabled when it should be. For
example, if you have a Web site configured to show a directory
listing (all files in the name space you are accessing), and
directory browsing is not enabled, this error message occurs.

Be sure that Read access is enabled on the site or directory where
users are browsing files. If directory browsing should be used (for a
file list), it must be specified on the properties of that directory or site
(a default document should not be used to prevent other problems if
this is the case).

## 403-3

The 403-3 error message will be displayed when you have enabled the capability to write or upload to your Web site, but this particular function has failed. These uploads are generally Web pages that are being published for use. The user will see the following information in the Web browser window:

▼ There is a problem trying to save the page to the Web site. This error can be caused if you attempt to upload to, or modify a file in, a directory that does not allow Write access.

■ Open the file:// home page, and then look for links to the information you want.

■ Click the Refresh button, or try again later.

▲ HTTP 403.3 – Forbidden: Write Access Forbidden.

This error can occur because of a problem in trying to save the Web page to the Web site. This can happen if you attempt to upload to or modify a file in a directory that does not allow Write access. This issue can result from a Web-publishing utility such as FrontPage. To resolve this problem, verify that the permissions to the directory or page are appropriate for the account that is attempting access.

To verify that the proper directory permissions are configured for Windows 2000:

1. Locate the destination folder where files will be posted.

2. Right-click the folder and click Properties.

3. Select the Security tab.

4. Click Add.

5. Add the account that needs permissions.

6. Click OK.

7. Select the appropriate rights to allow this user to write to this directory (Read/Write or Read/Write/Modify).

8. Click OK.

Also verify that the virtual directory has Write access granted for the users coming in. To verify permissions under Internet Information Server 5.0:

1. Open Internet Services Manager.

2. Expand Machine Name.

3. Expand the site where the upload directory exists.

4. Right-click the upload directory.

5. Click Properties.

6. On the Virtual Directory tab, click so that a check mark exists beside the Write option.

7. Click OK.

## 403-4

Error message 403-4 pertains to the Secure Sockets Layer (SSL) and the inability to access a Web site that is configured to use a secure connection. The user will see the following information:

▼ The page you are trying to view requires the use of "https" in the address.

■ Try again by typing **https://** at the beginning of the address you are attempting to reach.

▲ HTTP 403.4 – Forbidden: SSL required.

The first thing you will want to identify is that the user is typing the https prefix for the Web address. Https is required when accessing a secure Web site. When this prefix is used IIS knows to utilize the additional secure layer for Web site security.

If the https prefix is being used correctly, you will need to look at the IIS site to verify that SSL has been set up correctly. Once you enable the Require Secure Channel when accessing this resource (the Web site) option or the Require 128-bit Encryption option from the IIS HTML Admin (HTMLA), this error can occur. The HTML Admin (HTMLA) incorrectly allows you to enable Require Secure Channel when accessing this resource and Require 128-bit Encryption before an SSL certificate has been mapped to the Web site. The MMC does not allow you to enable either of these options until an SSL certificate has been assigned to the Web site using Key Manager. To resolve this problem, assign an SSL certificate to the Web site using the MMC.

If you do not have an SSL certificate to assign to the Web site, you will want to disable the options. You can disable the options by modifying the metabase using the adsutil.vbs admin script.

1. Open a Command Prompt window.

2. Change to the Adminsamples directory by typing (**\winnt\system32\inetsrv\adminsamples**).

3. Type **cscript adsutil.vbs set w3svc/1/root/AccessSSL false**, and then press ENTER.

4. Type **cscript adsutil.vbs set w3svc/1/root/AccessSSL128 false**, and then press ENTER.

5. Close the Command Prompt window and try to access the site again.

If you are still unable to access the Web site without receiving the HTTP Error 403 error, it is possible that SSL is enabled at a higher level in the metabase hierarchy. Repeat the previous steps, but execute the following commands instead:

▼ cscript adsutil.vbs set w3svc/1/AccessSSL false

■ cscript adsutil.vbs set w3svc/1/AccessSSL128 false

■ cscript adsutil.vbs set w3svc/AccessSSL false

▲ cscript adsutil.vbs set w3svc/AccessSSL128 false

If you are still unable to access the Web site without receiving HTTP Error 403, it is possible that SSL is enabled on a Web site instance other than the first instance. Repeat the previous steps but execute the Cscript command with the appropriate Web site instance number. For example, if SSL is enabled on the second Web site instance, the following Cscript commands will disable SSL:

▼   cscript adsutil.vbs set w3svc/4/AccessSSL false

▲   cscript adsutil.vbs set w3svc/4/AccessSSL128 false

## 403-5

The 403-5 error message generally indicates that the user's Web browser does not have the correct encryption coding. There are different encryption levels for Web browsers, which relate to the different levels of encryption methods that are legal for export to other countries. SSL provides the encryption levels for IIS and when a 128-bit method is being used, the visiting Web browser also must have this level installed.

When this error is reached, the user sees the following in the Web browser window:

▼   The page you are trying to view requires the use of a Web browser configured for 128-bit encryption.

■   Upgrade your Web browser to the 128-bit version.

■   If your Web browser does support 128-bit encryption, or if you believe you should be able to view this directory or page, please contact the Web site administrator by using the e-mail address or phone number listed on the file:// home page.

▲   HTTP 403.5 – Forbidden: SSL 128 required.

The easiest solution is to make sure that the user upgrades his or her Web browser to the appropriate version. If this is not feasible, the user will not be able to access the Web site. If encryption has been enabled erroneously you can use the instructions in the 403-4 section to disable the SSL certificate options.

## 403-6

The user will receive the 403-6 error message when the computer's IP address is not in the list of allowable IP addresses in the IIS security configuration. Each client has a unique IP address. If the server defines a list of IP addresses that are not allowed to access the site and the client's IP address is in this exclusion list, this error message will display. This is a feature that grants or denies specific users access to a Web site, directory, or file.

The user will see the following displayed in the Web browser:

▼ You do not have permission to view this directory or page from the Internet address of your Web browser.

■ If you believe you should be able to view this directory or page, please contact the Web site administrator by using the e-mail address or phone number listed on the file:// home page.

▲ HTTP 403.6 – Forbidden: IP address rejected.

There are two configuration settings in IIS that can prohibit a visiting IP address from being able to access the site. There are the Granted Access and Denied Access options. To modify the list:

1. Using the Internet Service Manager, select the Web site reporting the 403.6 error.

2. Right-click the Web site, virtual directory, or file where the error is occurring.

3. Click Properties to display the property sheet for that item.

4. Select the appropriate Directory Security or File Security property page.

5. Under IP Address and Domain Name Restrictions, click Edit.

6. In the IP Address and Domain Name Restrictions dialog box, if the Denied Access option is selected add the IP address, network ID, or domain of the computer that requires access to the exceptions list.

7. In the IP Address and Domain Name Restrictions dialog box, if the Granted Access option is selected, remove the IP address, network ID, or domain of the computer that requires access to the exceptions list.

## 403-7

When the Web site is configured to require a SSL client certificate and the certificate is not found or is not recognized, the 403-7 error message will be displayed. The user will see the following information in the Web browser window:

▼ The page you are trying to view requires the use of a client certificate.

■ Click the Refresh button to try again if you have installed your client certificate.

■ If you believe you should be able to view this directory or page, please contact the Web site administrator by using the e-mail address or phone number listed on the file:// home page.

■ HTTP 403.7 – Forbidden: Client certificate required.

▲ There are a few causes for this error message:

■ The Root Certificate of the server is not installed on the computer running IIS. If this is the case, download the Root Server Certificate into a browser on the server computer. Use the Certificate Wizard to download and install the certificate.

■ The Client Certificate has expired or the effective time has not been reached. Check the Effective Date on the client certificate and ensure that the time has arrived; also check the Expiration Date and ensure that the certificate has not expired.

■ The Client Certificate has been revoked. Check with your Certificate Authority to see if your certificate has expired.

## 403-8

Like the 403-6 error message, 403-8 indicates denied access to the Web site because of an inclusion or exclusion from a list. However, unlike 403-6, 403-8 actually uses the computer name where the Web browser is attempting access to the site. This list is configured similarly to the IP address list.

When this problem arises, the user sees the following in the Web browser:

▼ You do not have permission to view this directory or page from the Internet address of your Web browser.

■ If you believe you should be able to view this directory or page, please contact the Web site administrator by using the e-mail address or phone number listed on the file:// home page.

▲ HTTP 403.8 – Forbidden: Site access denied.

If the visitor should have access to the Web site, you will need to modify the list of computer names that are granted access to the site and remove the client's DNS name from the DNS restrictions on the IIS computer. To do this, open the properties on the Default Web site or the specific Web site in question:

1. Click the Directory Security tab.

2. Under IP Address and Domain Name Restrictions, click Edit.

3. Select the domain name that you want to remove in the Restrictions box.

4. Click Remove.

5. Do this for each domain that you want to remove.

**NOTE:** IP and Domain restrictions can also be set in the Master properties. You might have to perform the preceding steps under Master properties. To enter Master properties, right-click the server name in the Internet Services Manager and choose Properties. In the Master Properties box, click Edit.

## 403-9

When a 403-9 error is displayed to the visiting user, you can determine quickly that the Web site is being hammered by traffic. The 403-9 error message indicates that the Web site has reached the allowable connection limit. The following information is displayed to the user trying to access the site:

- ▼ There are too many people accessing the Web site at this time.
- ■ Click the Refresh button, or try again later.
- ■ Open the file:// home page; then look for links to the information you want.
- ▲ HTTP 403.9 – Access Forbidden: Too many users are connected to Internet Information Services.

To fix this issue, you will need to increase the number of maximum allowable users in the IIS settings, using the following instructions:

1. Open Internet Services Manager.
2. Right-click the Web site and choose Properties.
3. On the Web Site property page, select Connections.
4. Choose Unlimited or increase the Limited To: value.

## 403-11

The 403-11 error message is displayed when an authentication requires login and password information, and the user's password has expired, not been set, or has been locked out in the Windows 2000 Active Directory. The following information will be displayed when the error message is reached:

- ▼ You do not have permission to view this directory or page using the credentials you supplied.
- ■ Click the Refresh button to try again with different credentials.
- ■ If you believe you should be able to view this directory or page, please contact the Web site administrator by using the e-mail address or phone number listed on the file:// home page.
- ▲ HTTP 403.11 – Access Forbidden: Password change.

Verify the user's password information is available by looking in the Active Directory properties for the specific user account. If you are not the administrator of the Active Directory components (which is commonly the case), you will need to work with the administrator to get the issue resolved for the user.

## 403-12

403-12 is another error message that relates to the client's SSL certificate. However, unlike previous certificate-related error messages that could be either the server or the client certificate, error 403-12 is directed explicitly toward the client. The following information is displayed to the user in the Web browser window:

▼ The page you are trying to view requires the use of a valid client certificate. Your client certificate map has been denied access to this Web site.

■ Click the Refresh button to try again if you have changed your client certificate.

■ Contact the site administrator to establish client certificate permissions.

■ Change your client certificate and retry, if appropriate.

■ If you believe you should be able to view this directory or page, please contact the Web site administrator by using the e-mail address or phone number listed on the file:// home page.

▲ HTTP 403.12 – Access Forbidden: Mapper denied access.

On the client side, review the following items:

1. Check the effective date on the client certificate and ensure that the certificate is valid.

2. Check the expiration date and ensure that the certificate has not expired.

3. Check with the Certificate Authority that provided the certificate to see if the certificate has expired.

4. Verify that the certificate has not been explicitly denied access.

## 403-13

The 403-13 error message also pertains to the client certificate; however, in this instance the error identifies that indeed the certificate has been revoked. When this error occurs, the following information is displayed to the visiting user:

▼ The page you are trying to view requires the use of a valid client certificate. Your client certificate was revoked, or the revocation status could not be determined. The certificate is used for authenticating you as a valid user of the resource.

■ Click the Refresh button to try again, if you have a valid client certificate.

■ Contact the Web server's administrator to obtain a valid client certificate.

■ If you believe you should be able to view this directory or page, please contact the Web site administrator by using the e-mail address or phone number listed on the file:// home page.

▲ HTTP 403.13 – Forbidden: Client certificate revoked.

An HTTP 403.13 error message is returned when a resource that the user is attempting to access requires a valid client Secure Sockets Layer (SSL) certificate that the server recognizes. This client SSL certificate must be installed in the Web browser because it is used for authenticating the user of that browser as a valid user of the resource.

The error message also can occur if IIS is unable to contact the server that stores the Certificate Revocation List (CRL) when checking for revoked certificates. If a CRL server is unreachable, it is presumed that the certificates have been revoked. In the Web browser that is displaying the error, install a certificate from a recognized Certificate Authority (CA). If a certificate from a valid CA is installed, contact that CA to verify the certificate has not been revoked and that its CRL store is online.

> **NOTE:**   A CRL is a file that contains a list of revoked certificates, their serial numbers, and their revocation date. A CRL file also usually contains the name of the issuer of the CRL, effective date, and the next update date. A CDP is the location from which you can download the latest CRL; usually it is listed as "CRL Distribution Points" in the details of the certificate. It is common to list multiple CDPs using multiple access methods to ensure that applications (that is, browsers and Web servers) are always able to obtain the latest CRL.

## 403-15

When the error message 403-15 is displayed, generally there are too many users accessing the IIS server against the maximum allowable limit. The user's Web browser will display the following information:

▼   There are too many people accessing the Web site at this time.

■   Click the Refresh button, or try again later.

■   Open the file:// home page, and then look for links to the information you want.

▲   HTTP 403.15 – Forbidden: Client Access Licenses exceeded.

In addition to the Web browser displaying information, you will see the following information in the Windows 2000 Server event log files:

▼   Event ID: 27 Source: W3SVC Description: The server was unable to acquire a license for an SSL connection.

▲   Event ID: 201 Source: LicenseService Description: No license was available for user <username> using product IIS 5.0.

This issue can be caused by one of two things:

▼   The number of authenticated users has exceeded the number of Client Access Licenses (CALs).

▲ The number of Secure Sockets Layer (SSL) users (anonymous or authenticated) has exceeded the number of CALs installed on the server.

**NOTE:** If the Windows 2000 License Logging Service (LLS) is stopped, only 10 concurrent SSL connections are accepted. LLS is a Windows 2000 service that tracks the number of client licenses per server or per seat, depending on how many were purchased per the license contract with Microsoft.

To fix this issue, you can do one of two things: Start the License Logging Service and run IISReset from the command line to restart the Internet Information Server services or purchase more Client Access Licenses, add them to the Licensing application in the Windows 2000 Control Panel, and then run IISReset from the command line to restart the Internet Information Server services. However, you can configure a specific Windows 2000 registry key for SSL to never check LLS for CALs:

1. Start Registry Editor (Regedt32.exe).

2. Locate the following key in the registry:

   ```
   HKEY_LOCAL_MACHINE\System\CurrentControlSet\Services\
   W3SVC\Parameters
   ```

3. On the Edit menu, click Add Value; then add the following registry value:

   ```
   Value Name: EnableCAL
   Data Type: REG_DWORD
   Value: 0
   ```

4. Quit Registry Editor.

5. After you add this key, run IISReset from the command line to restart the services.

SSL actually counts the number of licenses that are available and decrements the amount each time a new license is requested and used. Each SSL connection decrements the SSL connections counter whether the authentication method is anonymous or NTLM. If the visiting user is authenticated through SSL, a CAL is used. When IIS is installed, the SSL connection counter is initialized using the retrieved number of CALs from the Windows 2000 configuration.

If there are 10 CALs installed on the Windows 2000 Server that hosts the Web site, the server will support up to 10 concurrent SSL connections. As long as the Web site allows anonymous access and there are no authentication methods such as logon pages, SSL certificate verifications, or access to network directories where an Active Directory login account and password is required, no CAL is issued. Only when there is some type of user authentication method in place will a CAL be used.

# 403-16

The 403-16 error message indicates that the client certificate being used is not valid for the IIS server. The IIS server accepts certain certificates but the one being used to access the site does not fall within the authorized parameters. The following information will be displayed in the user's Web browser:

▼ The page you are trying to view requires the use of a valid client certificate. Your client certificate is untrusted or invalid. The client certificate is used for authenticating you as a valid user of the resource.

■ Click the Refresh button to try again, if you have changed your client certificate.

■ Contact the Web server's administrator to obtain a valid client certificate.

■ If you believe you should be able to view this directory or page, please contact the Web site administrator by using the e-mail address or phone number listed on the file:// home page.

▲ HTTP 403.16 – Forbidden: Client certificate untrusted or invalid.

If the IIS server should trust the client's certificate, the issue could be with the Windows 2000 configuration itself. If the client certificate was created by a Certificate Authority that is trusted by the IIS computer, it is possible this error is caused by a known issue with Windows 2000 when it is configured to Trust Only Enterprise Root Stores. If this policy is enabled, the authentication will still fail, even if the CA is a Trusted Root Store.

To disable this configuration setting for Windows 2000:

1. On the Windows 2000 Server, start the Default Domain Policy Group Policy Editor; choose Start | Programs | Administrative Tools.

2. Select Computer Settings, choose Computer Configuration, and then select Windows Settings.

3. Choose Security Settings, select Public Key Policies and then choose Trusted Root Certification Authorities.

4. Right-click Trusted Root CA node, and then select Properties.

5. Disable the Trust Only Enterprise Root Stores option.

## 403-17

Error message 403-17 also relates to client certificate problems, but in this case it gives specific information to indicate that the certificate actually has expired or has not yet reached its date of validity. When certificates are assigned, they have a start and end date. Obviously, if the end date has been exceeded the certificate has expired; conversely, if the start date has not yet become current, the certificate will not work for authentication. When either of these scenarios happens, the following information is displayed to the user:

▼ The page you are trying to view requires the use of a valid client certificate. Your client certificate has expired or is not yet valid. The client certificate is used for identifying you as a valid user of the resource.

■ Click the Refresh button to try again if you have changed your client certificate.

■ Contact the Web server's administrator to obtain a valid client certificate.

- If you believe you should be able to view this directory or page, please contact the Web site administrator by using the e-mail address or phone number listed on the file:// home page.

▲ HTTP 403.17 – Forbidden: Client certificate has expired or is not yet valid.

As with any client certificate error message, the following steps should be taken in the listed order:

1. Check the Effective Date on the client certificate.
2. Ensure that the certificate is valid.
3. Check the Expiration Date on the client certificate.
4. Ensure that the certificate has not expired.
5. Verify that the Certificate Authority has not expired the certificate.
6. Request a new certificate from the Certificate Authority.

## 404-1

404-1 is the error message displayed when the Web site itself is unavailable to the client computer. This message specifically identifies a configuration error for IIS, where an IP address is not able to accept incoming connections. When this situation occurs, the following information will display in the user's Web browser window:

▼ The Web site you are looking for is unavailable due to its identification configuration settings.

- If you typed the page address in the Address bar, make sure that it is spelled correctly.

- Click the Back button to try another link.

▲ HTTP 404.1 – Web site not found.

To fix this issue, the user will want to verify that he or she has the correct site name or IP address for the Web server. If this information checks out, you will need to check the IIS configuration relating to using multiple identities.

1. In Internet Services Manager, open the properties for the Web site exhibiting the problem.

2. Under the Identification tab, verify that the correct IP address and port are listed in the Web Server's Web Site Identification.

3. If multiple Identities are listed, attempt to connect using one of the identities listed or remove the extra identities from the site.

## 404-b

The 404-b error message is a general information message that alludes to the attempted page not being available for one reason or another. You probably are more familiar with this message as a standard 404 error. The 404 (or 404-b) message can relate to a number of problems. When a 404-b error happens, the following information is displayed in the Web browser:

▼ The page you are looking for might have been removed, had its name changed, or is temporarily unavailable.

■ If you typed the page address in the Address bar, make sure that it is spelled correctly.

■ Open the file:// home page, and then look for links to the information you want.

■ Click the Back button to try another link.

▲ HTTP 404 – File not found.

The standard issues, such as typing in the wrong address and the accessed file being missing, are valid concerns. However, there are some IIS-specific errors that can produce this problem. Before delving too deeply into the IIS configuration, verify that the user is trying to access a valid URL or file. If these check out, you'll need to look at the IIS server to fix the problem.

On the IIS server, verify that the following conditions do not exist:

▼ The requested file has been renamed.

■ The requested file has been moved to another location or deleted.

■ The requested file is temporarily unavailable for maintenance, upgrades, or other unknown causes.

■ The requested file does not exist.

■ The requested filename does not exceed 256 characters.

**NOTE:** The Windows 2000 limitation on file naming conventions is 256 characters.

■ The directory being accessed is not hidden.

**NOTE:** Windows 2000 files and directories can be set with a Hidden attribute that effectively hides the resource from those that do not know of its existence.

▲ The file being accessed is not hidden.

## 405

A 405 error number indicates that the user is trying to access the Web site by typing in the Web address, but not specifying a specific document to open. This generally happens when a default document has not been set for the Web address. When this occurs, the user is presented with the following information in the Web browser window:

▼ The page you are looking for cannot be displayed because the page address is incorrect.

■ If you typed the page address in the Address bar, check that it is entered correctly.

■ Open the file:// home page and then look for links to the information you want.

▲ HTTP 405 – Resource not allowed.

For authorization purposes, you might not want a default document set for the Web site. This further ensures that only those people who know about the Web site will be able to access its information. Removing default document information in the IIS configuration settings forces the user to type in the full address along with a specific filename to open in order to gain access. If this scenario is not what you wanted or expected, you must assign a default document type in the IIS settings. To assign a default document:

1.  Run Internet Services Manager.
2.  Navigate to the Web site that is causing the error message.
3.  Right-click and choose Properties from the context menu.
4.  Add the appropriate startup document to the list.

## 406

The 406 error is included with IIS 5.0 for backward compatibility with earlier versions. There was an issue when accessing files other than standard HTML, such as image and audio files, without first browsing a Web page. If you receive this error, identify that the page being accessed has the appropriate HTML header in place.

When this error message becomes valid, the following will be displayed to the user:

▼ The resource you are looking for cannot be opened by your browser.

■ Click the Back button to try another link.

■ If you believe you should be able to view this directory or page, please contact the Web site administrator by using the e-mail address or phone number listed on the file:// home page.

▲ HTTP Error 406 – Not acceptable.

## 407

If a 407 error message is displayed, surely a proxy server is in use somewhere on the connection to the Web site. The following information will be displayed to the user in the Web browser window:

▼ You must authenticate with a proxy server before this request can be serviced.

■ Log on to your proxy server and try again.

■ If you believe you should be able to view this directory or page, please contact the Web site administrator by using the e-mail address or phone number listed on the file:// home page.

▲ HTTP 407 – Proxy Authentication Required.

This error is returned when access to a Web site is attempted through a proxy server that has access control turned on while using Basic Authentication. The Web proxy, through a 407 HTTP response, requests logon credentials from the browser client. The client provides the credentials or, in the case of a downstream Web proxy, the proxy server itself might provide the credentials. If the upstream proxy server does not allow the credentials used by the client or by the downstream proxy server, this error will be displayed.

**NOTE:** Proxy servers generally exist for companies to add security services for the network as it connects the company to the Internet. A downstream proxy server is the initial connection that travels out of the internal network; the upstream proxy server is the destination connection.

This issue can be resolved by passing the correct credentials to the proxy server. Contact the administrator of the proxy server and verify that the account has permission to use the proxy server. An ultimate solution would be to enable Anonymous authentication on the proxy server computer, but this might not be the preferred security method for the owner of the proxy server.

## 410

The 410 error message indicates that the Web site administrator has permanently removed the resource to which you are attempting access, and that he or she has issued a 410 error manually to let visitors know. The resource being accessed is not available on the Web server and will not be available in the future. When this situation occurs, the following information will be displayed to the user:

▼   The page you are looking for has been removed.

■   You might find the information you need by opening the file:// home page and then linking to a similar page.

▲   HTTP Error 410 – Permanently not available.

The 410 error is reserved for use by the Web server administrator to let the visitor know that the resource that is being requested will no longer be available at the URL that was used. This error should be used in instances where a typical HTTP 404 – Page Not Found message is not entirely correct because it is known that the resource will never be available at the specified URL again.

## 414

The 414 error should signal an alarm that the IIS server might be experiencing an attack from a hacker. When this situation exists, the following information will be displayed in the user's Web browser:

▼   There is a problem with the page you are trying to reach and it cannot be displayed.

■   Open the file:// home page; then look for links to the information you want.

■   Click the Refresh button or try again later.

▲   HTTP 414 – Request – URI Too Long.

Basically, the server is refusing to service the request because the Request – URI is too long. This rare condition is likely to occur in the following situations:

▼ A client has improperly converted a POST request to a GET request with long query information.

■ A client has encountered a redirection problem (for example, a redirected URL prefix that points to a suffix of itself).

▲ The server is under attack by a client attempting to exploit security holes present in some servers that use fixed-length buffers to read or manipulate the Request – URI.

IIS checks the string length of the URI and does not service a request when the URI is longer than expected. This is a security feature built into IIS 5.0, which attempts to identify and halt outside attacks on the Web site.

# 500

When an error message of 500 displays, you should be concerned because something is amiss with the IIS server itself. A 500 error indicates that configuration settings for the IIS server have been altered or have been set up incorrectly. The following information will be displayed to the user:

▼ There is a problem with the page you are trying to reach and it cannot be displayed.

■ Open the file:// home page, and then look for links to the information you want.

■ Click the Refresh button, or try again later.

▲ HTTP 500 – Internal server error.

This error message will generally indicate that something has changed on the Web site. An entire Web directory could have been deleted, security settings could have changed, or the Web services themselves may have stopped with an error and not started back up. Your best bet is to ask around and determine if anyone has manipulated the IIS server settings recently and find out what changes were made. Modify the settings that were changed back to the operable state, and then handcuff the responsible individual to a chair.

## 500-11

The 500-11 error message is a useful tool. With IIS 5.0 this error message indicates to the user that the server is being shut down and they should try later to access the Web site. This does not indicate that the server will be unavailable indefinitely; only that the server is shutting down for one reason or another—usually for a regular maintenance cycle. The following information will be displayed in the user's Web browser window:

▼ There is a problem with the page you are trying to reach and it cannot be displayed.

■ Click the Refresh button or try again later.

■ Open the file:// home page, and then look for links to the information you want.

▲ HTTP Error 500-11 – Server shutting down.

## 500-12

When the 500-12 error message is displayed to the user, the Web services are restarting or recycling and he or she should attempt access to the Web page relatively soon. When you are performing a recycle of the IIS services, this error message can help the user understand that the Web page will once again be available shortly. The following information will be displayed to the user as the services are restarting:

▼ There is a problem with the page you are trying to reach and it cannot be displayed.

■ Click the Refresh button or try again later; it does not normally take a long time for an application to restart.

■ Open the file:// home page; then look for links to the information you want.

▲ HTTP Error 500-12 – Application Restarting.

> *NOTE:* This error message also can be caused by anti-virus software with aggressive scanning turned on. When anti-virus software scans an IIS Web application, IIS might behave as if the global.asa has been modified and restart the Web application. Turning off virus scanning on the global.asa file might help resolve this issue. If a client GET request is made during this time, the Web server will return a 500-12 error.

## 500-13

If a user receives a 500-13 error message, you should immediately identify any performance issues the IIS Web server is experiencing. 500-13 indicates that the server is not able to handle the amount of incoming requests; the user will receive the following information:

▼ There is a problem with the page you are trying to reach and it cannot be displayed.

■ Open the file:// home page, and then look for links to the information you want.

■ Click the Refresh button, or try again later.

▲ HTTP Error 500-13 – Server too busy.

Identify the specific performance issues the IIS server might be experiencing by utilizing Windows 2000 Performance Monitor. Where performance inadequacies are found, you will want to either replace or upgrade equipment. For example, if the disk has become too full, you are running out of RAM, the network card is not keeping up with requests, or the processor is getting hit hard, you'll want to upgrade the specific component to continue to provide Web services. You also might want to consider this the time to implement load balancing.

## 500-15

If a user reports a 500-15 error message, keep an eye trained on them. This indicates that they have typed in the address for the Web site and also have included the global.asa file in the address line. The global.asa file is a site-wide configuration file that will not allow access via a Web browser. If this file has been entered into the Web address, the user might be attempting to hack into the Web site. The following information will display in the Web browser under this scenario:

▼ There is a problem with the page you are trying to reach and it cannot be displayed.

■ Edit the page address in the Address bar to remove global.asa and press ENTER.

■ If a link brought you to this Web page, contact that Web site's administrator.

■ Open the file:// home page; then look for links to the information you want.

■ If you believe you should be able to view this directory or page, please contact the Web site administrator by using the e-mail address or phone number listed on the file:// home page.

▲ HTTP Error 500-15 – Requests for global.asa not allowed.

## 500-100

When a 500-100 error message is displayed in the Web browser, there is some type of ASP connection problem on the IIS server. In fact, the 500-100 error message is generated by an ASP document. The following information will be displayed in the Web browser window:

▼ There is a problem with the page you are trying to reach and it cannot be displayed.

■ Click the Refresh button, or try again later.

■ Open the file:// home page, and then look for links to the information you want.

▲ HTTP 500-100 – Internal Server Error – ASP error.

This error occurs because a dynamic link library (DLL) that is required by the Microsoft Data Access Components is not registered.

To resolve the problem you will need to manually register the offending DLL with the operating system. To do this:

1. At a command prompt, change to the C:\Program Files\Common Files\System\OLE DB folder.

2. At a command prompt type the following command: **regsvr32 dllname.dll**.

3. You should receive confirmation that the DLL is registered successfully.

ASP can use several different DLL files for connection services. The specific DLL file will depend on the type of connection you are making. As an example, some of the more common DLL files and their locations are in the following list:

```
Microsoft ISAM 1.1 OLE DB Provider
Provider=Microsoft.ISAM.OLEDB.1.1
C:\WINNT\System32\Msisam11.dll
C:\WINNT\System32\Msuni11.dll

Microsoft Jet 3.51 OLE DB Provider
Provider=Microsoft.Jet.OLEDB.3.51
C:\Program Files\Common Files\System\OLE DB\Msjtor35.dll
C:\WINNT\System32\Msjt4jlt.dll
C:\WINNT\System32\Msjter35.dll
C:\WINNT\System32\Msjint35.dll

Microsoft Jet 4.0 OLE DB Provider
Provider=Microsoft.Jet.OLEDB.4.0
C:\WINNT\System32\Msjetoledb40.dll
C:\WINNT\System32\Msjet40.dll
C:\WINNT\System32\Mswstr10.dll
C:\WINNT\System32\Msjter40.dll
C:\WINNT\System32\Msjint40.dll

Microsoft OLE DB Provider for Indexing Service
Provider=MSIDXS.1
C:\WINNT\System32\Query.dll
```

Internet Publishing

Provider=MSDAIPP.DSO.1

C:\Program Files\Common Files\System\OLE DB\Msdaipp.dll

C:\WINNT\System32\Wininet.dll

C:\WINNT\System32\Shlwapi.dll

C:\WINNT\System32\Version.dll

C:\WINNT\System32\Lz32.dll

C:\WINNT\System32\Shell32.dll


Microsoft OLE DB Provider for ODBC Drivers

Provider=MSDASQL.1

C:\Program Files\Common Files\System\OLE DB\Msdasql.dll

C:\Program Files\Common Files\System\OLE DB\Msdatl2.dll

C:\Program Files\Common Files\System\OLE DB\Msdasqlr.dll

C:\Program Files\Common Files\System\Msadc\Msadce.dll

C:\Program Files\Common Files\system\Msadc\Msadcer.dll

C:\WINNT\System32\Odbc32.dll

C:\WINNT\System32\Comdlg32.dll

C:\WINNT\System32\Odbcint.dll


Microsoft OLE DB Provider for OLAP Services

Provider=MSOLAP.1

C:\Program Files\Common Files\System\OLE DB\MSOLAP.DLL

C:\Program Files\Common Files\System\OLE DB\Msolapr.dll

C:\Program Files\Common Files\system\OLE DB\msdaosp.dll

C:\WINNT\System32\Security.dll

C:\WINNT\System32\Sqlwoa.dll

C:\WINNT\System32\Sqlwid.dll

C:\WINNT\System32\Nddeapi.dll

C:\WINNT\System32\Winspool.drv

C:\WINNT\System32\Msv1_0.dll


Microsoft OLE DB Provider for Oracle

Provider=MSDAORA.1

C:\Program Files\Common Files\System\OLE DB\Msdaora.dll

C:\WINNT\System32\Mtxoci.dll

```
Microsoft OLE DB Provider for SQL Server
Provider=SQLOLEDB.1
C:\Program Files\Common Files\System\OLE DB\Sqloledb.dll
C:\WINNT\System32\Dbnmpntw.dll

MSDataShape
Provider=MSDataShape.1
C:\Program Files\Common Files\System\Msadc\Msadds.dll
C:\Program Files\Common Files\System\Msadc\Msaddsr.dll

OLE DB Provider for Microsoft Directory Services
Provider=ADsDSOObject
C:\WINNT\System32\Activeds.dll
C:\WINNT\System32\Adsldpc.dll
```

# 501

A 501 error message can indicate a couple different issues with the content available on the IIS server: one is an issue with downloading files; the other is the method that the Web page uses to fulfill the client request. When a 501 scenario happens, the following information will be displayed to the visitor:

▼ The page you are trying to reach cannot be retrieved.

■ Open the file:// home page, and then look for links to the information you want.

■ Click the Refresh button, or try again later.

▲ Error 501 – Not implemented.

To understand which issue is resulting in the 501 error message, you need only to identify what the user is attempting to do. If he or she is attempting to download a file, the size of the requested file is too large. IIS restricts file download size to 4GB. This file size actually is very large and in reality could take days to download. If the user needs to download a file that is larger than 4GB, consider minimizing the file size by using an industry application that uses compression algorithms to reduce the overall size. One popular compression application is WinZip (http://www.winzip.com) from WinZip Computing, Inc.

If the user is attempting only to access a Web page, there is something wrong with the HTML code in the Web page itself. IIS supports many different HTML tags and HTTP requests; however, there are restrictions on types. Table 16-1 represents the allowed IIS methods and protocols.

# 502

The 502 error message indicates there is an issue with a script that runs on the IIS server. The *Bad Gateway* message that accompanies the error number really relates to the *Common Gateway Interface* (CGI) component

| Method | Protocol | RFC |
|---|---|---|
| CONNECT | HTTP | 2616 |
| COPY | WEBDAV | 2518 |
| DELETE | HTTP | 2616 |
| GET | HTTP | 2616 |
| HEAD | HTTP | 2616 |
| LOCK | WEBDAV | 2518 |
| MKCOL | WEBDAV | 2518 |
| MOVE | WEBDAV | 2518 |
| OPTIONS | HTTP | 2616 |
| POST | HTTP | 2616 |
| PROPFIND | WEBDAV | 2518 |
| PROPPATCH | WEBDAV | 2518 |
| PUT | HTTP | 2616 |
| TRACE | HTTP | 2616 |
| UNLOCK | WEBDAV | 2518 |

**Table 16-1.** IIS Connection Restricted Methods and Protocols

instead of an actual network gateway, as it is sometimes assumed. When the 502 error occurs, the following information is displayed to the user in the Web browser window:

▼ There is a problem with the page you are trying to reach and it cannot be displayed.

■ Click the Refresh button, or try again later.

■ Open the file:// home page, and then look for links to the information you want.

■ If you believe you should be able to view this directory or page, please contact the Web site administrator by using the e-mail address or phone number listed on the file:// home page.

▲ HTTP 502 – Bad Gateway.

One issue that commonly results in a 502 error number is that the IIS server tries to run a VBScript under the CGI context. This occurs because the scripting engine typically is executed in the security context of the IUSR_MachineName account created by IIS when it is installed. However, Cscript.exe (the scripting engine) requires the presence of certain registry entries for the user context that it runs under. Because an HKEY_CURRENT_USER hive is created for the IUSR_Machine account, IIS loads the HKEY_USERS\.DEFAULT hive in its place. Still, the HKEY_USERS\.DEFAULT hive does not contain the necessary keys and entries for the scripting engine.

To fix this issue, follow these steps:

1. In the Registry Editor, create the following registry keys and entries:
   HKEY_USERS\.DEFAULT\Software\Microsoft\Windows Scripting Host
   HKEY_USERS\.DEFAULT\Software\Microsoft\Windows Scripting Host\Settings

2. Make sure that the Everyone group has Read access to these two registry keys.

3. Under the HKEY_USERS\.DEFAULT\Software\
   Microsoft\Windows Scripting Host\Settings registry
   key, add the following:

   ```
   BatchMode: REG_DWORD: 0
   DisplayLogo: REG_DWORD: 0
   Timeout: REG_DWORD: 0
   ```

4. Open a command window and go to the Inetpub\AdminScripts
   directory.

5. Type the following commands with the following syntax:

   ```
   cscript adsutil.vbs SET w3svc/CreateCGIWithNewConsole "1"
   cscript adsutil.vbs SET w3svc/CreateProcessAsUser "0"
   ```

6. Copy the .vbs script file to a virtual directory on the server
   that has execute/script permissions. By default, the Scripts
   directory has the necessary permissions.

## SUMMARY

Understandably, there will be problems with any Web server. Microsoft
has done an admirable job of isolating problems that can occur with
IIS 5.0 and providing descriptive information for determining where
the problem exists and how to fix it. But, to completely identify where
the problem exists, you have to understand the information that is
being relayed.

Using this chapter, you should be able to easily determine where
a problem lies, whether it resides with the client or with the IIS server.
Additionally, if it is an IIS server problem, you can quickly identify
the steps to resolve the problem. This chapter gives you a head start
for resolving issues that can creep up, by minimizing the time you need
to fix them. And, you will be able to better understand why those
users complain about not being able to connect to the Web site.

# CHAPTER 17

## IIS 5.0 Certification Requirements

The Microsoft Certified Systems Engineer (MCSE) qualification is one of the most sought-after industry certifications. With the majority of the industry running Microsoft products, becoming an MCSE is almost a requirement for anyone wanting to further his or her career. It seems that since the beginning of our history the American economy has been fueled by people who slave over textbooks late into the night, drink gallons of coffee, and take exams with eyes half-open (or half-closed, depending on your perception). The four-year college degree has been the cornerstone of hiring practices; potential employers generally have taken a stack of resumes and separated them into two distinct piles: those with a college degree, and those without.

A recent study by the Alexis de Tocqueville Institution (http://www.adti.net/) indicates that this business behavior and hiring practice might be steadily losing ground. The study shows that now companies are more willing to fill IT positions with MCSEs rather than people who have a four-year college degree. To complete the study, human resources managers in a few sectors of the corporate industry were randomly solicited by telemarketers; these sectors included the Fortune 500, the Inc. 500, and tech startups.

For this unique study the human resources managers were asked the following questions:

▼ Are you familiar with the MCSE program?

■ Is MCSE certification an acceptable qualification for positions in your organization?

■ Do you feel that MCSEs, when compared to employees with four-year college degrees, are More/Equally/or Less successful in tech careers at your company?

■ Does your company provide incentives for current employees to become certified?

▲ Are MCSEs successfully pursuing careers at your firm?

Based on this group of questions, only one received a score below 50 percent. That was number 4 (providing incentives to employees to become certified). Even more interesting, the study indicates that the Inc. 500 reflected the most positive answers. It further indicates that the older sect of corporate employees, those who entered the company with pen and paper, now are being replaced by people who are comfortable with the computer age and fluent in computer operations. The corporate world finally understands that technology is critical to business success; it is this evolved mindset that has contributed to the surge of certification requirements for hiring qualified technical staff.

The full study can be downloaded in Adobe Acrobat format from the Alexis de Tocqueville Institution Web site at the following link: http://www.adti.net/html_files/technology/mcsestudyfull.pdf. This study is a must-read for anyone in the technology field making an initial career decision or considering a change. Whether you are embarking on a new career or refreshing an old one, reading this full text will excite you about the options that are available.

# CHANGES IN IIS CERTIFICATION

When IIS 4.0 was the current revision of Microsoft's Internet server software, you had the option of including specific IIS components in the MCSE testing process. The MCSE + Internet certification enabled IT professionals to become current on Microsoft operating systems and gain Internet expertise. Employers who wanted to get their companies' Web presence online quickly or wanted to build efficient Intranets sought people with this certification.

Early in 2001, Microsoft announced that the MCSE + Internet certification would change. The primary reason for the change is the release of Windows 2000 and the insistence that Windows 2000 should be the operating system of choice for companies. Another reason for the change is the way Internet features are integrated into Windows 2000. Now, when you strive for your MCSE certification, you are required to become IIS proficient. Because IIS now is included with Windows 2000 as part of the operating system's installation, you must have some knowledge of IIS 5.0 to pass the MCSE certification path.

Microsoft's new certification path includes seven tests, broken down into four Core Exams, one Design Core Exam, and two Elective Exams. Basically, Microsoft requires the four Core Exams, but allows you to choose from a selection of Design Core Exams and Elective Exams. Use Table 17-1 to better understand the tests and courses available to help you attain your MCSE certification.

| Core Exams | | |
|---|---|---|
| **Test Number** | **Description** | **Course Number** |
| 70-210 | Installing, Configuring, and Administering Microsoft Windows 2000 Professional | 2151, 2152 |
| 70-215 | Installing, Configuring, and Administering Microsoft Windows 2000 Server | 2151, 2152 |
| 70-216 | Implementing and Administering a Microsoft Windows 2000 Network Infrastructure | 2153 |
| 70-217 | Implementing and Administering a Microsoft Windows 2000 Directory Services Infrastructure | 2154 |
| **Design Core Exams (Choose One)** | | |
| 70-219 | Designing a Microsoft Windows 2000 Directory Services Infrastructure | 1561 |
| 70-220 | Designing Security for a Microsoft Windows 2000 Network | 2150 |
| 70-221 | Designing a Microsoft Windows 2000 Network Infrastructure | 1562 |
| 70-226 | Designing Highly Available Web Solutions with Microsoft Windows 2000 Server Technologies | 2088 |

**Table 17-1.**    Microsoft MCSE Required and Optional Exams

| Test Number | Description | Course Number |
|---|---|---|
| | **Elective Exams (Choose Two)** | |
| 70-222 | Migrating from Microsoft Windows NT 4.0 to Microsoft Windows 2000 | 2010 |
| 70-223 | Installing, Configuring, and Administering Microsoft Clustering Services by Using Microsoft Windows 2000 Advanced Server | 2087 |
| 70-224 | Installing, Configuring, and Administering Microsoft Exchange 2000 | 1572 |
| 70-228 | Installing, Configuring, and Administering Microsoft SQL Server 2000 Enterprise Edition | 2072 |

**Table 17-1.**    Microsoft MCSE Required and Optional Exams *(continued)*

**NOTE:**   For those candidates who have passed the NT 4.0 exams 70-067, 70-068, and 70-073, Microsoft offers a Windows 2000 Accelerated Exam (70-240). Utilizing this exam enables those who have worked hard to pass the NT exams to upgrade their certifications without taking all four Core Exams. Be prepared! The accelerated exam is not an easy way into the Windows 2000 certification. You still must be proficient in the topics covered in the Core Exam Courses to pass this test. In addition, you can take the exam free of charge *only* once, no matter whether you pass or fail.

If you look closely at Table 17-1, in the Design Core Exams section you will see a specific exam and course that pertains to IIS 5.0: Designing Highly Available Web Solutions with Microsoft Windows 2000 Server Technologies. This exam explicitly replaces the Internet exams included in the old MCSE + Internet MCSE track. As of this writing, the new exam is in beta with a public availability slated for August 2001.

When you decide to trek down the MCSE path, keep a goal in mind. You should choose Design Core Exams and Electives based on your current job requirements or a job that you have your eye on. For example, if your current job would be enhanced by in-depth Web expertise with database connections, choose the following:

▼ Core Exams

■ Designing Highly Available Web Solutions with Microsoft Windows 2000 Server Technologies

■ Installing, Configuring, and Administering Microsoft Clustering Services by Using Microsoft Windows 2000 Advanced Server

▲ Installing, Configuring, and Administering Microsoft SQL Server 2000 Enterprise Edition

## DESIGNING HIGHLY AVAILABLE WEB SOLUTIONS WITH MICROSOFT WINDOWS 2000 SERVER TECHNOLOGIES

If your goal is to become proficient in Microsoft's Web technologies, you not only need to understand IIS 5.0; you must become very comfortable with Windows 2000. Taking the MCSE track to be a Web professional can lead to a rewarding job, both mentally and monetarily. The Internet is everywhere. It is being ported to different types of devices such as cell phones, pagers, and *personal digital assistants* (PDAs). Becoming certified in Internet technologies is a smart career decision as the Internet is constantly evolving and expanding, and will be an industry force for a long time to come. Because Microsoft basically has reinvented its own offerings to have a direct Internet flair, and because Microsoft has such a large market share, it makes complete sense to select MCSE as the Internet certification of choice.

As described in the previous section of this chapter, the Designing Highly Available Web Solutions with Microsoft Windows 2000 Server Technologies course and exam is the Design Core selection you will want to focus on to achieve the MCSE Internet certification. In the remainder of this chapter you will find the topics that this course covers and the knowledge you must obtain to pass the exam.

Passing this exam is a tough accomplishment—one that takes more effort than simply cramming the night before your scheduled sitting. The exam takes everything you have learned about Windows 2000 in the previous Core Exams and applies the knowledge toward Web solutions. You can never be confident how your particular test will be arranged—each one is different—so you need to be prepared in all of the applicable areas outlined in the rest of this chapter. Most of the following topics are covered in previous chapters of this book; however, there are some items that are specific to Windows 2000 that can be found only in offerings specific to the topic. If you find anything that piques your interest and you definitely would like to learn more, purchasing a book that is specific to the topic will give you an edge that will carry over into studying and passing the exam.

# Designing Cluster and Server Architectures for Web Solutions

One of the first items you will be faced with when taking the Windows 2000 Web course is designing a clustering environment. As outlined previously, Network Load Balancing and Server Clustering are key technologies that extend the performance and availability of the Web server. It's no surprise that a course and exam on designing highly available Web solutions would require you to finally come to terms with these technologies.

Some of the general topics that are covered include designing Network Load Balancing solutions to improve availability, scalability, and fault tolerance. Some specific components considerations to tuck away into your long-term memory are the number of hosts, the number of clusters, the placement of servers, multicast versus unicast, failover strategy, priority, affinity, filtering, load weighting, and application types. Each of these topics is covered in course number 2088.

## Design Cluster Service Cluster Solutions to Improve Fault Tolerance

In addition to the general topics of server clustering and load balancing, you should earmark specific considerations for designing cluster solutions for fault tolerance issues. These issues include the number of nodes, the placement of servers on the network, cluster resource groups, fail-over and failback strategies, active/active, active/passive, application types, and dependencies. You should be prepared to exhibit a brief understanding of the technologies and you will be required to provide details of the specific components that make up the technologies.

## Design Data Storage for High Availability

Once you have mastered the knowledge for server clustering and network load balancing, it's on to learning about designing a data warehouse capable of providing long-term access and massive storage capability. Some considerations include *Redundant Array of Independent Disks* (RAID) and *storage area networks* (SANs).

RAID is a type of redundant disk organization technology. RAID offers many advantages, including a safe means of storing data, easy addition of disk capacity, and enhanced disk drive performance. RAID brings improved performance and reliability to a system's hard disk subsystem.

SANs are multiserver, multistorage networks and can grow larger than 400 terrabytes. A SAN acts as a secondary network to a LAN. Every server that needs access to the SAN has a fiber channel connection to the SAN. This secondary network relieves the main network of massive data transfer loads because backup traffic occurs between storage devices inside the SAN.

## Design a System Management and Monitoring Strategy

Any high-level system in which efficient and reliable operation is critical needs some type of proactive monitoring and reporting mechanism in place. Imagine the phone ringing in the middle of the night because the Web site is down. Now, imagine a full night's sleep because you were alerted to a potential problem earlier in the day and you spent an extra 10 minutes after work to alleviate the issues. Part of passing the exam is knowing how to design and implement a mechanism that ensures this level of monitoring and alerting.

To pass this exam you must be familiar with performance monitoring, event monitoring, Windows 2000 services, data analysis, and Windows Management Instrumentation (WMI). Understanding these key components will ensure your success when attaining your Web certification.

### Design a Disaster Recovery Strategy

Because of the state of industry technology, even when you have taken the most tedious steps to ensure you have the best hardware and software and that it is all configured optimally, outages can happen. *Never trust technology.* Use that statement and build a disaster recovery strategy around it. To pass the Web exam you must be able to proficiently create a plan that minimizes your Web server's downtime in the event of a disaster. There's nothing like a flawless backup and recovery scheme to keep you employed, and retaining this knowledge is critical to passing the exam.

## Designing a Highly Available Network Infrastructure

In addition to creating a server environment that ensures the highest possible availability for your Web site, the Web exam requires that you retain the knowledge for building a network infrastructure capable of supporting a multitude of traffic. The exam highlights several key areas of the network infrastructure that you should have covered in more detail in the Core Exams. These areas include designing a TCP/IP network, designing a highly available network topology, planning server configurations, and analyzing and designing end-to-end bandwidth requirements.

### Design a TCP/IP Network Infrastructure

Part of designing a Windows 2000 infrastructure is understanding the TCP/IP services built into it. To pass the Web exam you must have developed this knowledge. Internet sites rely on TCP/IP as the communication method to and from the connected client. To pass the exam for this area you will need a deep understanding of subnet addressing, DNS hierarchy and naming, DHCP server environment, and routed and switched environments.

## Design a Highly Available Network Topology

Building a TCP/IP network infrastructure is only part of building a highly available Web site, so the exam requires that you also be comfortable with building redundancy into the infrastructure. Additional pieces of the TCP/IP component include designing redundant paths, redundant services, and redundant components. Putting this knowledge to use during the exam will help you attain your MCSE certification for Web services.

## Plan Server Configurations

Any network infrastructure needs a final connection point. Providing end-to-end connections is nothing unless there is a destination. In studying for the Web exam you also have to cover specific server configurations that help make the overall network scheme work. This part of the network infrastructure includes network adapters, cluster communication, connectivity, and bandwidth as they relate to the Web server itself. Consider these questions:

▼ What kind of network adapters will maximize connectivity to the Web site?

■ How will your server configuration improve server clustering?

▲ What steps can you take to ensure that the server can handle the number requests flowing from the network?

# Planning Capacity Requirements

In addition to designing a network and server configuration that mesh correctly to provide high capacity, you also will be required to show a working knowledge of how to formulate the requirements. Primarily, you will need to prove your suggestions are correct by outlining a few key elements.

## Calculate Network, Server, and Cluster Capacity

One aspect of proving your network and server evaluations are correct is to show the calculations that accurately represent the proper size of the network, server, and clustering. Some of the important topics to cover in this area are the server memory, CPU, total cost, flexibility, manageability, application scalability, and client/server and server/server communications.

## Design an Upgrade Strategy for Networks, Servers, and Clusters

As part of the overall capacity planning, you should be familiar with new installations and upgrades of the current infrastructure. Some things to consider for this area are showing the knowledge of how to scale up and scale out. This means you should know how to increase the size of the network and server, and understand how these can be further improved by building redundancy in separate locations. For example, if you are upgrading a current Intranet, it would make sense to offload some of the Web service processing to locations closer to the connecting user. Replicating, or mirroring, your Web server content to different locations allow the user to minimize the number of hops to access data stored in a Web environment.

## Calculate Storage Requirements

As mentioned earlier, it's important to have a good understanding of the storage requirements for the Web server. Taking this even further, the Web exam will require you to have in-depth knowledge of how to calculate the storage requirements. Other considerations related to this section of the exam include disk placement, the correct RAID level for the situation, and redundancy.

## Design Directory Services

Important to the overall capacity requirements is the directory services that you implement. The server and network capacity requirements will change depending on the directory type you use. The exam will ask you to demonstrate good working knowledge of the different directory types and the different configurations for optimizing each one. The considerations for this portion of the exam include understanding the Windows 2000 Active Directory, the *Lightweight Directory Access Protocol* (LDAP), optimizing availability for these directory types, providing continued and prompt authentication, and the proper server sizing to accommodate the different directories.

# Designing Security Strategies for Web Solutions

It seems the hottest topic on the Internet these days is how to secure your Web site against hackers. How secure is your Web site? It should come as no surprise that Microsoft requires a thorough knowledge of security mechanisms to pass the Web exam. One of the more commonly headlined causes of a sabotaged Web site is a poorly implemented or nonexistent security plan. The Web exam requires you to become proficient in the most critical areas of Web security.

## Design an Authentication Strategy

As part of the overall security requirements for the exam, you should become very familiar with the different authentication methods available in IIS 5.0. These authentication methods are based on Internet standards and encompass the spectrum of basic security. For the exam you will need to understand and be able to communicate the following components:

▼ Certificates

■ Anonymous access

■ Directory services

■ Kerberos

▲ Public Key Infrastructure (PKI)

## Design an Authorization Strategy

As well as understanding the different authentication methods, you should concentrate on applying the methods into the real world by being able to design an authorization plan. Different organizations will require the implementation of different methods. You must be able to develop a strategy based on the different scenarios. Focus on such items as group membership, IP blocking, access control lists, and Web content zones.

## Design an Encryption Strategy

In tandem with the authorization methods you must be able to grasp the concepts of encryption to increase the security of communications over the Internet. The underlying network does not provide the best security mechanisms to let it stand on its own. You will need to implement technologies available in IIS 5.0 to provide the most secure Web environment. Passing the Web exam will require that you understand the following technologies:

▼ Internet Protocol Security (IPSec)

■ Secure Socket Layer (SSL)

■ Certificates

■ Encrypting File System (EFS)

▲ Point-to-Point Tunneling Protocol (PPTP)

## Design a Firewall Strategy

Providing security through authentication, authorization methods, and encryption covers only the options local to the Web server. To ensure optimum security you must learn the concepts for configuring the connection between the Web server and the Internet. Understanding how firewalls work ultimately will enable you to diagnose potential security breaches and make decisions that will keep the Web server protected from outside forces.

The Web exam requires you to have in-depth comprehension of the many facets of firewall security. There are a multitude of components that must be considered when creating an overall firewall protection strategy. The Web exam will test you on your ability to develop a solid plan for protecting the Web server at the juncture between the internal network and the outside world. To pass the Web exam you must be very familiar with packet filters, proxy servers, protocol settings, Network Address Translation (NAT), and perimeter networks (also known as *Demilitarized Zones*, DMZs).

### Design a Security Auditing Strategy

Knowing how to build a secure Web environment will enhance your chances for passing the Web exam the first time. However, the MCSE test goes a bit further than just designing the technologies. It also requires that you know how to check and test for possible security breaches. When studying for this portion of the exam, keep these terms close to the cuff: intrusion detection, security, performance, denial of service, logging, auditing, and data risk assessments. Providing an overall auditing strategy is a service that many companies look for. By stuffing this knowledge in your technology toolbox, you'll increase your chances for passing the Web exam and gain a rounded set of abilities that will be an essential requirement for employment in a large number of companies.

## Designing Application and Service Infrastructures for Web Solutions

When building a Web environment that needs to offer high availability, one can assume that there is critical data involved and that front-end applications will serve as the transport between the client and the Web server. The MCSE Web exam also assumes this and requires that you become familiar with some of the Microsoft applications as they pertain to the Web scenario. The topics in this section outline key Microsoft technologies for extending the functionality of the Web as well as technologies that are common among popular Web sites. Placing additional Web-enabled applications on top of the Web services will offer a shortcut to providing rich functionality. For example, creating a Web application that allows employees to record their time and expenses online instead of utilizing an old paper method will prove its worth in a short period of time.

### Design a Microsoft Exchange Messaging Web Integration Strategy

As part of the Web exam you must become familiar with Microsoft Exchange messaging and how you can implement this server application as a Web-enabled service. This portion of the exam focuses specifically on the browser's capability to access the Exchange Web services and configuring *Wireless Access Protocol* (WAP) gateways. WAP gateways enable communication between Exchange Web services and devices that can access the Web through a wireless connection. These devices include cell phones, laptops, and PDAs.

## Design a Database Web Integration Strategy

As described previously, consolidating data using a robust database server such as Microsoft SQL server will allow for centralized administration and the capability to use a Web interface to interact with critical data. When perusing the information in this course, make sure to identify the methods for database access and authentication.

## Design Content and Application Topology

Providing a Web environment that is always accessible is a common concept in the Web course. However, when applications are integrated into the Web service, you also must provide high availability for the applications themselves. The Web exam takes this into account and requires you to explain methods for applying the same concepts of high availability to the installed applications. Pay special attention to factors such as scaling out, load balancing, fault tolerance, deploying and synchronizing Web applications, state management, service placement, and log shipping.

## Design an Application Management and Monitoring Strategy

As we've discussed, a proactive approach to Web monitoring and systems management is a key component to know for passing the Web exam. In accordance, Microsoft requires that you have a full understanding of how to apply this same concept to the applications made available on the Web server. If the Web server is continually available but the applications providing access to data fail, the visiting user will still think that the entire Web site is down.

In this day and age, proactive management is a hotbed topic; those who provide this service will ensure long relationships with their employers. Microsoft understands this; therefore it requires that you become knowledgeable in the area of application monitoring. When studying for this portion of the exam, identify areas that will allow you to successfully describe how to detect failed applications as well as utilize a mechanism to be notified when the failure occurs.

## SUMMARY

Exam 70-226, Designing Highly Available Web Solutions with Microsoft Windows 2000 Server Technologies, is a tough exam. For those interested in obtaining IIS 5.0 Web expertise it is a key component in obtaining the MCSE certification. As you can see from the information contained in this chapter, Microsoft is serious about integrating Web technologies into their products. There are numerous subjects that can be understood only by first having a full comprehension of the Windows 2000 operating system and its associated components. However, anyone who installs, implements, and administers an IIS 5.0 Web server must have expertise in Windows 2000.

# APPENDIX A

## Windows 2000
## Events for IIS 5.0

IIS 5.0 uses its logging features to provide data that will help troubleshoot site problems. Depending on the configuration you use, the logs can be very comprehensive. However, this is just one step in identifying issues. Built on the Windows 2000 platform, when IIS 5.0 enters an error state specific information also is logged in the Windows 2000 Event log files. Utilizing both the IIS 5.0 logs and the Windows 2000 Event logs you can more quickly reach a resolution for error conditions.

The Windows 2000 Event Viewer is the mechanism that records informational, warning, and error events that are communicated by the operating system. The Event Viewer can be accessed by choosing Start | Programs | Administrative Tools | Event Viewer. There are three logs you should be aware of: System, Security, and Application. Each log is accessible using the Event Viewer. IIS 5.0 takes full advantage of these logs because it is tied so closely to the Windows 2000 operating system.

Whenever Windows 2000 starts, logging begins automatically. This is because event logging is an actual Windows 2000 service. You can view the available Windows 2000 services by right-clicking the My Computer icon on the Windows 2000 desktop, choosing Manage, expanding the Services and Applications section, and then highlighting the Services sub-section. The Event Log service is shown in Figure A-1.

The Event Log service is one of the few Windows 2000 services in which you cannot stop, start, or alter its startup parameters. There is a very good reason for this: If logging is not available to the operating system and errors occur that make the computer unusable, you will have no way of knowing what caused the problem; hence, no way of resolving the issue. Because logging is available for determining possible IIS 5.0–related errors, you should have a point of reference to understand the impact of these error messages. Keep the following references handy: the error numbers and meanings associated with Web service events, FTP service events, and Active Server Pages events.

Keep in mind that Windows 2000 logs *everything*. If you are perusing the Event logs and see a large number of recorded events,

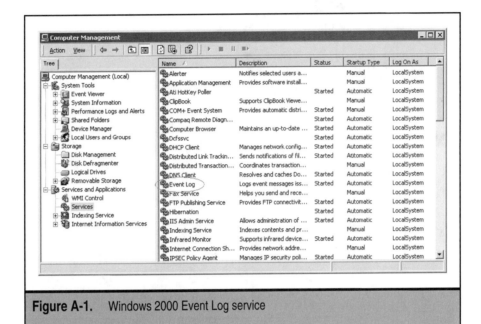

**Figure A-1.**    Windows 2000 Event Log service

don't unnecessarily become alarmed unless you are sure that the IIS server is in an error state. Informational messages are recorded more regularly than error and warning messages. If you would rather not see the informational messages you can use the filtering capabilities of the Event Viewer to configure certain Event ID numbers to prevent them from displaying. To filter out specific Event IDs:

1. Open the Event Viewer program.
2. Right-click the specific log file (Application, Security, or System) and choose Properties from the context menu.
3. Click the Filter tab.
4. Select the Event Source you want to filter.
5. Enter the ID number you want to exclude from displaying in the Event ID field.

The example shown in Figure A-2 filters the Web service ID 16.

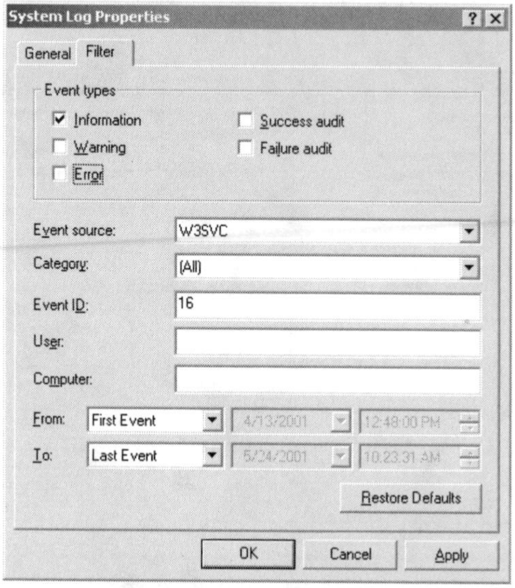

**Figure A-2.** Excluding Event ID

# WEB SERVICE WINDOWS 2000 LOG EVENTS

The IIS 5.0 Web service contains many components. The diagrams in the following sections are broken down by component for quick reference.

## Authentication

The following table represents the Event IDs assigned to the Authentication component of the Web service.

| Windows 2000 Event ID Number | Description |
|---|---|
| 1 | Error loading the map file. |
| 2 | Login failed for a specific user. |
| 3 | Digest authentication: invalid authentication method for a specific user. |

| Windows 2000 Event ID Number | Description |
| --- | --- |
| 4 | Digest authentication: a specific user was not recognized. |
| 5 | Digest authentication: authentication for a specific user has timed out. |

# Logging

The following table includes the Event IDs associated with the logging portion of the Web service.

| Windows 2000 Event ID Number | Description |
| --- | --- |
| 1 | IIS logging has been shut down because a disk full error was encountered. |
| 2 | IIS logging was unable to create a specific directory. |
| 3 | IIS logging was unable to create a specific file. |
| 4 | IIS logging has resumed. |
| 5 | IIS ODBC logging failed to connect to the data source. |
| 100 | The IIS server was unable to log on using a specific Windows account. |
| 101 | The IIS server was unable to access the virtual root for a specific directory. |
| 102 | SQL Logging failed because the IIS server was unable to load the ODBC32.DLL file. |
| 103 | The IIS server was unable to open the ODBC data source using a specific user name. |
| 104 | The logging parameters are too long. |
| 105 | The IIS server administration tool was unable to connect. The server will be unavailable for viewing in the administration tool. |
| 106 | The InetLog Context failed to be created. |

| Windows 2000 Event ID Number | Description |
|---|---|
| 107 | The log object could not be created and logging has failed. This could be because of an incorrect log configuration. |
| 108 | The IIS server was unable to locate the log file directory. |
| 109 | A log record was unable to be written so the IIS server has suspended logging requests. |
| 110 | The IIS server has resumed request logging. |
| 111 | The socket library could not be initialized. |
| 112 | The logging service could not find a specific module to start. |
| 113 | A specific instance has an invalid binding descriptor. |
| 114 | A specific instance has an invalid secure binding descriptor. |
| 115 | The service could not bind a specific instance. |
| 116 | The metabase path could not be opened. |

## Metabase

The following table lists the Metabase Event IDs reported by the Web service.

| Windows 2000 Event ID Number | Description |
|---|---|
| 1 | Cannot access the IIS metabase for a specific server. |
| 2 | The IIS server is not responding to an HTTP query. |
| 800 | MetaData has not been initialized. |
| 801 | The specified metadata was not found. |
| 802 | The version number specified in the metadata storage was not recognized. |
| 803 | The specified meta object path was not found. |

| Windows 2000 Event ID Number | Description |
| --- | --- |
| 804 | A meta object or metadata was specified numerous times and the duplicates were ignored. |
| 805 | Invalid metadata was specified and ignored. |
| 806 | A secure communications path could not be established with the targeted server. |
| 807 | The request could not complete because the path was not inserted into the string. |
| 808 | The GetData method was used to remove the METADATA_SECURE attribute when the DeleteData method should have been used. |
| 809 | Saving the metadata failed prior to backup. |

# ODBC Logging

The Web service's ODBC Logging Event IDs are available in the following table.

| Windows 2000 Event ID Number | Description |
| --- | --- |
| 1 | Unable to perform the query. |
| 2 | The form that was filled in is missing information in a required field. |
| 3 | A query file could not be opened because either it was not found or you have insufficient permissions to access it. |
| 4 | The template file could not be opened; either the file does not exist or your permissions do not allow access to the file. |
| 5 | The template file being accessed contains an else tag without a corresponding if tag. |
| 6 | The template file being accessed contains an endif tag without a corresponding if tag. |

| Windows 2000 Event ID Number | Description |
|---|---|
| 7 | The template being accessed contains an expression that is comparing different types of data. |
| 8 | The template file contains an expression that uses the CONTAINS operator, but the value that is being acted upon is not a string value. |
| 9 | The template file contains an expression that uses a quoted string value, but the close quote is missing. |
| 10 | The template file contains an expression that is unrecognized. |
| 11 | The query file contains an unrecognized field. |
| 12 | The query file contains no data in the Datasource and SQLStatement fields. |
| 13 | The Odbc32.dll library could not be loaded to execute the query. ODBC most likely is not properly installed on the server. |
| 14 | The HTTP method being used is not supported. POST and GET are the only supported methods. |
| 15 | Error executing the query. |
| 16 | The maximum number of SQLStatement fields has been exceeded. |

## Server-Side Includes

The following table lists the Event IDs associated with the Web service's server-side includes (SSI).

| Windows 2000 Event ID Number | Description |
|---|---|
| 1 | Cannot resolve the virtual path. |
| 2 | Error in processing the SSI file. |
| 3 | Invalid SSI tag. |
| 4 | Cannot perform flastmod. |
| 5 | Cannot perform fsize. |

| Windows 2000 Event ID Number | Description |
|---|---|
| 6 | A specific variable cannot be found. |
| 7 | A specific variable cannot be evaluated. |
| 8 | SSI feature not supported. |
| 9 | There was an error handling the SSI file. |
| 10 | The server successfully processed the SSI file. |
| 11 | Failure in processing the SSI file. |
| 12 | Failed to execute a specified command. |
| 13 | A script failed to execute. |
| 14 | An ISAPI extension failed to execute. |
| 16 | The document being accessed has been moved to the specified location. |
| 17 | The child process environment could not be set up. |
| 18 | The child process pipes could not be set up. |
| 19 | A process could not be created. |
| 20 | The #EXEC command timed out. |
| 21 | The #EXEC ISAPI application failed. |
| 22 | The ISAPI application attempted to redirect to a specified location. |
| 23 | #EXEC could be run because the Execute permission was not assigned. |
| 24 | A specific action could not be processed because of permission problems. |
| 25 | The maximum depth of server-side includes has exceeded the allowable number. |
| 26 | An unsupported ServerSupportFunction() has been used. |
| 27 | The CMD option is not enabled for the #EXEC calls in use. |
| 28 | #EXEC calls have been disabled for the virtual path being accessed. |
| 29 | A recursive #INCLUDE chain is being accessed. |

# Web Services

The following table lists the Windows 2000 Event IDs for the Web services.

| Windows 2000 Event ID Number | Description |
|---|---|
| 1 | The HTTP server could not initialize security. |
| 3 | The HTTP server could not initialize the socket library. |
| 4 | The HTTP server could not initialize because of a shortage in available memory. |
| 6 | The HTTP server could not initialize the main connection. |
| 8 | The HTTP server could create a client connection for the specified user. |
| 14 | The DLL used to filter HTTP requests failed. |
| 16 | The script requested for execution failed because of a timeout. |
| 18 | An error occurred when the HTTP server tried to process a specific service-side include file. |
| 19 | An ISAPI application caused an exception that could not be handled by the HTTP server. |
| 20 | The HTTP server could not load the specified ISAPI application. |
| 21 | A server-side include file has exceeded the maximum depth of configured server-side includes. |
| 22 | An attempt to load a filter failed because the SF_NOTIFY_READ_RAW_DATA filter notification was not used. |
| 23 | A global filter was loaded from the server's registry to accommodate compatibility with previous versions of IIS. |
| 26 | Lack of the proper access permissions kept the server from reading a specific file. |
| 27 | The server could not acquire a necessary license for an SSL connection. |

| Windows 2000 Event ID Number | Description |
|---|---|
| 28 | The server halted processing of the application's requests because the out-of-process crashes exceeded the maximum limit. |
| 29 | The server failed to shut down a specific application. |
| 30 | The server was unable to read a specific file because it does not exist. |
| 31 | The server was unable to read a specific file. The description in the Event ID will list a specific Windows error message. |
| 32 | The server was unable to read a specific file because the file exceeds the maximum allowable size. |
| 33 | The server could not allocate a free buffer to read the specific file. |
| 34 | The server was unable to use the PUT function for the specified URL. A backup copy was saved. |
| 35 | The server was unable to use the PUT function for the specified URL. A backup copy could not be saved. |
| 36 | The server failed to load a specific application. |
| 37 | An out-of-process application shut down unexpectedly. |

# Web Application Manager (WAM)

The table in this section describes the Event IDs associated with the Web Application Manager of the Web service.

| Windows 2000 Event ID Number | Description |
|---|---|
| 201 | A WAM instance was started with a specific Process ID. |
| 202 | A WAM instance failed to start. |
| 203 | A WAM instance was shut down. |
| 204 | While processing an ISAPI application the HTTP server encountered an exception it could not handle. |

| Windows 2000 Event ID Number | Description |
| --- | --- |
| 205 | The HTTP server could not load the specific ISAPI application. |

# FTP SERVICE WINDOWS 2000 LOG EVENTS

The following table lists and describes the Windows 2000 Event IDs for the FTP service.

| Windows 2000 Event ID Number | Description |
| --- | --- |
| 1 | The FTP server could not initialize security. |
| 3 | The FTP server could not initialize the socket library. |
| 4 | The FTP server could not initialize because of insufficient usable memory. |
| 5 | The FTP server could not locate the installed FTP/TCP Windows 2000 service. |
| 6 | The FTP server could not create a socket for the main connection services. |
| 7 | The FTP server could not create a thread to service the main connection. |
| 8 | The FTP server could not create a thread to service the connecting user. The user's connection has been terminated. |
| 9 | A call to a system service failed. |
| 10 | A specific user connection has timed out after a precise number of seconds. |
| 11 | An anonymous login request was received from a specific user. |
| 12 | A user logon request was received from a specific user. |
| 13 | A specific user could not log on because access to the home directory could not be established. |

| Windows 2000 Event ID Number | Description |
| --- | --- |
| 14 | A specific user was denied access to the requested directory due to a security change. |
| 1000 | The FTP performance statistics were unable to be collected. |

# ACTIVE SERVER PAGES WINDOWS 2000 LOG EVENTS

The table in this section contains the Event IDs available for specific Active Server Pages messages.

| Windows 2000 Event ID Number | Description |
| --- | --- |
| 100 | The server is out of free memory to process the ASP page. |
| 101 | Unexpected error. |
| 102 | The function expected a string input but none was received. |
| 103 | The function expected a number as the input but a string was used. |
| 104 | The requested operation is not allowed. |
| 105 | An array index is out of the allowable range. |
| 106 | A type mismatch was identified. |
| 107 | Stack overflow. |
| 108 | The specified object could not be created. |
| 109 | Member not found. |
| 110 | An unknown name was identified. |
| 111 | There was an attempt to access an unknown interface. |
| 112 | A missing parameter was detected. |

| Windows 2000 Event ID Number | Description |
| --- | --- |
| 113 | The executed script exceeded the maximum timeout setting. |
| 114 | The application object encountered an incoming object that was not free-threaded. |
| 115 | An external object produced an unexpected error and halted the running script. |
| 116 | The script close tag, %>, was missing from the end of the block. |
| 117 | The running script lacks either of the close script tags (</SCRIPT> or >). |
| 118 | The object close tag is missing from the end of the object block (</OBJECT> or >). |
| 119 | The ClassID or ProgID attribute is missing. |
| 120 | Invalid Runat attribute. |
| 121 | The object tag has an invalid scope. It must be created in the Global.asa file. |
| 122 | The object tag has an invalid scope. |
| 123 | The required ID attribute of the Object tag is missing. |
| 124 | The required Language attribute has not been defined in the Script tag. |
| 125 | The value of a specific attribute has no parameter to define a close. |
| 126 | A specific include file was not found. |
| 127 | The HTML close tag (-->) is missing. |
| 128 | A missing File or Virtual attribute was detected. |
| 129 | The specified scripting language is not installed on the server. |
| 130 | The specified File attribute cannot start with a forward slash or a backslash. |
| 131 | The specified Include file cannot contain '..' to indicate a parent directory. |
| 132 | The selected Active Server Page could not be processed normally. |

| Windows 2000 Event ID Number | Description |
| --- | --- |
| 133 | The object tag has a specific invalid ClassID. |
| 134 | The object has a specific invalid ProgID. |
| 135 | A specific file is included by itself. |
| 136 | A specific object instance is trying to use a name that has been reserved by the system. |
| 137 | An attempt was made to retrieve the Web site's Global script. Script blocks must be contained in the Global.asa procedures. |
| 138 | A nested script block was detected. One script block cannot be positioned inside another script block. |
| 139 | A nested object was detected. One object tag cannot be placed inside another object tag. |
| 140 | The page command (@) is out of order. |
| 141 | The page command (@) has been repeated and can only be used once in each Active Server Page. |
| 142 | A thread token failed to open. |
| 143 | The application attempting to run cannot be found because of an incorrect name. |
| 144 | An initialization error occurred because the page level objects list failed. |
| 145 | The specified new application could not be added. |
| 146 | The specified new session could not be added. |
| 147 | Server error. |
| 148 | The server is too busy to process requests. |
| 149 | The request cannot be completed because the application is restarting. |
| 150 | The Application directory could not be opened. |
| 151 | A change notification event was requested and it could not be created. |
| 152 | An error occurred during the processing of a user's security credentials. |
| 153 | The creation of a new thread failed. |

| Windows 2000 Event ID Number | Description |
|---|---|
| 154 | The specified HTTP headers could not be written or displayed to the client's Web browser. |
| 155 | The requested page's content could not be written or displayed to the client's Web browser. |
| 156 | A header error because of an attempt to resend them when they were already being displayed in the client's Web browser. |
| 157 | Buffering is turned on and cannot be turned off. |
| 158 | An URL is required to complete the request. |
| 159 | Buffering is off and must be turned on to complete the request. |
| 160 | Writing to the log file failed. |
| 161 | The data is mismatched and the conversion of a variant to a string variable failed. |
| 162 | The cookie name "ASPSessionID" is a reserved cookie name and cannot be modified. |
| 163 | A comma was used as a delimiter in a log file. Commas cannot be used within a log entry. |
| 164 | An invalid TimeOut value was specified. |
| 165 | A new SessionID string could not be created. |
| 166 | A request was made to access an object that has not first been initialized. |
| 167 | The Session object could not be initialized. |
| 168 | An attempt was made to store a base object within a Session object. |
| 169 | The information for an object is incomplete and cannot be stored within the Session object in that state. |
| 170 | The session did not delete. |
| 171 | Missing path information was detected. |
| 172 | A physical path cannot be used to define a path parameter; only a virtual path. |

| Windows 2000 Event ID Number | Description |
|---|---|
| 173 | An invalid character was used to define a path parameter. |
| 174 | Either / or \\ was used to define a path parameter; these are disallowed characters. |
| 175 | The '..' characters were used to define a parent path. These are disallowed characters. |
| 176 | A known path was not specified for the MapPath method. |
| 177 | The Server.CreateObject method failed. |
| 178 | The Server.CreateObject method does not have the proper permissions to complete the request. |
| 179 | The Application object could not be initialized. |
| 180 | A base object cannot be stored within the Application object. |
| 181 | An object using the apartment threading model was attempting storage within the Application object. |
| 182 | An object with missing information was attempting storage within the Application object. |
| 183 | An empty cookie was detected. Cookies with empty keys cannot be stored. |
| 184 | The specified cookie is missing a required name. |
| 185 | A default property has not been set for the specified object. |
| 186 | An error occurred while parsing a certificate. |
| 187 | The application was locked by another request so the requested object addition failed. |
| 188 | Objects created using object tags cannot be added to the base session. |
| 189 | Objects created using object tags cannot be added to the base application. |
| 190 | An error occurred while an external object was released. |

| Windows 2000 Event ID Number | Description |
| --- | --- |
| 191 | A trappable error occurred during the OnStartPage method of the external object. |
| 192 | A trappable error occurred during the OnEndPage method of the external object. |
| 193 | An error occurred during the OnStartPage method of the external object. |
| 194 | An error occurred during the OnEndPage method of the external object. |
| 195 | An invalid server method all was established. |
| 197 | An object with the apartment model behavior cannot be added to the base application object. |
| 198 | The request cannot be processed because the server is currently shutting down. |
| 199 | JScript objects cannot be added to the session. |
| 200 | The date specified exceeds the allowable range. The date cannot be before January 1, 1980 or after January 19, 2038. |
| 201 | The scripting language specified in the server's registry cannot be found installed on the server. |
| 202 | The attribute for code page is missing. |
| 203 | The code page attribute that is specified is invalid. |
| 205 | An event for a change notification could not be created. |
| 206 | The BinaryRead method could not be used. |
| 207 | The Request.Form collection cannot be used following a BinaryRead method. |
| 208 | The common version of the Request collection cannot be used following a BinaryRead method. |
| 209 | An unsupported value for the TRANSACTION property was specified. |
| 210 | The method in use has not yet been implemented. |
| 211 | An ASP object was specified that is no longer available. |
| 212 | The buffer cannot be cleared when the Response.Clear method is used after the Response.Flush. |

| Windows 2000 Event ID Number | Description |
| --- | --- |
| 214 | The Path information exceeds the maximum allowable length. |
| 215 | The SESSION property can have a value of only TRUE or FALSE; another value was specified. |
| 216 | The MSDTC service is not running or is not installed. |
| 217 | An object tag contains an invalid scope. Allowable scopes are Page, Session, or Application. |
| 218 | The LCID attribute is missing. |
| 219 | The LCID that was specified is not available. |
| 220 | A location request was made to the GLOBAL.ASA. |
| 221 | The command specified is unknown. |
| 222 | The metadata tab contains information that has an invalid Type Library designation. |
| 223 | The metadata tag contains a Type Library specification that does not correspond with a registry value. |
| 224 | The specified Type Library could not be loaded. |
| 225 | A Type Library Wrapper object could not be created using the information specified in the metadata tags. |
| 226 | An attempt was made to edit the StaticObjects collection at runtime. |
| 227 | The Server.Execute call failed. |
| 228 | The Server.Execute call failed while the page was loading. |
| 229 | The Server.Transfer call failed. |
| 230 | The Server.Transfer call failed while the page was loading. |
| 231 | Server.Execute – An Invalid URL, or a fully qualified absolute URL was used; only relative URLs can be used. |
| 232 | The metadata tag contains invalid cookie information. |

| Windows 2000 Event ID Number | Description |
|---|---|
| 233 | The cookie script source file specified in the metadata tag could not be loaded. |
| 234 | An invalid include directive occurred. |
| 235 | Server.Transfer – An Invalid URL, or a fully-qualified absolute URL was used; only relative URLs can be used. |
| 236 | The metadata tag contains invalid or missing information for the SRC of a cookie. |
| 237 | The metadata tag contains invalid or missing information for the name of a cookie. |
| 238 | No value was specified for a specific attribute. |
| 239 | There was an attempt to use a Unicode ASP file. Unicode files are not supported. |
| 240 | A ScriptEngine created an exception. |
| 241 | The CreateObject created an exception. |
| 242 | A query for either the OnStartPage or OnEndPage failed with an exception. |

# APPENDIX B

## IIS Registry Settings

T he key configuration settings for IIS 5.0 have been migrated to the Metabase, a convenient storage object in the file system, making it easier to back up and restore than when all of the settings were housed in the computer's registry. All of a Web site's personality exists in the Metabase, enabling you to move the entire Web to another computer if necessary. The registry still does house some specific service settings that you should be aware of; modifying this information can help you tweak the global configuration of IIS.

The registry is a hidden database that contains a multitude of settings specific to the operating system and the installed applications. It is a tree-like structure, much like the directory or folder structure you see in Windows Explorer. For example, if you want to identify the last person to log on to the computer, you would navigate down through the registry following this path: HKEY_LOCAL_MACHINE\ SOFTWARE\Microsoft\Windows NT\CurrentVersion\Winlogon\ DefaultUserName. The registry is critical to the computer's operation. Altering one setting could keep the computer from ever booting again, so you have to be careful when sifting through the data.

Access to the registry is accomplished through the Windows 2000 Registry Editor. There are two versions of the Registry Editor on a Windows 2000 computer: Regedt32.exe and Regedit.exe. To access both editors click the Start button, choose Run, type the specific command in the Open field, and click OK.

**NOTE:** Alternatively, you can access each Registry Editor by typing its command in an MS-DOS window.

Regedit.exe is a leftover command from the Windows 9x days, whereas Regedt32.exe is specific to the Windows NT and Windows 2000 operating systems. Although each editor displays the same registry information, there is a big difference between them; this difference is key to choosing which one to use. Folks that use the Regedit.exe version are generally the same people that still use File Manager instead of Windows Explorer in Windows NT (unfortunately, for those people, Microsoft left File Manager out of Windows 2000).

Regedit.exe became a comfortable tool, and everyone knows how hard it is to learn new tricks.

Regedt32.exe was created specifically for the Windows NT and Windows 2000 operating systems, and should be the Registry Editor of choice. Regedt32.exe contains many more options than Regedit.exe. It enables you to print and save registry information whereas Regedit.exe does not. It also includes a Security menu for modifying who has access to the information contained therein. However, probably the best, most useful feature (and the primary reason you should choose this editor) is the Read Only mode. As you become comfortable with the registry, its structure, and the data contained therein, turning on the Read Only mode (shown in Figure B-1) will enable you to safely surf through the registry's many levels without causing excessive harm to the computer's configuration.

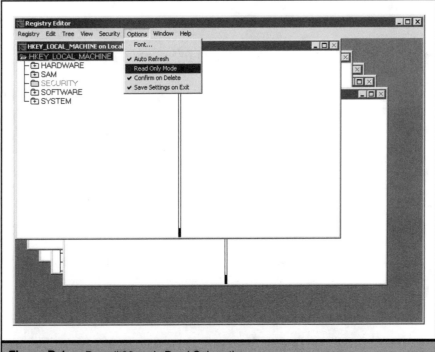

**Figure B-1.**    Regedit32.exe's Read Only option

As the name suggests, the Registry Editor allows you to edit settings contained in the hierarchal database. This means you can add, modify, and delete information displayed in the editor. Data that is stored in the registry comes in five different formats: REG_BINARY, REG_DWORD, REG_EXPAND_SZ, REG_MULTI_SZ, and REG_SZ. It is extremely important to understand these formats, as the computer recognizes the information only when it is in the correct pattern. Table B-1 describes the different registry data types.

The remainder of this appendix lists the registry values assigned to IIS 5.0 and describes what function is attributed to each one.

| Registry Data Type | Description |
| --- | --- |
| REG_BINARY | A base-2 number system in which values are expressed as combinations of two digits: 0 and 1. |
| REG_DWORD | A data type composed of hexadecimal data with a maximum allotted space of 4 bytes. |
| REG_SZ | A group of characters or character bytes handled as a single entity. Computer programs use strings to store and transmit data and commands. Most programming languages consider strings (such as "2674:gstmn") to be distinct from numeric values (such as "470924"). |
| REG_EXPAND_SZ | A REG_SZ that can have expanded value entries. |
| REG_MULTI_SZ | A REG_SZ that can contain multiple value entries. |

**Table B-1.** Registry Data Types

# GLOBAL

The following Global registry entries can be found by navigating to HKEY_LOCAL_MACHINE\SYSTEM\CurrentControlSet\Services\InetInfo\Parameters.

| Identifier | Data Type | Description |
|---|---|---|
| CacheSecurity Descriptor | REG_DWORD | The value can be either a 0 or a 1, with 1 (on) as the default. This registry identifier enables IIS to cache the security information for an object. This allows quicker access to the object because security does not have to be checked every time the object is accessed. |
| CheckCert Revocation | REG_DWORD | The value can be either a 0 or a 1, with 0 (off) as the default. This registry identifier indicates whether or not the IIS 5.0 server itself should check to see if a certificate has been revoked. Normally this is performed over the Internet. Enabling this feature will have a severe performance impact on the server. It should be used only if you are issuing your own certificates. |
| DisableMemory Cache | REG_DWORD | This identifier has a valid value of 0 or 1, with 0 (off) as the default. This value turns on and off server global server caching. |

| Identifier | Data Type | Description |
| --- | --- | --- |
| ListenBackLog | REG_DWORD | This identifier has a valid range of 1-250, with 15 as the default. The value determines the number of active connections remaining in the queue until the server can process them. |
| MaxConcurrency | REG_DWORD | This identifier has a valid range of 0-unlimited, with a default value of 0. The value configures the number of threads assigned to each processor for handling input-output (I/O) functions. |
| MaxPoolThreads | REG_DWORD | This identifier has a valid range of 0-unlimited, with a default value of 4. In this instance, a pool is a group of threads. The value determines how many pools are configured for each processor. For performance reasons you should never set this figure above 20. |
| PoolThreadLimit | REG_DWORD | This identifier has a valid range of 0-unlimited. The default value is calculated by multiplying the specified amount of RAM times 2. This value configures the maximum number of pool threads that can be created. |

| Identifier | Data Type | Description |
|---|---|---|
| MinFileKbSec | REG_DWORD | This identifier has a valid range of 1-8192, with a default value of 1000. The value indicates the length of time the IIS server will wait before disconnecting when sending a file to a client. The total value is calculated by adding the maximum Connection Timeout setting to the size of the actual file; then dividing it by the MinFileKbSec entry. |
| ObjectCacheTTL | REG_DWORD | This identifier has a valid range of 0-unlimited, with a default value of 30 seconds. This value determines the length of time (TTL—time to live) that objects are held in cached memory. |
| ThreadTimeout | REG_DWORD | This identifier has a valid range of 0-unlimited, with a default of 24 * 60 * 60 (24 hours). The value configures the number of seconds that the input-output thread will be held when there is no I/O activity detected by the system. |

| Identifier | Data Type | Description |
|---|---|---|
| UserTokenTTL | REG_DWORD | This identifier has a valid range of 0-0*7FFFFFFF, with a default value of 15 * 60 (15 minutes). When a user authenticates with the system, a token is given that is cached in memory so authentication needs to happen only once per session. The entry indicates the amount of time (in seconds) that the user token is cached after the connection has ended. |

# SERVICE

The Service registry information deals with specific IIS service information that impacts the service itself. These values fall under their own ServiceName value in the HKEY_LOCAL_MACHINE\ SYSTEM\CurrentControlSet\Services\*ServiceName*\Parameters path. In the previous path, the *ServiceName* will be replaced by the actual name of the service. For example, the WWW Service is W3SVC, whereas the FTP Service is MSFTPSVC. Each of the identifiers listed in the following table are attributable to each IIS service.

| Identifier | Data Type | Description |
|---|---|---|
| AllowGuest Access | REG_DWORD | This identifier allows a value of either 1 or 0, with 1 (on) as the default. The value contained in this identifier indicates whether Guest access is allowed for the Web site. You might want to consider setting this to 0 (off) to bolster security. |

| Identifier | Data Type | Description |
|---|---|---|
| EnableSvcLoc | REG_DWORD | This identifier allows a value of 1 or 0, with the default being a 1 (on). When the IIS snap-in is run, each service visible in the console has been registered with the system through a service locator (when the value is 1). This enables the MMC to find the service and load it. |
| Language Engines | REG_SZ | This identifier accepts a string of text. The value in this identifier portrays a specific scripting language installed that does not support the standard Object.Method syntax of the Active Server Pages. |

**NOTE:**   The LanguageEngines identifier is not installed into the registry by default. If you want to use this value you must create it manually. To do so, you must:

1.  Create the specific registry key: HKEY_LOCAL_MACHINE\SYSTEM\CurrentControlSet\Services\W3SVC\ASP\LanguageEngines\*LanguageName.*

2.  Add the following values:

    ■  Identifier: Write

        ■  Data type: REG_SZ

        ■  Value: Response.WriteEquiv |

    ■  Identifier: WriteBlock

        ■  Data type: REG_SZ

        ■  Value: Response.WriteBlockEquiv |

# WWW SERVICE

The following table outlines the registry entries that pertain specifically to the WWW service. These entries are located at: HKEY_LOCAL_MACHINE\SYSTEM\CurrentControlSet\Services\W3SVC\Parameters.

| Identifier | Data Type | Description |
| --- | --- | --- |
| AcceptByteRanges | REG_DWORD | This identifier allows a value of either 1 or 0, with 1 (on) as the default. The value indicates whether the HTTP server will process the Internet standard Range header information for type bytes. |
| AllowSpecial CharsInShell | REG_DWORD | This identifier allows a value of 1 or 0, with 0 (off) as the default. The value determines whether specific file characters can be used in batch and cmd files run on the server. These characters (,;%<>) can pose a serious security risk to the Web site so it's best to leave this as the default. |
| DLCSupport | REG_DWORD | This identifier allows a value of 1 or 0, with 0 (off) as the default. The value configures support for downlevel clients. With this identifier downlevel clients (clients with older Web browsers) can access multiple Web sites sharing a single IP address. |
| DLCCookie NameString | REG_SZ | This identifier accepts a string of text. The value contains the name of a specific Web site that stores a downlevel host menu. |

| Identifier | Data Type | Description |
|---|---|---|
| DLCCookieMenu DocumentString | REG_SZ | This identifier accepts a string of text. The value indicates a specific file name for clients that do not support cookies. This file is attached to all requests (like a cookie) until the session is ended. |
| DLCMungeMenu DocumentString | REG_SZ | This identifier accepts a string of text. The value indicates a specific file name for clients that do not support cookies. This file helps downlevel clients resolve URLs by embedding the host name in the URL. |
| DLCMenuString | REG_SZ | This identifier accepts a string of text. The value stores a special prefix for downlevel clients to better access the URL. |
| LogSuccessful Requests | REG_DWORD | This identifier allows input of a 1 or 0, with a 1 (on) as the default. The value indicates whether the server will log all successful activities on the server. |

| Identifier | Data Type | Description |
|---|---|---|
| SSIEnableCmd Directive | REG_DWORD | This identifier allows input of a 1 or 0, with a 0 (off) as the default. The value is not installed by default so it must be manually created in the registry. This value enables and disables the capability for #exec cmd to be used on the server. The method can be used by hackers to destroy the server, so you will want to consider implementing this registry value. |
| TryExceptDisable | REG_DWORD | This identifier accepts a 1 or 0, with a 0 (off) as the default. Setting this value to 1 is helpful should you need to debug an ISAPI application. With the value set to 1, anytime an ISAPI application causes an exception, the server will stop functioning. |
| UploadReadAhead | REG_DWORD | This identifier allows a range of 0-0*80000000, with a default value of 48 KB. The value indicates the amount of data that will be read by the server before it passes the data to the application. In essence, it stores the specified size of data in memory before releasing it to the server for processing. If you increase this value, consider increasing server RAM. |

| Identifier | Data Type | Description |
|---|---|---|
| UsePoolThreadFor CGI | REG_DWORD | This identifier allows input of a 1 or 0, with a 1 (on) as the default. The value determines whether the IIS 5.0 server allocates a pool thread for CGI processing. |

# FTP SERVICE

The table in this section identifies those registry settings specific to the FTP service. To find these settings navigate to: HKEY_LOCAL_ MACHINE\SYSTEM\CurrentControlSet\Services\MSFTPSVC\ Parameters.

| Identifier | Data Type | Description |
|---|---|---|
| Annotate Directories | REG_DWORD | This identifier accepts a value of 1 or 0, with 0 as the default value. The value determines whether the FTP service will include annotations for the directories contained in the virtual FTP server. These annotations enable administrators to provide better descriptions to visiting users. When this is enabled, the annotations are stored in a file called: ~ftpsvc~.ckm. |

| Identifier | Data Type | Description |
|---|---|---|
| EnablePort Attack | REG_DWORD | This identifier allows the entry of a 1 or 0, with 0 (off) as the default. The default value configures the FTP server to utilize only the default port for connections; thus blocking off all other ports to attack. Enable this only if you want users to connect to the FTP site using alternate ports. |
| LowercaseFiles | REG_DWORD | This identifier accepts a value of 1 or 0, with 0 (off) as the default. With the default value selected for this identifier, files and folder names on the FTP site will keep the letter case under which they were originally stored. |

# APPENDIX C

## WebDAV Publishing

The Web Distributed Authoring and Versioning (WebDAV) technology enables you to install a publishing directory on an IIS 5.0 server. The publishing directory allows easy access to a type of virtual directory to those who are granted authorization. Utilizing WebDAV gives your organization the value of a Web site that accepts documents from many different vehicles. This technology enables you to extend the capabilities of the computers to easily port company information to Web-based services. It also is the tool to use for building a collaborative model within the company.

WebDAV extends the HTTP 1.1 protocol, so it does not work with other services such as FTP. This extension enables clients to publish, lock, and manage resources on a specified Web site. When WebDAV is implemented, a client can easily access the virtual directory as if it were a mapped drive on his or her computer. The WebDAV directory actually is available (to those granted access) through the My Network Places applet on a Windows 2000 computer. Because WebDAV is integrated so tightly with Windows 2000 and IIS 5.0, it can be utilized only if Windows 2000 is running on both the client and the network server. For a client this would mean that Windows 2000 Professional is the minimum operating system requirement.

Because WebDAV enables clients to interact with the publishing directory as if it were a standard mapped network drive, the connected client can

▼ Move and copy files in the WebDAV directory

■ Retrieve and write to a file's properties

■ Lock and unlock a file so that numerous users can share the same file

▲ Use the Search function of the computer to find files with specific attributes

## CREATING THE PUBLISHING DIRECTORY

Installation of WebDAV is performed automatically when IIS 5.0 is installed. Once the WebDAV component is installed you must create your first publishing directory. To create a publishing directory, follow these steps:

1. Create a physical directory on the Windows 2000/IIS 5.0 Server, giving it any name you choose.

**NOTE:**   You can create the physical directory anywhere on the IIS 5.0 server, except in the WWWRoot directory. The WWWRoot directory has specific security permissions that disallow the creation of virtual directories underneath.

2. Open Internet Services Manager and walk through the steps for creating a virtual directory.

3. During the virtual directory setup, make sure to type **WebDAV** as the alias for the virtual directory and link to the physical directory you created.

4. Once the virtual directory is configured you must modify the permissions to allow users to publish. The permissions required for publishing are Read, Write, and Browse.

WebDAV uses the security features of both IIS 5.0 and Windows 2000; thus you can create Windows 2000 Server groups to add user accounts for access to the publishing directory. Taking careful steps to ensure the appropriate permissions are in place can give the required security to the publishing directory. As part of the overall publishing directory configuration, you will need to identify how you wish the clients to connect.

WebDAV uses the specific IIS 5.0 authentication methods for connection. Verify that the IIS 5.0 authentication offerings are configured for optimum security. For example, you probably do not want to allow anonymous access to the publishing directory. This would allow anyone accessing the Web server through a browser to connect and use the publishing directory. Most organizations use WebDAV as a way for separate departments to collaborate and publish Web documents. For this reason you would be required to create a different publishing directory for each department. Leaving the Anonymous access enabled would allow all departments to manipulate all publishing directories. Consider implementing the IIS 5.0 Integrated Windows Authentication method and utilizing the Windows 2000 NTFS security features for access to each publishing directory.

Depending on your requirements, there will be different scenarios to ponder before determining the publishing directory security. The following examples give you a few ideas of what thought processes to take for identifying your Windows 2000 NTFS security needs:

▼ If you require that clients be able to see files and directories, modify and manipulate them; and also be able to perform their own publishing, enable Read, Write, and Directory Browsing.

■ If you require that clients be able to publish information, but no one else should view the published documents, configure the publishing directory with Write *enabled*; Read and Directory Browsing *disabled*.

▲ If you require that clients be able to publish and read Web documents, but force them to know where a file is located without browsing, configure the directory with *Read* and Write *enabled*; Directory Browsing *disabled*.

**NOTE:** Keep in mind that when a Windows 2000 directory share is created, the group Everyone has the Full Control enabled automatically. You will want to remove this group immediately.

## SEARCHING THE PUBLISHING DIRECTORY

In addition to applying the appropriate Windows 2000 and IIS 5.0 rights, if you plan to allow clients to search the publishing directory, you must enable the Indexing Service. The Indexing Service runs in the background on the Windows 2000 Server. It constantly updates a file directory cache so that searches can be performed, and performed more quickly. To enable the Indexing Service, complete the following tasks:

1. The Component Services applet (choose Start | Programs | Administrative Tools).

2. The Computer Management applet (choose Start | Programs | Administrative Tools).

3. The Services applet (select Start | Programs | Administrative Tools).

4. Right-click the My Computer icon and choose Manage from the context menu.

5. In an MS-DOS command window, type **net start cisvc**.

You will need to allow the Indexing Service to run for a period of time the first time it is enabled. This gives the Windows 2000 Server the necessary time to gather file and directory information. The length of time required for the initial gathering of information will depend on the number of files that exist on the Windows 2000 Server. After the Indexing Service has completed its initial run it will continue to update its cache as files are created, deleted, and modified. The impact on the server from the Indexing Service is minimal. Once the catalog has been created, make sure that the Index This Resource and the Read IIS 5.0 permissions are enabled on the virtual directory. Index This Resource causes the Web server to create a catalog file from the Indexing Service; Read enables clients to view the results of a search.

# PUBLISHING TOOLS

WebDAV makes the Web site feature rich, allowing access to the publishing directory through Windows 2000, Internet Explorer version 5 or higher, and Office 2000 or better. To further extend your capabilities it helps to understand how each can serve as a publishing agent. Although each agent can effectively Web-enable collaboration for your organization, you should be able to determine which one is the best tool for each scenario. To help with troubleshooting potential publishing problems, you will want to consider pinpointing one tool as the company standard. This will give you an advantage if users have trouble. It also helps keep the costs of training to a minimum because the user would need to become proficient with only one tool.

## Windows 2000

Publishing through Windows 2000 is as simple as accessing a directory on the network server. Most users are generally familiar with mapped drives in Windows Explorer, so this might be the method of choice, particularly if Internet Explorer is not the company standard Web browser and Office 2000 has not been selected as the organization's productivity suite.

To publish using Windows 2000, follow these steps:

1. Find the My Network Places icon on the Windows 2000 desktop and double-click it.

2. Double-click the Add Network Place icon, shown in Figure C-1.

3. In the Add Network Place Wizard, enter the URL of the WebDAV directory that is being used for publishing, as shown in Figure C-2.

4. Click the Next button.

5. On the last page of the wizard type a name for the publishing directory. Make the name something memorable and something that will distinguish it from the other available publishing directories. See Figure C-3.

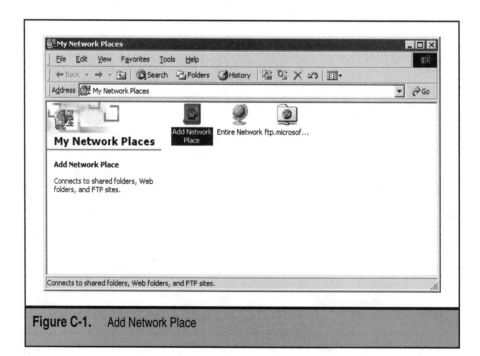

**Figure C-1.** Add Network Place

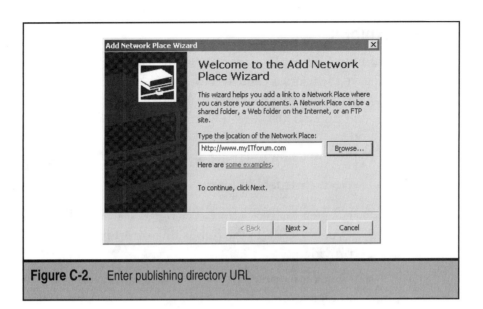

**Figure C-2.**    Enter publishing directory URL

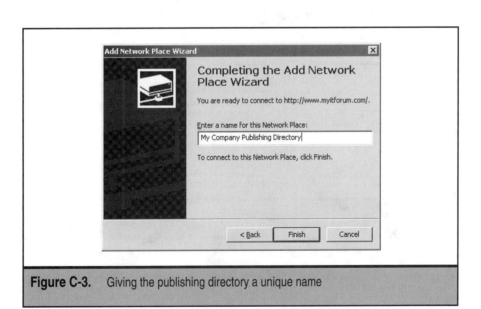

**Figure C-3.**    Giving the publishing directory a unique name

## Internet Explorer

If you use Internet Explorer as the publishing agent of choice, you will give the users a vehicle they probably are completely familiar with. Using Internet Explorer (5.0 or higher), you can manipulate files and publish just as you would using the Windows 2000 Explorer method.

To publish using Internet Explorer, follow these steps:

1. Open Internet Explorer.

2. On the File menu, click the Open option.

3. Type the URL to the publishing directory in the space provided.

4. Check the option to open the URL as a Web folder, as shown in Figure C-4.

Because of the functionality of Internet Explorer 5.0 or later, by enabling an URL to open as a Web Folder, the Internet Explorer window utilizes the same features of Windows Explorer. You can open files and drag-and-drop files from the local computer.

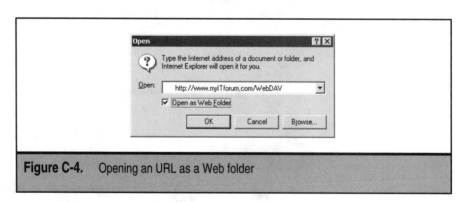

**Figure C-4.**  Opening an URL as a Web folder

## Office 2000

If the Microsoft Office suite of applications is your company standard, you might find programs such as Word and Excel easy methods of publishing Web documents. Companies generally spend a lot of money training employees to use the application suite effectively, so using this method you would see an immediate return on investment. Publishing using Office 2000 or better utilizes the same features with which you are already familiar.

To use Office 2000 to publish Web documents, use the following steps:

1.  Create a document in any Office 2000 application. For this example I used Microsoft Word.

2.  When the document is complete, on the File menu choose Save As.

3.  On the left side of the Save As menu, click the My Network Places icon.

4.  Select the WebDAV shortcut in the list (shown in Figure C-5) and click the Open button.

5.  If Integrated Windows Security is the authentication method, you will be prompted for your login credentials.

6.  Once the publishing directory is open, click the Save button to publish the document.

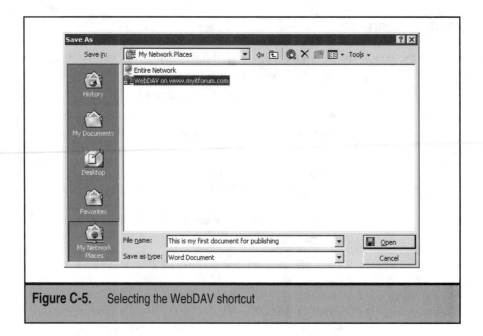

**Figure C-5.** Selecting the WebDAV shortcut

It's that easy. Saving the file using the methods you are already comfortable with enables you to publish documents quickly and securely.

# INDEX

## X–Z